Win the Money War

Clear Investing Advice for Service Members

James D. Redwine

DEDICATION

For Gina, Nick, Elyse, and Charlie.

CONTENTS

Part I

INTRODUCTION

This section discusses the audience that inspired the writing of this book and the manner in which the book's information appears.

Chapter 1: Purpose

This book tells you how to build wealth. Building wealth will improve your financial security. You will receive specific recommendations for what to do with your paycheck. A significant portion of these recommendations will include aggressive investing techniques that typical financial advisors will not share with you. You will quickly get your money working for you, while you stay focused on your career. You will be able to execute this book's advice, regardless of your experience with money. Executing this advice will strengthen your family, improve your career, and enhance your retirement.

This book is primarily for service members (SMs) and their families. Most of this book's readers will be soldiers, sailors, airmen, coastguardsmen, or marines. Nonetheless, even civilians will benefit from this book's advice. Readers of this book will possess few, if any, complex business or commercial real estate interests. I will make some recommendations concerning business and real estate, but I will limit my recommendations to what a career SM can reasonably accomplish. Most likely, the readers of this book will simply wish to become more financially secure, without jeopardizing their military careers and losing any more time with their families than deployments have already taken.

Even more specifically, this book is for "do-it-yourself" (DITY) investors. DITY investors are extremely conscious of their expenses. DITY investors believe that the advantages of reducing their expenses outweigh the advantages that paid assistance might accrue. Until their finances attain greater sizes and complexities, this may be true. Indeed, "Win the Money war" will provide enough information for a SM to get his finances growing.

Nonetheless, once the SM's portfolio of investments begins enjoying reasonable growth, the SM may wish to hire a financial advisor (FA). The FA will charge a fee but will identify advanced techniques for further expanding and fully protecting the SM's wealth. Of course, SMs that are nearing or are already in retirement will possess even more complex financial situations. FAs can help retirees preserve the growth of their wealth, while the retirees are withdrawing money from their investments for living expenses. Additionally, FAs can help protect the retirees' estates for the eventual transfer of those estates to the retirees' descendents.

"Win the Money War" is not a comprehensive listing of the latest changes in the rules and regulations that govern your pay and benefits. Besides being dull, such a book would be obsolete within a year of its publication. More importantly, such a book would fail to present the methods for significantly expanding your wealth. Its advice would be too "tactical". Your financial plan would lack a long-term "strategic" focus. A strategic focus is what will move you out of the trenches of living from paycheck to paycheck.

Too often, financial articles bury us in theory while leaving us baffled as to what we should actually do. For SMs, this is particularly annoying. Ever between deployments, we simply do not possess the time to muse about hazy financial concepts. Instead, we quickly toss a few bucks into an investment or two, before grabbing our rucks and running to wherever the bad guys are next waiting for us. The unfortunate result of this approach is that we possess ramshackle portfolios that offer poor returns. Our finances become a shambles. Poor finances lead to unhappy spouses. Unhappy spouses create weak marriages. Weak marriages end in divorce. Divorces devastate SMs' emotional and financial health. Emotionally and financially devastated SMs weaken units. Weakened units are less capable of accomplishing missions. Failed missions lead to lost wars.

A rushed approach to your finances may lead to your accepting advice from poorly qualified personnel. Such personnel are your military buddies who are dispensing "hot tips" in the smoking area. Acting on their advice will result in your possessing a hodgepodge of investments that chase the latest investing fads. These fads will pass, and you will be left with a mess of investments that fail to work in harmony toward your attainment of long-term wealth.

Being apathetic is even worse than being rushed. Many SMs toss a few bucks here and there with nary a thought toward the future. They figure they will simply "work till they drop". They know that they cannot take their money with them, so they spend every penny of their paychecks and pick up any slack with the magic of "plastic". We all know that SMs occasionally get chaptered, miss a promotion, or suffer other financial setbacks. We know that many SMs become disillusioned with or exhausted by the military and then quit. However, we are confident that our superlative performances, youthful vitality, and love for the military will persist. These disasters will not happen to us. Unfortunately, such a Pollyanna's approach to our finances jeopardizes our futures.

At the worst, we may regard financial planning with actual contempt. We may detest fellow SMs who pay close attention to their investments. We might consider such attention an improper or even immoral focus for a SM. If this attitude is yours, change it. I am confident that you would not serve in the military for free. If getting a paycheck is important to you, then properly investing that paycheck should also be important. If you are simply above such matters, then at least learn how to advise your subordinates in the means for improving their finances.

I sincerely hope that the commanders and leaders among you will recommend this book to your subordinates. I will appreciate the added book sales, and you will appreciate the effect on your units' combat readiness. Improving your subordinates' finances will free them from the anxieties of caring for their families with too few assets. With strong personal finances behind them, SMs will focus on the enemies in front of them. In both Iraq Wars, I dealt with SMs whose finances were in such trouble that we considered pulling the SMs from the line. Their financial problems at home made them less effective in war. From experience, I assure you that improving your subordinates' personal finances is a force sustainment imperative.

Chapter 2: Formats

This book uses formats that many SMs will find familiar. The U.S. military's "WARNO", short for "Warning Order", is an informal tool that military leaders use to alert their troops to an impending mission. The U.S. military's "OPORD", short for "Operations Order", is the formal tool that military leaders use to organize and convey their plans for completing that mission. In the case of this book, the mission is to increase your wealth. A variety of financial instruments will be your weapons, and a host of financial challenges will be the enemy forces that you must overcome.

WARNO

After receiving missions, leaders immediately publish WARNOs to their troops. WARNOs can be verbal or written. WARNOs are brief; they are not large, detailed transmissions. WARNOs give troops quick estimates of the situations, rough ideas of the impending missions, and some initial tasks to accomplish. WARNOs are time savers. WARNOs enable the troops to immediately start preparing themselves and their equipment. After issuing WARNOs, leaders return to the task of finalizing the more detailed OPORDs. At later hours, leaders will issue the completed OPORDs to their troops. The OPORDs will be detailed and, hopefully, well considered plans.

While a standard format exists for the OPORD, no standard format exists for the WARNO. Many leaders simply publish skeletal versions of the OPORD. Other leaders develop their own WARNO formats, altogether. I fell into the latter category. My own WARNO possessed three sections: General Situation, Draft Mission Statement, and Immediate Instructions. This format enabled me to convey enough information to my men to get the ball rolling. After issuing my WARNO, I returned to the task of crafting the detailed OPORD.

In this case, the WARNO will alert your family to a number of financial tasks that they can immediately execute. Your family need not wait until you have absorbed every bit of this book's material and have presented a detailed financial OPORD. Some financial tasks can receive your family's immediate attention.

What follows is a "financial" WARNO for your family. The impending mission is to improve your family's financial readiness. You should immediately share this WARNO with your family. The WARNO will enable your family and you to immediately execute a number of simple tasks for improving your cash flow and for increasing your savings. Once you have shared the WARNO with your family, you can finish reading this book. The remainder of the book will give you precise recommendations for increasing your long-term wealth.

Personal Finance WARNO

1. General Situation

    a. Enemy Forces
        i. Taxes
        ii. National Problems
        iii. Excessive Mutual Fund Fees
        iv. Briefly Owned Homes

    b. Friendly Forces
        i. Income
        ii. Thrift Savings Plan (TSP) or 401(k)
        iii. Individual Retirement Accounts (IRAs)

    iv.   Social Security

2. Draft Mission Statement: You must quickly initiate an investment strategy that improves your family's financial ability to defeat a variety of economic threats.

3. Immediate Instructions

    a. You
        i.   Know what you earn, and discover where it is going.
        ii.   Learn where your earnings *should* be going.
       iii.   Propose family budget cuts, weather the storm of resistance, kill a cut or two, and then demand adherence to the surviving cuts.
       iv.   Calculate the savings that your cuts will net.
       v.   Automatically deposit those savings into a partially liquid account.
       vi.   Eliminate bad debt, ASAP. Accept no further bad debt.
       vii.   Calculate net savings after bad debt elimination.
      viii.   Calculate minimum cash in-flows required from earnings to sustain the family's immutable, or non-discretionary, expenses.
       ix.   Ask financial institutions how to establish your investments. Do not ask financial institutions *what* investments they recommend. After reading this book, you will tell the institutions what you want.
       x.   Dollar-cost-average investment contributions that you cannot lump-sum-invest.
       xi.   Monitor the progress of savings accounts and investments to determine how you can expand them.

xii. Chair periodic financial discussions with your family.
  1. Get your family to enumerate their desires and dreams.
  2. Update your family on the performance of your savings and investments.
  3. Propose more budget cuts.
xiii. Ensure your spouse knows where the savings and investments are and how to get them, in the event of your death.

b. Spouse
  i. Maintain the checkbook.
    1. Pay off bills for family expenses that are necessary for survival.
    2. Pay off superfluous bills, but do not recreate these expenses.
    3. Balance checkbook, monthly.
    4. Do not bounce checks.
  ii. Pay off credit cards in full. Never carry a balance – ever.
  iii. Only use credit cards for emergencies. Pay with checks or, ideally, with cash.
  iv. Faithfully transfer savings into investments. Accept no attrition of your contributions.
  v. Develop a detailed budget. Accurately track all cash flows.
  vi. Identify and eliminate non-essential expenses.

c. Children
  i. Think, "Scholarships!"
    1. Achieve the best possible academic scores.
    2. Obtain at least one varsity letter. The type of sport is irrelevant.
    3. Participate in official, socially rounding activities.

ii. Participate in a legal, after-school income producing pursuit.

iii. Open a savings account with limited check cashing privileges and overdraft protection. Balance your checkbook.

iv. Avoid illegal substances and pranks that invite the Law's wrath.

v. Drive safely.

vi. Learn what your parents are doing, and repeat it.

d. Entire Family

i. Embrace the concept of delayed, rather than immediate, gratification.

ii. Applaud one another's financial successes (e.g. increased savings, expanded cuts, established investments, eliminated debts, and achieved academic excellence).

iii. Enthusiastically participate in family budgeting sessions. Aim to expand savings and investments. Do not push for individual gratification (e.g. new bass boat, new diamond, or new phone).

The WARNO transmission is now complete. At this point, your family can immediately initiate movement in the direction of improving your household's finances. Later, your family will get more detailed instructions from you. You will get these more detailed instructions from the formal OPORD that you are about to receive.

Your family now possesses some idea of the impending mission. Your spouse and children are busily examining the checking account, credit cards, scholarship opportunities, and the consequences of changing their spending habits. At this point, you can leave to attend the formal OPORD.

Personal Finance OPORD

The military's formal OPORD contains five sections: Situation, Mission, Execution, Service Support, and Command & Signal. I distributed the relevant components of this book among these five sections. While each of these sections officially contains several sub-sections, I did not bother to use most of these sub-sections. You did not purchase this book to learn the craft of writing military OPORDs. As such, I will briefly explain the functions of only the OPORD's five, main paragraphs and will then resume the task of telling you how to maximize your paycheck.

The OPORD will explain what the economic enemy forces are doing and how their actions hinder your financial success. The OPORD will explain how various friendly forces can assist you. The OPORD will formalize your mission. The OPORD will give you the precise steps to execute to overcome the enemy forces and to capitalize on the friendly forces, in order to achieve your mission. The final sections of the OPORD will discuss resources that are available to support your efforts.

1. Situation

The title of the first section of the military's OPORD is "Situation". The Situation includes those elements with which we must contend. "Enemy Forces" are those elements that deter our success. They are obstacles to the completion of our mission. "Friendly Forces" are elements that assist us in the completion of our mission.

2. Mission

The title of the second section is "Mission". It is the shortest but the most important section in the OPORD. Were the OPORD an essay, the Mission would be its thesis. Like an essay's thesis, all other sections of the OPORD must support the Mission. The Mission is a single sentence that states our objective using the "5 Ws" – who, when, what, where, and why.

3. Execution

The title of the third section is "Execution". While the Mission states what we must do, the Execution section conveys how we intend to do it. The Execution section establishes our intended maneuvers. These maneuvers must lead to our accomplishment of the Mission, while contending with each of the Situation section's forces.

4. Service Support

The title of the fourth section is "Service Support". The Service Support section explains the administrative and logistical resources that are available to support the maneuvers that we devised in the Execution section.

5. Command & Signal

The title of the fifth and final section is "Command & Signal". This section establishes who is in charge of the operation. This section also explains how we will communicate.

You should now be familiar with the OPORD's format. The Financial OPORD that you are about to receive will be much longer and more detailed than the WARNO that you received and issued to your family. The OPORD will give you the information that you need to accomplish your mission. You must carefully study the OPORD's information and then execute a financial plan that capitalizes on that information.

The remaining chapters of this book will follow the OPORD format. OPORD aficionados will note that the chapters' numbers do not quite match the sections' numbers in an actual military OPORD. Hopefully, you can overlook this numeric inconsistency.

Part II

SITUATION (ENEMY FORCES)

This section of the OPORD discusses the economic enemies that oppose your pursuit of the mission.

Chapter 3: Taxes

Taxes are essential. Taxes pay for the governmental functions necessary to keep a nation civilized and secure. They pay for the public works that no individual could hope to finance but that every civilized society must possess. Paying taxes is your civic duty. To do otherwise is selfish, unlawful, and un-American. That said, to pay any more taxes than what constitutes your fair share is foolish.

For the purposes of this book, taxes are an enemy force. You cannot annihilate this particular enemy, but you can minimize this enemy's ability to annihilate you. In fact, avoiding unnecessary taxes is also your civic duty. A few thousand dollars that you erroneously grant to the U.S. Government will do little to help the Government cover its trillions of dollars in financial obligations. On the other hand, your properly investing those few thousand dollars will do much to reduce your chances of requiring government subsidies. You will avoid economic woes that would necessitate the Government's adding you to its already immense debt. You will avoid becoming part of the problem. In fact, your invested dollars will fuel the nation's economic growth, making you a part of the solution. With righteous zeal, you should make every effort to legally reduce your taxes.

Ordinary Federal Income Taxes

Ordinary federal income taxes refer to the rates that the IRS applies to such incomes as salaries, interest, and business revenue. It also applies to dividends from stocks or mutual funds that investors have not held long enough to qualify for more favorable tax rates.

Understanding ordinary federal income taxes' most immediate effects on you necessitates your understanding the ordinary federal income tax brackets. Currently, the U.S. has a "progressive" tax system. As taxpayers' incomes increase, taxpayers lose greater percentages of their incomes to taxes. The tax brackets' current rates are a result of the tax reforms that former President George W. Bush signed into law. Congress approved a 2-year extension of those reforms until the end of 2012. After 2012, the tax brackets may return to the higher levels that they occupied before Bush's presidency. Two of the 2012 filing statuses and their associated tax rates (brackets) are as follows:

Tax Rate	Married Filing Jointly	Single
10%	Up to $17,400	Up to $8700
15%	$17,401 to $70,700	$8701 to $35,350
25%	$70,701 to $142,700	$35,351 to $85,650
28%	$142,701 to $217,450	$85,651 to $178,650
33%	$217,451 to $388,350	$178,651 to $388,350
35%	$388,351 and above	$388,351 and above

When the tax brackets return to their pre-Bush era versions, we will only have five brackets, not the current six. The percentages will be 15%, 28%, 31%, 36%, and 39.6%. Unfortunately, we can only speculate what the income thresholds will be, at each of these levels. For the purposes of this book, I will use the existing brackets for my examples that deal with ordinary income. At a minimum, this will illuminate the relevant processes.

Marginal versus Average Tax Rates

Two terms are important for understanding the tax brackets: "marginal tax rate" and "average tax rate". Your "marginal tax rate" refers to the tax rate of the highest tax bracket into which your taxable income falls. Your taxable income is your Modified Adjusted Gross Income (MAGI). Your MAGI is your income after deductions and exemptions. The IRS only applies the marginal tax rate to that portion of your MAGI that falls into that marginal tax bracket. The IRS does not apply the marginal tax rate to your entire MAGI. Like individually buttering a stack of pancakes, the IRS taxes each portion of your MAGI at a different rate. The top pancake receives the most butter (the highest rate). The sum of the dollar amounts that result from these individual taxations is your total tax liability.

Dividing your total tax liability by your gross income (not your MAGI) yields your "average tax rate". When a person declines a higher paying job for fear that the higher salary will place him in a higher tax bracket, he shoots himself in the foot. Only that portion – that margin – of his increased MAGI that falls into that new, higher tax bracket is what the IRS will tax at that new, higher rate.

Example: Determining marginal versus average taxes.

Situation

Assume that in 2011, your spouse and you claimed "Married Filing Jointly" status on your tax forms and that your family's gross income was $87,000. Assuming that you had no kids and that you claimed two exemptions, your MAGI would have been about $67,500. This MAGI would have placed you in the 15% marginal tax bracket.

Calculations

In 2012, you are considering a new job that will increase your gross income to $100,000. As such, your MAGI will increase to about $80,500. This MAGI will place you in the 25% marginal tax bracket. However, the IRS will only tax $80,500 – $70,700 – $9800 of your MAGI at the new 25% marginal tax rate. The IRS will continue to tax the previous $70,700 – $17,400 = $53,300 of your MAGI at the 15% rate, and the IRS will continue to tax the original $17,400 of your MAGI at the 10% rate. Your total federal income tax liability will be (25% X $9800) + (15% X $53,300) + (10% X $17,400) = $12,185. Your average tax rate will be $12,185 total tax liability / $100,000 gross income = 0.12185, or about 12.2%.

Investors use the marginal tax rate to determine exactly how much they will get out of each dollar of their impending income increases. If your family's MAGI happened to be precisely $142,700 and you anticipated a $10,000 income increase in the coming year, you would know that that $10,000 margin of your income would only produce (100% income – 28% marginal tax rate) X $10,000 = $7200 worth of investment capital.

Alternatively, you can use your marginal tax rate to determine how much you will save by increasing your deductions, provided that you itemize those deductions. Assume that your MAGI is $60,000, placing you in the 15% marginal tax bracket. You are considering purchasing a home. You plan to use a mortgage that will enable you to deduct $12,000 in interest payments for the first year. Your $12,000 deduction will save you 15% marginal tax rate X $12,000 = $1800 in taxes.

FICA Taxes

Unfortunately, ordinary income taxes are not the only taxes that SMs suffer. The Government also pulls Social Security and Medicare taxes from SMs' incomes. Social Security and Medicare taxes are known as "FICA" taxes. FICA stands for "Federal Insurance Contributions Act". This is the act that authorizes the

Government to levy Social Security and Medicare taxes.

Unlike our ordinary income taxes' progressive system, FICA Social Security and Medicare taxes are "flat" taxes. In "flat" tax systems, all taxpayers pay the same percentages, regardless of the sizes of their incomes. Since the late 1990s through 2010, FICA Social Security and Medicare taxes have been 6.2% and 1.45%, respectively, for all taxpayers. Starting with the 2011 tax year, the rate for FICA Social Security taxes dropped to 4.2%. The rate for Medicare remained 1.45%. The drop in the FICA Social Security tax rate was a stimulus initiative by the Obama Administration. Nonetheless, the 6.2% rate will return in 2013, unless Congress enacts new legislation.

The IRS applies the FICA tax rates to your gross income, not to your MAGI. The "W-2 Wage and Tax Statement" that the military sends to you after each tax year shows your total FICA taxes. If you bother to do the math, you will see that Box 4 (Social Security tax) is exactly 4.2% of Box 3 (Social Security wages), and Box 6 (Medicare tax) is exactly 1.45% of Box 5 (Medicare wages). You might also notice that Boxes 3 and 5 include every dollar of your income – even your contributions to the Government's Traditional Thrift Savings Plan (TSP). Contributions to a Traditional TSP get no relief from FICA taxes, only from ordinary federal income taxes. We will discuss Traditional and Roth TSPs in Chapter 8.

Interestingly, a $110,100 cap exists on the gross income against which the IRS can apply FICA Social Security taxes for 2012. This means that even the President will pay a tax of no more than $110,100 gross income X 4.2% = $4624.20. The rest of the Boss' 2012 income will be FICA Social Security tax-free. In essence, this cap turns FICA Social Security taxes into "regressive" taxes. The greater your income, the smaller the percentage of that income you will pay in FICA Social Security taxes.

Unlike FICA Social Security, no cap exists on taxable FICA Medicare wages. Regardless of the size of your income, you will pay 1.45% of that income in FICA Medicare taxes.

The value of all this FICA tax stuff is to make you aware that you must consider more than simply your ordinary federal income tax rate, when determining how much you will net from your income. You must also account for FICA taxes. For example, if a husband and wife anticipated an annual income of $76,000, their average tax rate would be 10.01% for a total federal income tax liability of $7605 (see the "Marginal Tax Rate" calculator at http://www.dinkytown.net/java/TaxMargin.html). However, their FICA taxes would claim another (4.2% + 1.45%) X $76,000 = $4294. Failing to account for another $4294 in taxes could be a serious error, when anticipating their annual solvency.

Fortunately, once you begin taking your Social Security benefits, you will stop paying FICA taxes. Nonetheless, you might still owe ordinary federal income taxes, if your combined income exceeds certain thresholds.

Capital Gains Taxes

When you purchase an asset at a given price and later sell that asset at a higher price, you enjoy a capital gain. Typical assets that produce capital gains are stocks, mutual funds, and homes. You must hold an asset for at least 12 months, before you can sell the asset and qualify for the capital gains tax rate. Currently, the capital gains tax rate for taxpayers with marginal income tax rates of 25% or higher is 15%. For taxpayers in the 10% or 15% marginal income tax brackets, the capital gains tax rate is actually 0%. Unfortunately, the 0% and 15% capital gains tax rates will disappear by 2013, if Congress does not extend the Bush era tax cuts. The capital gains tax rates will increase to 10% for taxpayers in the 15% income tax bracket and to 20% for taxpayers in the higher income tax brackets.

This is another time when knowing your marginal income tax rate becomes useful. If your MAGI just lands you in the 28% income tax bracket and you sell an asset that produces a $50,000 capital gain, whether you held the asset for one month or for one year will make a big difference. If you only held the asset for one month, the IRS will regard your capital gain as ordinary income and will tax your gain at your marginal income tax rate. Your after tax return will be (100% income – 28% marginal income tax) X $50,000 = $36,000. On the other hand, if you held the asset for more than a year, your after tax return will be (100% income – 15% capital gains tax) X $50,000 = $42,500.

Thankfully, FICA taxes do not apply to capital gains. This fact enables investing-savvy SMs to significantly reduce their tax burdens, relative to SMs who rely solely on fixed incomes. Investors in taxable accounts can generate substantial incomes that suffer capital gains taxes but suffer neither ordinary federal income nor FICA taxes. Properly liquidating accounts to generate income from a combination of capital gains and principal can produce dramatically lower tax liabilities, while amply covering expenses[i]. In the Execution section, we will discuss this process in more detail. True, the impending 20% capital gains tax rate will increase the challenge of capitalizing on capital gains' being exempt from FICA taxes. Nonetheless, even with the jump from 15% to 20%, generating income from investments in taxable accounts will continue to offer tax advantages over relying on fixed incomes.

Chapter 4: National Problems

From individual Americans' perspectives, taxes are an enemy force. Taxes take dollars that we need for personal expenses. From the nation's perspective, taxes are a friendly force. Taxes pay for the mechanisms that prevent anarchy. However, several forces exist that are enemies from both a personal and a national perspective.

Inflation

The forces of demand and supply drive inflation. Domestic and international consumers' desires for our nation's products coupled with manufacturers' abilities to meet those demands determine whether prices will inflate or deflate. Producing too few products for the demand will cause prices to inflate. Producing too many products causes prices to deflate. From a national perspective, a slight degree of inflation is good. It means our products are in demand. This demand spurs economic growth that leads to more jobs. However, too much inflation will cause manufacturers' equipment replacement costs to rise. This rise will lower profits. Falling profits will lead to budget cuts, layoffs, and, ultimately, lower stock prices. On a personal level, inflation is definitely an enemy force from the very beginning. Unless we compensate for it, we will be unable to enjoy the goods that our nation produces.

Inflation's most immediate effect is to force you to spend more dollars for an item, this year, than you would have spent for the same item, last year. Many economists use the 3.1% average Consumer Price Index (CPI) as their inflation estimate[ii]. Using this estimate, we can assume that, every year, goods will cost about 3.1% more than they did in the preceding year. We can use the U.S. Bureau of Labor Statistic's Inflation Calculator to determine the effect of inflation on our purchasing power, over any period[iii]. For example, an item that cost $100 in 1980 cost over $264 in 2010. In those 30 years, our purchasing power dropped over 2 and 1/2 times. When developing one's financial plan, failing to compensate for the effects of inflation is a disastrous mistake.

Dollar Devaluation

Inflation and dollar devaluation look the same, but they are different. In contrast to inflation, dollar devaluation refers to the declining purchasing power of the U.S. dollar. While the reduced supply of products drives inflation, the increased supply of dollars, themselves, drives dollar devaluation. Dollar devaluation is the result of our Government's continually printing more dollars (currency notes) to pay for growing financial obligations that current sources of revenue are insufficient to cover.

An article published by the National Center for Policy Analysis reported that the U.S. Government's unfunded liability for Social Security and Medicare had already climbed to $107 trillion by 2009[iv]. The same article reported that this $107 trillion liability was approximately seven times the nation's Gross Domestic Product (GDP). This is similar to your promising to pay for an expensive item while knowing that you do not now, nor might you ever, have the money to do so. However, the Government has an advantage that you do not have.

The Government has the authority to print money. Unfortunately, in 1971, that authority lost a critical control mechanism. In that year, President Richard M. Nixon took America off the Gold Standard. This move ended the system that chained the value of a U.S. dollar to a specific weight of gold. From a national perspective, eliminating this control measure may have seemed sensible. Unfortunately, the nation's abandonment of the Gold Standard has permitted the consistent erosion of the value of your hard-earned dollars. To cover its persistently growing financial challenges, the U.S. Government continues to print larger numbers of U.S. dollars (legal counterfeiting). This increases the global supply of U.S. dollars. As the total supply of U.S. dollars increases, the value of individual U.S. dollars decreases.

Obligations for Social Security, for Health Care, for global military operations, and for paying federal employees are tempting the Government to jeopardize our nation's financial future. By printing more dollars to cover these obligations, the Government leads us closer to the disaster suffered by Germany, shortly after the First World War. Merely buying one's groceries cost millions of Reich marks.

At the level of the individual SM, dollar devaluation looks the same as inflation. Things cost more. However, understanding the difference between dollar devaluation and inflation is important. Compensating for these enemy forces requires different tactics.

National Debt

The nation's annual revenue deficits add up to the nation's total debt – the "national debt". The Government's own operating costs produce those deficits. Unfortunately, those deficits are increasing without equal increases in revenues. By early 2012, the national debt exceeded $15 trillion, making the size of U.S. debt greater than the U.S. economy[v]. Unless our Government slashes its operating costs while increasing its revenues, its debt will remain and will increase. Note that the national debt is *in addition to* obligations for Social Security and Medicare.

Raising taxes might help the Government reduce the national debt, but this approach would merely push the problem forward. Higher taxes would mean less spending money for individuals and less investment capital for businesses. Recession would result. Recession opposes the solution that the Government seeks. A recession would mean a lowering of consumer spending which would force a reduction in industrial production. Less capital would flow, fewer profits would appear, and the Government could levy fewer taxes.

The long-term solution will necessitate the development of incentives that stimulate economic growth. Economic growth will provide more taxable corporate revenues and will make individual Americans more self-sufficient. Until this solution exists, the Government must pay its debts with something. The interim solution will be to print more money. Of course, this brings us back to dollar devaluation.

Consumer Mentality

This enemy force could well be your most challenging opponent. It has almost certainly infiltrated your position and is now manipulating your financial choices. If you suffer too much of a consumer mentality, you will possess a predisposition to spend money. This penetration of your defenses was not entirely your fault. Your own U.S. Government consciously promoted your consumer mentality. Consumer spending is the life-blood of the Keynesian economic model that guided our leaders' post World War II fiscal policies and, arguably, made the U.S. a global super-power. Our Government crafted policies and instituted measures that promoted consumer spending. Avoiding reductions in consumer spending was essential for motivating manufacturers to seek ways to expand their productivity. Effectively, Uncle Sam made spending money your patriotic duty.

Today, we are so faithfully executing our duty that we are failing to accumulate any personal wealth. Consumer spending data in March 2010 showed that Americans' spending rates increased 0.6% while their incomes increased a mere 0.3%[vi]. Our Cold War leaders unwittingly saddled our current leaders with a population that is incapable of building wealth. Such a population requires government subsidies to survive in retirement.

Our Cold War leaders were not the only culprits goading us to freely spend our hard-earned cash. Today's advertisements and peer pressures add supporting fires to the consumer mentality's assault. Advertisers bombard us with wondrous luxuries that will scratch our every itch. Peers flaunt possessions that stir our envy.

These supporting fires tempt us to spend our money, rather than invest our money. We grow too impatient to embrace the virtues of delaying gratification. We rob the future to enjoy the moment.

Short of becoming hermits, we cannot halt our exposure to advertisements. We can only remind ourselves that we did not need nor desire these luxuries, before the TV blasted them into our living rooms. Are the short-term pleasures from these luxuries worth the long-term wealth that the purchases of these luxuries will sacrifice?

Controlling your envy of your neighbors' toys is challenging. Your buddy has a new sports car; why should you not have a new sports car? The reason is the same as for resisting advertisements. Your buddy's sports car is simply an advertisement. Before seeing your buddy's sports car, did you really need a sports car? More accurately, your buddy's sports car is a proclamation. He is proclaiming that he prefers immediate pleasure to future wealth. He is broadcasting the fact that his eventual net worth will be less than it could be. Viewing your buddy's purchase in this light may lessen your need to emulate him. You might opt to channel your money into investments.

Interest Payments

Since we often buy toys with credit, we often make interest payments. Receiving interest income and making interest payments are different sides of the same coin. The former is good, provided that taxes do not overly reduce it. The latter is generally bad but can, at times, be unavoidable. Unavoidable interest payments are those that we make for such things as home mortgages and installment loans for cars. Few people can pay for a home without financing at least some portion of the home's price. Nonetheless, just about everyone needs a home. Similarly, a car is a necessity for commuting between home and work. However, too many of us succumb to the temptation to buy substantially more car than we need. Such temptation exists in the housing market, as well. The difference is that a home will last and might appreciate in value. A car will do neither.

The unequivocally bad form of interest payment is that for credit card debt. Few laws restrict the interest rates that credit card companies can charge. Credit card companies take advantage of this fact to charge interest rates as high as 20% or more. The daily compounding of these rates makes the percentages even higher. Credit card companies lure you by offering low, minimum monthly payments. Unfortunately for you, nearly every dollar of the minimum payment services the interest on your debt. Little goes toward the principal. The principal is the actual amount that you charged against your credit card for the good or service. Since you only marginally reduce your principal with each minimum payment, your credit card debt continues for many years.

Only making minimum payments for several years will result in a debt juggernaut. The daily compounding of a credit card's interest rate will force you to accumulate more interest payments on the interest, itself. Taking the full life of the loan to pay off your credit card debt can easily result in your paying well over double the amount that you originally charged. The fact that the Government regards credit card debt as being simple consumer debt leads to the final insult. Unlike home mortgage interest, you cannot deduct credit card interest from your taxes.

Liabilities and Assets

Our propensity to consume leads us to acquire many items that we do not need. Wasting money on items that we do not need reduces our wealth. The fact that we often use credit to acquire these superfluous items compounds our losses.

Items that we do not need are items that generate negative cash flows. Items that generate negative cash flows and do not appreciate in value are liabilities. For example, a bass boat is almost certainly a liability. Even if your bass boat was a gift, it is still a liability. You must pay for this gift's maintenance, spare parts, fuel, licensing, and taxes. Unless you are using the boat to catch fish that you sell for a profit, the boat is a liability, not an asset.

Assets are items that generate positive cash flows. Wealth comes from positive cash flows and increases in value. As for the bass boat, you are losing money for the privilege of owning it. This is a negative cash flow. Cash flows toward items or systems that stand little or no chance of one day generating positive cash flows are bad. Cash flows toward items that might appreciate in value can be good, depending on the circumstances.

Net Worth

The difference between your liabilities and your assets determines your net worth. So long as your spending rate matches or exceeds your savings rate and your possessions fail to appreciate in value, your net worth will be zero or less. Net worth is a truer measure of one's wealth than is one's income. A person can earn a large income, while possessing a negative net worth. Such a person spends every dollar of his paycheck and then uses credit cards to make even more purchases. Because he possesses many toys and is able to cover his minimum payments, he assumes he is wealthy or, at the very least, is comfortable. Unfortunately, such a person possesses a false sense of security. His "wealth" is a façade.

Having many toys does not mean that you have many assets. Anything that fails to appreciate in value and fails to generate income is a liability, not an asset. Cars, boats, pools, vacation homes, timeshares, and RVs are great offenders that many people proudly display as assets when, in fact, they are liabilities[vii]. They cost money to own.

Why should you care about your net worth? What purpose does money serve, if not to buy toys? Undoubtedly, toys are benefits of wealth. However, having toys without wealth puts the cart before the horse. Spending to the limit and beyond of your earnings leaves nothing for the day when you can earn no more. This day will most assuredly come. The reasons for your being incapable of generating income will vary from exhaustion to coercion. Unfortunately, unless the reason is death, your bills will persist. The obsolete toys that you purchased will not pay those bills. You will require subsidies from either the Government or from your family. Your options will be limited, your self-esteem will suffer, and your legacy will be inglorious. A further disadvantage of having a negative net worth is that it will adversely impact your ability to obtain favorable terms on any loans for which you apply. In contrast, possessing a positive net worth will give you something on which to draw when that day of reckoning arrives.

Chapter 5: Excessive Mutual Fund Fees

This book will recommend financial instruments that are easy to understand, easy to establish, and easy to manage. For the most part, these instruments will be mutual funds. Mutual funds fall into two major categories: index mutual funds, or simply "index funds", and managed mutual funds. Index funds are passively managed. Little buying and selling of index funds' underlying securities occurs. As such, index funds' expenses are low. Managed mutual funds are actively managed. Frequent buying and selling of managed mutual funds' underlying securities occurs. As such, managed mutual funds' expenses are higher than index funds' expenses. Managed mutual funds possess teams of analysts. These analysts buy and sell the funds' underlying securities in efforts to beat the various markets' rates of return.

All mutual funds charge various expenses, fees, and loads. For mutual funds to benefit you, you should choose funds that minimize these loads, fees, and expenses. Additionally, you should choose funds that execute fewer turnovers and maintain minimal cash reserves. Index funds generally meet these goals but forfeit the opportunities that actively managed funds can exploit. Managed mutual funds suffer higher rates of turnover and sit on larger cash reserves but can occasionally exploit an impending market condition to produce an acute gain or lessen a loss. You can evaluate all of these factors for nearly any fund by visiting a website such as "Morningstar" at http://www.morningstar.com/.

What Are Mutual Funds?

Mutual funds do the direct stock buying work for you. A mutual fund's managers will buy stock in various companies whose operations match whatever investing philosophy the fund follows. The managers will buy these stocks using other investors' and your pooled money. When you send money to a mutual fund, you are purchasing shares of the fund. You are not directly purchasing stocks of the individual companies. The collective value of the fund's various company stocks divided by the number of shares held by all investors in the fund determines the value of each share of the fund. Investment companies refer to this value as the share's "Net Asset Value" (NAV). The NAV of a fund's shares is what actually matters to a mutual fund investor, not the individual values of the stocks that the fund holds.

Mutual funds offer the safety of diversity. When you buy shares of a mutual fund, you are buying shares of a fund that owns a multitude of companies' stocks. Each of your mutual fund shares represents the sum of the performances of all of those companies, not solely the performance of a single company. The failure of a single company whose stock is owned by a mutual fund will only fractionally affect the NAV of that fund's shares. Owning a multitude of companies within every share of your mutual fund gives you the diversity to better survive market swings.

Mutual funds are extremely liquid. You can easily sell a mutual fund. You are simply liquidating your shares of the fund. You are not trying to sell a specific stock. Specific stocks may be unpopular at the time you choose to sell them. No buyers may exist. You may be stuck with those stocks, or you may be forced to sell them at a sizable loss. I learned this lesson the hard way. When "Boston Chicken" went bankrupt, my individual Boston Chicken stocks became worthless. Nobody wanted them. I received nothing for my Boston Chicken stocks. In contrast, the inherent diversity of a mutual fund's shares means that little chance exists that the shares' NAV will be zero. Should circumstances force you to sell your mutual fund's shares during a depressed market, you will almost certainly get at least some money for your shares.

Nearly anyone can afford to invest in mutual funds. A mutual fund's price of entry can be as low as $1000, depending on the brokerage that offers the fund. Further, mutual funds allow you to add almost any sum of cash, on a regular basis. Individual stocks possess specific prices. You must pay that price to get that stock. If you want 10 shares of stock in XYZ Company, you must work with a broker to pay exactly 10 times the current price of XYZ Company stock. In contrast, mutual funds permit you to contribute nearly any sums of cash. Mutual fund companies will automatically adjust your account to reflect the increase in the number of your shares.

Why Should Mutual Fund Costs Be Low?

The more you pay for an investment, the higher must be your returns for you to enjoy a profit on that investment. All mutual funds come with a variety of sales charges, marketing fees, and management fees. The returns from your investments must exceed these charges and fees before you will see any profit. Mutual fund companies are eager for your dollars. If you jump at the offers of the first sales representatives you encounter, you could pay loads (sales charges) as high as 8.5%, marketing fees (12b-1 fees) as high as 1%, and management fees of over 1.5%.

Loads are sales charges and are classified as "front end", "back end", or "level". Loads are in addition to other expenses and fees. Loaded mutual funds charge these chunks of cash when you first purchase the funds, when you exit the funds, or over the entire times that you own the funds. In the last case, a single load is charged in small bites over time, not continuously re-charged in full. The Motley Fool website quoted Morningstar as having determined that loaded funds produced no better returns than did funds without loads, over the past 3 to 5 years[viii]. In many cases, this determination is true. However, not all loaded funds are bad. Some loaded funds have good track records. In such funds, the loads are modest, and the managers are excellent. However, finding such finds requires expert assistance. For DITY investors, avoiding loaded funds is normally the best approach.

Advertising and management fees exist for the lives of your funds. You must pay these fees every year, regardless of your funds' performances. This is "risk transference" – the mutual fund companies transfer 100% of their risks to you. You put up 100% of the capital with the hope that the mutual fund managers will skilfully invest it and return profits to you. Regardless of whether that happens, the mutual fund companies' advertisers and managers will get their full fees.

Fortunately, not every mutual fund charges a full 1% advertising fee, and some funds charge no such fees, at all. Avoiding funds that charge high 12b-1 fees will improve your returns. On the other hand, all mutual funds do, indeed, charge management fees. Your challenge is to keep 12b-1 and management fees as low as possible.

Chapter 6: Briefly Owned Homes

While you may have already accepted that your cars, boats, and pools were liabilities, the true status of your home might have eluded you. You may have assumed that your home was an asset. Every financial magazine and article that you read encourages you to build equity in a home. Unfortunately, while buying homes may benefit civilians with careers that permit sedentary existences, buying homes will not necessarily benefit SMs. Our military careers force us to frequently move our families and sell our homes after no more than three years. SMs represent less than 1% of the U.S. population. Those magazines and articles' advice is aimed at the other 99% of the population.

Until the 2008 bursting of the housing bubble, the value of houses seemed all but guaranteed to appreciate. Everybody knew somebody who made a killing when selling a home. Prior to 2008, the national average for annual home appreciations was approximately 5%[ix]. This 5% average yielded respectable appreciations in value after only three years of compounding. The value of a $300,000 home that appreciated 5% for each of three years was over $347,000. SMs who sold their homes after only three years of such steady appreciations in value appeared to profit.

Unfortunately, those profits were not quite as large as you might expect. Even during those pre-2008 "boom" years, people who sold homes after just a few years of ownership enjoyed modest profits. This was due to the fact that calculating the profit from the sale of a home is not nearly as simple as just subtracting the home's purchase price from the home's sale price. A multitude of administrative costs profoundly influence the difference between a seller's revenue (cash flow before expenses) and profit (cash flow after expenses). For SMs who move every three years, too little time passes for modest value appreciations to overcome these myriad expenses.

Appraised Value

When you sell your home, you must pay off the rest of your mortgage before you can calculate any profit. If you must sell your home after only a few years of ownership, the size of the remaining mortgage might dwarf whatever equity you have obtained. SMs are particularly vulnerable to this problem due to our frequent moves. "Equity" is that portion of the home that the buyer truly owns. Unfortunately for buyers, while the size of a home's mortgage remains constant, the size of the buyer's equity fluctuates with the home's market value. Real estate appraisers quantify your home's market value by estimating what your home is worth.

The appraiser will base his appraisal of a home's value on the size and quality of the home, relative to the local housing market. Understanding that a home's value is based on local market conditions is important. While popular magazines may claim that home ownership is a guaranteed homerun, local market conditions can make home ownership a strikeout. The value of a home in one town can be drastically lower than the value of a similar home in a neighboring town. A host of economic, political, geographic, demographic, and topographic factors enter the equation. One town has an excellent school system, whereas the next town has a poor school system and a drug problem. In contrast to home values, the price of a share of Microsoft stock is the same for all buyers, regardless of the buyers' geographies.

The host of factors that affect home values can whimsically change. One day, a huge company builds a factory in your town, creating hundreds of jobs. People come to your town to fill those jobs. These people increase the demand for local housing. This rise in demand increases your home's value. For a while, your home appears to be a good investment. Unfortunately, something like "globalization" eventually comes along, enabling your company's competitors to ship factories overseas, employ native workers at slave wages, and slash prices well below your locally based company's ability to profitably manufacture products. Your company folds, jobs are lost, housing demand dies, and your home's value plummets.

Example: The effects on profits of changing home values.

Situation

A SM (buyer) just bought a home. He will only own the home for three years. He wants to know the effects of varying market conditions on the home's value. He wants to know whether he will profit when he sells the home.

1. Appraised value of the home is $300,000.

2. Price buyer paid for that home is $300,000 [see Note 1, at bottom of example].

3. Money that the buyer put down (his starting equity) was $60,000. This figure does not include the buyer's closing costs. Closing costs are extra.

4. Mortgage is $300,000 – $60,000 = $240,000.

5. Term that the buyer chose was 30 years at a 4.5% fixed interest rate.

Scenario #1

Assume that the home's value appreciates roughly 5% per year, all 3 years.

1. Newly appraised value is $347,000.

2. Change in home's value equals change in owner's equity and is $347,000 appraised value – $300,000 original purchase price = $47,000 gain.

3. Mortgage balance is $240,000 original loan – $12,000 worth of principal payments over 3 years = $228,000 [Note 2; Note 3].

4. Owner's equity in home is $60,000 down payment + $12,000 worth of principal payments over 3 years + $47,000 increase in home's value = $119,000.

5. If the owner sells the home for $347,000 in that third year, the owner (seller) will make $347,000 appraised value – $228,000 mortgage remainder = $119,000 gross revenue. Note that this is the same figure as his increased equity, above.

6. In essence, the $119,000 that the owner gets from selling the home will reimburse his $72,000 in equity payments. These payments equal his $60,000 down payment plus $12,000 worth of principal payments. This gives him $119,000 gross revenue – $72,000 in equity payments = $47,000 adjusted revenue.

7. The seller's revenue after sales expenses is $47,000 adjusted revenue – $26,000 closing costs & realtor fees = $21,000 [Note 4].

8. Assume the owner will spend about $9000 in maintenance costs, over 3 years [Note 5]. His revenue after sales expenses and maintenance becomes $21,000 revenue after sales expenses – $9000 maintenance = $12,000 [Note 6].

9. However, the seller also paid $31,600 in interest over 3 years [Note 2]. By itemizing his deductions, he might enjoy as much as a third of this figure in tax savings. Effectively, the interest that he paid will drop to $31,600 – ($31,600 X 33%) = $20,224.

10. The seller's profit becomes $12,000 revenue after sales expenses and maintenance − $20,224 interest = -$8224 (a loss).

Scenario #2

Assume the home's value stays the same, all 3 years.

1. Continuing appraised value is $300,000.

2. Change in home's value is $300,000 appraised value − $300,000 purchase price = 0.

3. Mortgage balance is $240,000 original loan − $12,000 worth of principal payments over 3 years = $228,000.

4. Owner's equity in home is $60,000 down payment + $12,000 worth of principal payments over 3 years + 0 increase in home's value = $72,000.

5. If the owner sells the home for $300,000 in that third year, the owner will initially get $300,000 − $228,000 mortgage remainder = $72,000 gross revenue.

6. In essence, the $72,000 that the seller gets will reimburse his $72,000 in equity payments. Adjusted revenue is $72,000 gross revenue − $72,000 in equity payments = 0.

7. Unfortunately, his revenue after sales expenses will be 0 adjusted revenue − $22,500 closing costs & realtor fees = -$22,500 (a loss).

8. His revenue after sales expenses and maintenance becomes -$22,500 revenue after sales expenses − $9000 maintenance = -$31,500 (a bigger loss).

9. Again, the seller will have effectively paid $20,224 in interest over 3 years.

10. The seller's profit becomes -$31,500 revenue after sales expenses and maintenance – $20,224 interest = -$51,724 (an even bigger loss).

Scenario #3

Assume the home's value depreciates roughly 3% per year, all 3 years.

1. Newly appraised value is $274,000.

2. Change in home's value is $274,000 appraised value – $300,000 purchase price = -$26,000 (a decrease).

3. Mortgage balance is $240,000 original loan – $12,000 worth of principal payments over 3 years = $228,000. Note that this number has been constant. The banker will get his loan payments, regardless of what happens to your equity.

4. Owner's equity in home is $60,000 down payment + $12,000 worth of principal payments over 3 years – $26,000 decrease in value = $46,000. [Note 7]

5. If the owner sells the home for $274,000 in that third year, the owner will make $274,000 – $228,000 mortgage remainder = $46,000 gross revenue.

6. In essence, the $46,000 that the seller gets will reimburse that much of his $72,000 in equity payments. Adjusted revenue is $46,000 gross revenue – $72,000 in equity payments = -$26,000 (a loss).

7. Revenue after sales expenses is -$26,000 adjusted revenue – $20,500 closing costs & realtor fees = -$46,500 (a bigger loss).

8. His revenue after sales expenses and maintenance becomes -$46,500 revenue after sales expenses – $9000 maintenance = -$55,500 (an even bigger loss).

9. Yet again, the seller will have effectively paid $20,224 in interest over 3 years.

10. The seller's profit becomes -$55,500 revenue after sales expenses and maintenance – $20,224 interest = -$75,724 (a huge loss).

Analysis

The situation and its three scenarios show that selling your home after a mere three years of ownership can hurt you, regardless of whether you enjoy typical appreciations in value. Many "hidden" costs enter home buying equations.

I am not suggesting that you eschew home ownership. Obtaining a home is essential for all but beach bums. I am simply saying that SMs should not assume that buying a home guarantees a profit. Homes do not produce positive cash flows, and homes' appreciations are not guaranteed. Even if a home does appreciate, your profit from its sale may not meet your expectations. An added negative is that you must obtain another residence. Most SMs cannot simply sell their homes and then pitch tents. Any new residence that you obtain could easily consume whatever gain you enjoyed from your first home's sale. In this way, homes greatly differ from true assets. You can sell true assets without lowering your quality of life.

Note 1

In most scenarios, buyers will not pay more for a home than the home's currently appraised value. From year to year, this value can change. To fill tax coffers, local governments commission appraisers to go about estimating what homes are worth. Local market conditions determine housing demand, and appraisers effectively quantify that demand with their estimates. These estimates can suddenly change the size of your equity in a home. If an appraiser declares that your home's value has increased, then your equity will increase. Unfortunately, your property taxes will also increase. Your home's changing equity is similar to the changing value of a company's stock or of a mutual fund's share. Stocks and shares' values change in response to the stock market's assessment of what those stocks and shares are worth. This assessment is a quantification of the public's demand for the products and services of the company that sold that certificate of stock or for the companies in the fund that sold the share.

Note 2

The $12,000 worth of principal payments comes from the "Mortgage Calculator" on the Bankrate.com website at http://www.bankrate.com/calculators/mortgages/mortgage-calculator.aspx. The calculator's inputs for our example are the $240,000 mortgage amount, the 30-year mortgage term, and the 4.5% interest rate, per year. After calculating the monthly mortgage payment ($1216.04 in our SM's case), selecting the calculator's "Amortization Table" brings up the total interest and principal payments. A spreadsheet containing 30 years' worth of payment data appears. Scroll down 36 months and then go to the far right column's "Balance" figure to find the remaining mortgage ($227,842.99). Subtract the remaining mortgage from the original loan of $240,000 to get the 3 years' worth of equity payments that the SM will have made. I rounded this result to $12,000. Also, just to the left of the Amortization Table's "Balance" column is the "Total Interest" column. This column's numbers are the total amount of interest paid, up to whatever month you select. For our SM, the three years' worth of interest paid is over $31,600.

Note 3

The $240,000 of the original loan is the bank's equity in the home. Until you pay off the mortgage, you and the bank jointly own the home. However, the bank does not really want the home; the bank wants interest payments. You want the home, but you do not have enough money to pay for it. As such, the bank agrees to immediately cover your shortfall, in exchange for your agreement to gradually reimburse the bank with interest. Over the years, every reimbursing payment that you send to the bank will contain an amount for the equity plus an amount for the interest. Initially, the amount for equity is small, and the amount for interest is large. As time passes, the equity amounts will increase, while the interest amounts will decrease. The bank gets more interest toward the start of the loan; the buyer gets more equity toward the end of the loan. This arrangement protects the bank by ensuring the bank gets its interest, as soon as possible. The bank is hedging its bet against the possibility that some financial disaster will eventually make the buyer incapable of honoring the loan agreement.

Note 4

"Closing costs" include the title and transfer taxes, as well as the administrative and legal fees. These costs add another 1 – 3% of a home's total sale price to a seller's costs. "Realtor's fees" add yet another 5 – 7% of a home's sale price to a seller's costs. Both the seller and the buyer pay various closing costs and, possibly, realtor's fees, but the seller's expenses are generally higher. For this example, I assumed the seller's closing costs would equal 1.5% and the seller's realtor's fees would equal 6%, for a total of 7.5%. Thus, 7.5% X $347,000 = $26,000. I rounded the result to the nearest thousand. An important point to remember is that a buyer's closing costs are in addition to the buyer's down payment.

Note 5

A rule of thumb is to assume that maintenance costs will annually be about 1% of a home's sale price. This estimate assumes the home is in good condition. Costs for older homes and "fixer-uppers" can be substantially higher.

Note 6

The seller's true profit will be even lower, if the seller spends money for improvements to the home. The returns from large-scale improvements rarely warrant their costs, unless such improvements are necessary to ensure that a home's basic functions (e.g. plumbing) are fully functional[x]. Spending another $10,000 on kitchen counter-tops in hopes that you can raise a home's sale price by $15,000 is a risky venture. Save your $10,000. SMs own homes too briefly to warrant spending large sums of money on improvements. Improvements are only sensible for long-term homeowners who are interested in their improvements' intrinsic values. These long-term homeowners accept that their improvements are mostly sunk costs. SMs are short-term homeowners. Short-term homeowners should focus on simple "curb appeal": pick up the trash, mow and clip the yard, vacuum the dog hair, and paint over the crayon marks.

Note 7

Although the buyer made $72,000 worth of equity payments, his equity no longer equals $72,000. If you sell your home, you must pay off the mortgage balance before taking anything for yourself. The mortgage balance does not fluctuate with the value of the home. Your equity is what fluctuates. This is good for the bank but bad for you. Your home's equity is analogous to your stocks' values. You may have handed over $10,000 to buy stock in a company, but that does not guarantee that your company's stock will always be worth $10,000. If you borrowed any money, say $5000, to make up that $10,000 price tag, you must still repay that full $5000 to the lender, regardless of the final value of your stock – even if it is zero.

Standard Deduction versus Mortgage Deduction

Everybody says that a home's mortgage interest deduction is the best gig going. They clamor that renting forfeits the ability to claim that deduction. However, getting that mortgage deduction that people have badgered you into believing only an idiot would forego might undermine your best interests. Renting may actually be better, in some circumstances.

In 2012, the standard deduction for single taxpayers is $5950. For married taxpayers filing jointly, the standard deduction is $11,900. The interest deduction for a home does not become an advantage to the homebuyer until the combination of that home's interest deduction and other itemized deductions is greater than the homebuyer's applicable standard deduction. All couples can get at least $11,900 in deductions, even if they do not own a home. You might conclude that the obvious solution is to purchase a bigger house and, hence, get a bigger mortgage. Yes, you will get a bigger home interest deduction, but your cash flow will suffer. Further, if your home's value decreases, you may find yourself underwater – owing more than your home is worth – just as your PCS orders arrive.

The following example highlights the effect of a typical home's mortgage interest deduction on a homebuyer's cash flow. The example's outputs come from the mortgage tax deduction calculator at the "Bankrate.com" website at http://www.bankrate.com/calculators/mortgages/loan-tax-deduction-calculator.aspx.

Example: Mortgage deduction versus standard deduction.

Situation

A SM wants to buy a home and wants to take 30 years to do it. He wants to know which option will give him more tax savings: buying or renting.

Inputs

1. Home's selling price is $300,000.

2. Minimum down payment to avoid paying Private Mortgage Insurance (PMI) is 20% X $300,000 = $60,000 [see Note 1, below].

3. Mortgage is $300,000 selling price – $60,000 down payment = $240,000.

4. Term that SM chooses to pay off his mortgage is 30 years.

5. Interest Rate for 30-year mortgage is 4.5% [Note 2].

6. Combined Taxes are 31% [Note 3].

7. Closing Costs are $3200 [Note 4].

8. Standard Deduction, if SM decides to rent is $11,900.

Outputs (for the buyer's first year of mortgage payments)

1. Monthly mortgage payment is $893.40 interest + $322.64 principal = $1216.04.

2. Total interest paid is $893.40 interest X 12 months = $10,720.79.

3. Home interest deduction equals the $10,720.79 in total interest paid [Note 5].

4. Tax savings for the SM's first year of home ownership are 31% combined taxes X $10,720.79 home interest deduction = $3323.44.

5. Average annual tax savings over the 30-year life of the SM's mortgage are $2043.71.

6. Tax savings, if SM decides to rent are $11,900 standard deduction X 31% = $3689.00.

Analysis

In this example, the tax savings from the home's mortgage interest deduction for the first year are actually $3689.00 – $3323.44 = $365.56 less than the tax savings from the standard deduction. Over the full 30-year term of the loan, the SM's tax savings will average $3689 – $2043.71 = $1645.29 less than what the SM would enjoy with the standard deduction. For the first year, the SM has a negative cash flow of $1216.04 monthly mortgage payment X 12 months = $14,592.48. If he rents a place for, say, $1200 per month, his negative cash flow would become $1200 monthly rental payment X 12 months = $14,400. Renting a place would allow him to keep $14,592.48 – $14,400 = $192.48 more than buying a home. Therefore, if the SM decides to rent, his total cash savings for the year will be $365.56 + $192.48 = $558.04 more than if he buys a home.

While this example appears to favor renting over buying, a more equitable assessment would account for a buyer's other itemized deductions. The addition of the buyer's other itemized deductions to the buyer's home mortgage interest deduction would increase the tax savings associated with buying a home. Nonetheless, this example should illuminate the fact that, by itself, the mortgage interest deduction will not necessarily justify purchasing a home. This is all the more true if a reasonable chance exists that the home's value will depreciate over the three years that a SM is likely to own it. The combined effects of lost equity and sales expenses will annihilate any tax savings that the mortgage interest deduction might have produced.

Note 1

PMI is a special, added insurance expense. It hits buyers who use conventional loans and finance more than 80% of their homes' prices. However, SMs have access to Veterans' Administration (VA) loans. VA loans enable SMs to avoid PMI, even if SMs finance 100% of a home's price.

Note 2

Interest rates in the summer of 2012 have been even lower than 4.5% for a 30-year mortgage. Nonetheless, I chose to use a rate for my example that is closer to what I expect rates to eventually be.

Note 3

The 31% figure assumes the SM is in a 25% federal income tax bracket and that he pays 8% state income taxes. The 31% figure accounts for the deduction of those state income taxes from his federal income taxes.

Note 4

The $3200 amount assumes a 1% origination fee plus $800 in filing fees. I have assumed that the SM will not pay for any "Discount Points". Each Discount Point costs another 1% of the loan. The advantage of Discount Points is that they slightly reduce mortgage interest rates. However, the SM will probably PCS in three years. Three years is not enough time to benefit from the purchase of a Discount Point. Discount Points usually lower your interest rate by only about .125%[xi]. This amount would change the SM's interest rate to 4.5% – .125% = 4.375%. To get this 4.375% rate, the SM would pay an additional 1% X $240,000 = $2400 to the bank. That $2400 would be in addition to his original $3200 closing costs and his $60,000 down payment. Discount Points will rarely make sense for SMs. SMs PCS too quickly to recoup the prices of points. In this example, if the SM paid another $2400 to lower his interest rate to 4.375%, his monthly payment would drop from $1216.04 to $1198.28. Unfortunately, recouping this $17.76 per month difference would require the SM to keep his home for at least $2400 / $17.76 = 135 months, or 11.25 years.

Note 5

      For tax reporting purposes, the SM's home mortgage interest deduction is only the cumulative interest that he paid for the year. The deduction does not include the portions of his mortgage payments that covered his equity. The SM's home mortgage interest deduction will become less, each year, as his monthly payments include larger portions of equity and smaller portions of interest. While his increasing equity is good, the SM's tax savings will shrink. Mortgage lenders want their interest as soon as possible. As such, they structure loan agreements to weight the majority of a borrower's early mortgage payments toward the lender's interest. Toward the latter years of a home's term of ownership, the Standard Deduction will become larger than the home's mortgage interest deduction.

Full Cost of Home Ownership

      In the above scenario, the SM's tax savings from the standard deduction and his monthly rental savings would put $558.04 more in his pocket each year, relative to accepting a mortgage. The SM might well regard this figure as insignificant and decide that buying a home is still preferable to renting. However, the SM has more analysis to do. Thus far, we have only discussed the home's mortgage payment. Our mortgage payment included only the principal and interest. Other costs exist. Homeowners must also pay for taxes and insurance. We refer to a home's principal, interest, taxes, and insurance as the home's "PITI". Coupling the PITI with a home's fluctuating, yet inevitable maintenance costs gives a better estimate of what a SM's full cash outflow will be, when owning a home. Yet another cost that can reduce a homeowner's cash flow is Private Mortgage Insurance (PMI). Lastly, utilities add costs, but utility costs exist for both buying and renting. As such, I will ignore them, in this section.

Property Taxes

Property taxes are a persistent threat to home ownership. Unlike your mortgage that will someday amortize (die), local governments will tax your home, forever. To make matters worse, local governments will gradually increase your home's property taxes. Property taxes vary from state-to-state, from county-to-county, and even from town-to-town. Most homes will suffer a property tax of somewhere between 1% and 2% of the homes' appraised values. However, higher rates exist, and the locations for some of these higher rates may surprise you.

States that do not charge income taxes are popular among SMs. However, SMs should evaluate a prospective state's total tax burden, before settling in that state. All states must pay their bills. Doing so forces states to levy taxes in one place or another. If a state charges no income taxes, the state is almost certain to compensate by charging a high tax on something else. Property taxes are a common choice.

Insurance

Insurance costs are more predictable. Insurance typically costs around half a percent of the home's price.

Maintenance

Maintenance costs are impossible to predict. You have no way of knowing when your pipes will break. The rule of thumb is to assume that routine maintenance will cost 1% of your home's value, per year, for a new home. An older home will cost more.

Private Mortgage Insurance (PMI)

PMI is an additional insurance payment that lenders will require from buyers who borrow more than 80% of a home's purchase price. For example, if a buyer could only manage a down payment of 10% of a home's price ($30,000 in our examples), then a typical PMI calculation might be (0.5% / 12 months) X $270,000 mortgage = $112.50 per month. The greater the percentage borrowed, the greater the PMI. PMI calculations vary, depending on the lender. Whatever the calculation, the borrower must pay PMI to the lender until the ratio of the borrower's remaining mortgage balance to the home's appraised value is 80% or less.

To avoid paying PMI, a buyer must make a full 20% down payment on the home. Of course, the buyer must also cover his closing costs. In our mortgage deduction example, the buyer would have to pay at least $60,000 down payment + $3200 closing costs = $63,200 to avoid PMI payments.

PMI payments apply to conventional loans, only. An alternative to paying PMI that is available to SMs is using Veterans' Administration (VA) loans. VA loans allow SMs to purchase homes with little or no down payment. Nonetheless, VA loans carry pitfalls of their own.

Example: Full cost of home ownership.

Situation

A SM wants to purchase a $300,000 home. The property tax rate in his home's location is 1.4%. The home is less than 5 years old. He wants to know what his true costs will be.

Assumptions

1. Property tax liabilities are 1.4% X $300,000 appraised value = $4200 per year ($350 per month).

2. Insurance costs are 0.5% X $300,000 appraised value = $1500 per year ($125 per month).

3. Maintenance costs are 1% X $300,000 appraised value = $3000 per year ($250 per month).

4. PMI cost is 0. A SM who cannot meet the 20% minimum down payment will simply use a "zero-money-down" VA loan. Nonetheless, VA loans inflict "VA Funding Fees" on SMs. These fees can add anywhere from 1.25% to 3.3% of a home's mortgage to a SM's closing costs. If the SM in this example uses a VA loan but cannot pay the full VA Funding Fee upon closing, the SM will have to roll the VA Funding Fee into his mortgage. That will actually increase the "Principal and Interest" costs shown below. For this example, I am assuming that the SM pays the full VA Funding Fee upon closing.

5. Including utility costs is not necessary. Both homeowners and renters will pay roughly similar costs.

Total monthly cost of home ownership:

Item	Cost
Principal and Interest	1216
Taxes	350
Insurance	125
Maintenance	250
PMI	0
Total	$1941

Analysis

The SM's total monthly cost for owning the home would be $1941. Per year, the SM must produce $23,292 to pay for his home.

Unless the SM had a clear vision of the effects that his home's appreciation would have on his finances, buying the home might not be in his best interest. That clear vision must include knowledge of how many years the SM will remain in his home and knowledge of whether his home's value will appreciate. Such sites as www.zillow.com and www.trulia.com can help you determine if a home is likely to appreciate or depreciate. A local, licensed realtor can also provide such information, but keep in mind that the realtor's agenda is to sell homes. If the SM will be able to hold the home for many years and the home will steadily appreciate, then purchasing the home might be okay. Barring such knowledge, the SM might be wiser to rent.

Although I excluded the costs of utilities, some rental agreements will actually include the costs of various utilities in the rent payment. This possibility could add another advantage to renting.

Veterans' Administration Loans and Funding Fees

When making a down payment is impossible, SMs can use a Veterans' Administration (VA) loan. Eligible SMs can get a home mortgage through the Veterans' Administration with zero money down. Zero-money-down VA loans enable SMs to avoid paying for PMI. A VA loan is a good tool for military families to quickly obtain a home. Nonetheless, while SMs will quickly get a home with zero money down, they will pay for that privilege.

For SMs wishing to use VA loans, the VA can guarantee up to 25% of a housing loan, provided the entire loan does not exceed $417,000[xii]. Thus, SMs who meet the VA's eligibility criteria might qualify for up to $104,250 in loan guarantees. These guarantees serve the same purpose as 20% down payments and thus eliminate the need for SMs to pay for PMI. Private lenders actually craft the VA loan arrangements. The VA's loan guarantees protect lenders from financial disasters in which SMs fail to repay their loans.

Using a zero-money-down VA loan is tempting, but this choice has a drawback. VA loans charge "VA Funding Fees". These fees are unique to VA loans. The purpose of these fees is to reimburse America's taxpayers for the costs of the VA loan program. These fees range from a high of 3.3% to a low of 1.25% of the loan amount. Second time VA loan users who put zero money down suffer the highest fee of 3.3%. First time VA loan users who put zero money down suffer a 2.15% fee. Both second time and first time VA loan users who make down payments of at least 5% but less than 10% suffer a fee of only 1.5%. To enjoy the lowest 1.25% fee, second time and first time VA loan users must put down 10% or more. Possessing a qualified disability rating – something that most active duty SMs will not have – is the only means for eliminating the VA Funding Fee. VA Funding Fees are in addition to all of a SM's other closing costs and realtor's fees. The SM can pay the VA Funding Fee in full, at closing. Alternatively, the SM can simply roll the fee into his loan. Beware that the latter option will increase the SM's interest payments.

For 30-year terms, mortgage interest rates for VA loans are about 0.25% lower than conventional loans' 30-year rates. On the other hand, VA loans' rates for 15-year terms are often higher than conventional loans' 15-year rates. Conventional loans are actually better choices for SMs who can afford 20% or more down payments and can afford the monthly PITI for 15-year terms.

What should be evident is that the purpose of a VA loan is not necessarily to provide SMs with great deals on homes. VA loans are more for the purpose of enabling SMs to get into homes, quickly. The Government does not want its redeploying veterans living on the streets. VA loans offer SMs the ability to purchase homes with minimal cash. Nonetheless, SMs should be aware that VA loans offer shelter at a cost.

Mortgage Terms

When using a mortgage to buy a home, you must choose how many years you will take to pay off that mortgage. The term that you choose affects the size of your mortgage interest rate. As the term lengthens, your rate increases. The most commonly chosen terms are 15 years and 30 years. Choosing a 15-year term to pay off your mortgage will force you to make larger monthly payments but will result in your paying substantially less interest, overall. Choosing a 30-year term to pay off your mortgage will enable you to enjoy smaller monthly payments but will result in your paying substantially more interest, overall. If your positive monthly cash flow is strong enough to absorb the larger monthly payments, then choosing a 15-year term is usually the better choice.

Interest rates for 15-year terms are normally between one half and one full percentage point lower than interest rates for 30-year terms. Other terms do exist. Terms as short as 10 years are available, and terms as long as 40 years are available. Whether choosing these less common terms makes sense depends on your particular situation. Paying less interest over the life of a loan is always appealing. However, the shorter the term, the greater will be the monthly payment. Increasing your monthly negative cash flow might endanger your ability to cover your other expenses.

Extending your term beyond 30 years rarely makes sense. A SM will pay more in interest, alone, than the original price of his home. Additionally, the SM might stay in debt until his 80s. A poor plan is one that assumes you will be able to make mortgage payments well into your full retirement. True, the smaller monthly payments that a lengthy term permits will enable a more positive cash flow. The SM might be able to shrewdly invest the relative savings. Nonetheless, no guarantee exists that the performance of the SM's investments will, indeed, surpass the size of the SM's total interest payments. The only guarantee is that the lending institution will get its interest from the SM, or the lending institution will get the SM's home.

Example: 15-year term mortgage versus 30-year term mortgage.

Situation

A SM wishes to know the total quantity of interest that he will pay with either a 15-year term or a 30-year term. This example uses the "Mortgage Comparison: 15 years vs. 30 years" calculator at http://www.dinkytown.net/java/MortgageCompare.html.

Calculations

1. Mortgage Amount = $240,000

2. 15-year Loan

    a. Rate = 3.75%

    b. Monthly payment = $1745

  c. Total interest paid over life of loan = $74,160

 3. 30-year Loan

   a. Rate = 4.5%

   b. Monthly payment = $1216

   c. Total interest paid over life of loan = $197,778

Analysis

  Taking 15 years to pay his $240,000 mortgage forces the SM to make monthly payments of $1745. However, his mortgage interest rate will be lower than the rate that he will get for a 30-year term. The lower rate and the shorter term will result in his paying only $74,160 in interest, over the life of the loan.

  On the other hand, taking 30 years to pay his $240,000 mortgage enables the SM to make monthly payments of only $1216. These lower payments come at a cost. The SM will pay $197,778 in interest, over the life of the loan. Due to the effects of compounding, the overall interest charges on a 30-year loan are more than double the overall interest charges on a 15-year loan. In both cases, the total interest charges will be in addition to the SM's $240,000 in principal payments.

Conclusion

  The monthly payment for the 15-year term is nearly 44% more than the monthly payment for the 30-year term. Nonetheless, if the SM's cash flow can safely absorb this increase, paying less than half the total interest and amortizing the loan prior to the SM's full retirement age normally make his choosing a 15-year loan the wiser move.

Part III

SITUATION
(FRIENDLY FORCES)

This section of the OPORD discusses tools that can assist you in the pursuit of your mission.

Chapter 7: Income

Your income is the money that your various pursuits bring into your hands. This money can come from a variety of sources, such as your employment, your cash producing assets, or your investments in fixed income instruments.

The difference between your income and your expenses is your cash flow. Most of us will calculate our cash flow on a per month basis. If your income exceeds your expenses, you will have a positive cash flow (in flow) and will accumulate wealth. If your expenses exceed your income, you will have a negative cash flow (out flow) and will accumulate debt.

Expenses can be either obligatory or discretionary. Obligatory expenses are the bills that enable you to keep your home, your car, and your insurance. Discretionary expenses are the bills that enable you to enjoy cable TV, to provide unlimited texting for your children, and to dine out. You must pay both types of bills, but you can avoid the items that generate the discretionary bills. The absence of these items will not "put you on the street".

Secondary Income

Online businesses, multi-level marketing (MLM) operations, and rental properties are typical sources of secondary income for SMs. Such operations often require substantial investments of time and effort. Identifying a target market, developing a web portal, ensuring secure payment methods, responding to buy-and-sell alerts, and shipping goods to customers can turn online businesses into full-time jobs. Directly marketing your products, developing and servicing customer bases, shipping and returning products, and recruiting and training down-line distributors can make MLM operations intensive propositions. Researching where the best rental properties lie, negotiating the purchase prices, screening tenants, establishing payment mechanisms, collecting rents, evicting deadbeats, and maintaining the properties are among the many items that can make being a landlord quite laborious. Nonetheless, for all of their requirements of your time and effort, such secondary sources of income can improve your financial security.

Online businesses are often home-based. This fact enables you to take tax deductions for some of the space, power, and equipment that you use in your home, in connection with these ventures. Online businesses allow you to work from your living room, while possessing the power of the World Wide Web to research demographics and globally market your products. The availability of virtually free desktop video conferencing tools offers the option to conduct instantaneous face-to-face meetings in real time with nearly anyone on the planet.

MLM operations offer the advantages of franchising for virtually insignificant investments. Unfortunately, well-known franchises, such as McDonald's, require astronomically large investments. In contrast, MLM operations rarely cost more than a few hundred bucks. A franchise is a successful business that benefits from others' purchasing the right to copy that business. The owner of the original business is the "franchisor". The owners of the copies are "franchisees". The franchisor accrues royalties from the successes of the franchisees. This is a fair deal for both parties. The franchisees owe their successes to the proven business model that the franchisor shared with them.

Rental properties are expensive but can, indeed, produce income. Besides the obvious advantage of your tenants' monthly payments' increasing your monthly cash flow, rental properties offer several other advantages. Tax breaks for depreciation, tenants' amortizing your properties' mortgages, and appreciation of your properties' values can make rental properties profitable.

Nonetheless, SMs should be aware that obtaining rental properties can require very large amounts of money. Using most of your money to purchase a rental property can tie your financial fortunes to this single asset class. If this asset class suffers extended, adverse economic conditions, your net worth will suffer.

Assets

Items that generate positive cash flows are assets. Items that do not generate positive cash flows but do appreciate in value can also be assets, provided that their liquidation does not decrease your quality of life. As stated earlier, bass boats are not assets. They cost money to maintain, and their values depreciate after purchase. A home is not necessarily an asset, either. A home's value might appreciate, but selling the home forces you to buy another one.

Collectibles that you might sell at an on-line auction for more than you paid to acquire them are, indeed, assets. Military families' frequent overseas assignments give them opportunities to acquire many items that could sell for sizable gains in the U.S. Of course, this assumes that such families are not paying substantial warehousing fees to store their collectibles and that the weight of their collectibles is not throwing these families over their limits for PCS moves, thus forcing them to pay penalties.

Savings Deposit Program (SDP)

The SDP is an income instrument that is unique to the military. SMs who are serving in designated combat zones can use the SDP. Upon reaching a theater, SMs can go to the nearest finance office and deposit up to $10,000 in the SDP. SMs can contribute this money by allotment, check, or cash. Deposits in the SDP will earn a guaranteed 10% per year, with 2.5% coming each quarter. The best financial wizards in the country would take this deal. Mathematically, if a SM could get all $10,000 into the SDP on the first day of a one year deployment and kept that money in the SDP for the full year plus the 90 days on top of that year that the rules allow, the SM would earn $1250 in interest income.

Getting to the full $10,000 will require a few months for most SMs. The rules prohibit depositing more than a month's base pay, per month. However, the dollars that SMs contribute to the SDP can come from anywhere. If you are deploying and you have money languishing in a checking account or low interest earning savings account, put those dollars in the SDP. The quantity of those dollars may not exceed your base pay, but that does not mean that those dollars must come *from* your base pay. Contact your local military pay office about the SDP's details, as soon as you learn that you are deploying.

Chapter 8: Thrift Savings Plan (TSP)

The Government's TSP is similar to civilian employers' 401(k) plans. The TSP and 401(k) plans are saving and investment plans that offer tax advantages to SMs and civilians who contribute to these plans. We call these plans "defined contribution" plans. SMs and civilians can contribute dollar amounts to these plans, up to the IRS-defined limits for a given year. These contributions will go into baskets of investments (commonly mutual funds) that the Government and civilian employers establish. The sums of the SMs' or civilians' contributions and the growths of these contributions will determine the sizes of the retirement incomes that the TSP and 401(k) plans will produce.

With defined contribution plans, all investment risks lie on the shoulders of the employees (the SMs and civilians). The employees must choose their own investments within the baskets of funds that that the TSP and 401(k) plans offer. If the employees choose poorly, the employees will suffer poor returns. In contrast to defined contribution plans, your military pension is a "defined benefit" plan in which the Government assumes all investment risk. Depending on your rank and your years of service, you know exactly what your retirement income will be. The Government, not you, must worry about how to ensure that the plan will possess enough money to pay your monthly checks.

Both Traditional and Roth versions of the TSP and 401(k) plans exist. The primary difference between the two versions is when you must pay taxes on your contributions. With Traditional versions, your contributions grow tax-deferred. You do not pay taxes on your contributions until you withdraw them. With Roth versions, you pay the taxes before you contribute your money, but your money grows tax-exempt. The IRS limits the annual amount that you can contribute to these plans. You may contribute to both plans, but your total cannot exceed the IRS' limit. For 2013, the limit will be $17,500, per Internal Revenue Code (IRC) Section 402(g).

The TSP and 401(k) plans are long-term investment tools. You may not withdraw money from a TSP or 401(k) investment until you are 59.5 years old. If you do pull money out of a TSP or 401(k) before you are 59.5 years old, you will pay a 10% penalty plus ordinary income taxes.

On the other hand, once you reach 70.5 years old, the IRS forces you to take Required Minimum Distributions (RMDs) from both traditional and Roth versions of TSP and 401(k) plans. You may not leave all of your money in these accounts, forever. Actuarial data and the size of your account will dictate the precise size of the RMDs that you must take. For Traditional TSP and Traditional 401(k) accounts, you must pay taxes on the amount of the RMD for that year. For Roth versions of these accounts, taking the RMD does not create a taxable event, but you must still take the RMD. This requirement is due to the IRS' rules that govern employer-sponsored retirement plans. Nonetheless, you can legally overcome this requirement by rolling your entire Roth TSP balance into a Roth Individual Retirement Account (IRA), prior to the year that you turn 70 years old.

Unlike many 401(k) plans that civilian employers provide, the Government's TSP allows you to take RMDs and then leave the remainder of your money in your TSP account. Many 401(k) plans force employees to remove their entire balances, no later than when the employees turn 70.5 years old. In the case of a Traditional 401(k), specifically, simply taking a check for the entire balance can result in a massive tax hit.

Fortunately, rather than dumping single, massive checks into taxable bank accounts, civilian employees can transfer the balances of their 401(k) accounts into Rollover IRAs that brokerages offer. Transfers of tax advantaged account balances to Rollover IRAs are not taxable events, provided the transfers take less than 60 days to complete. However, Rollover IRA account holders must still take annual RMDs, once they turn 70.5 years old. The amounts in these eventual RMDs are, indeed, taxable. Nonetheless, the account holders will avoid the pain of immediately paying taxes on their entire Traditional 401(k) balances. Another benefit of the Rollover IRA option is that brokerages might offer investment choices that are better than the choices in the civilian employers' 401(k) plans.

Traditional TSP and Traditional 401(k) Plans

Traditional TSP and Traditional 401(k) plans reduce your taxable income by the amounts that you contribute. To illustrate the advantage of reducing your taxable income, assume that you will be in the 25% tax bracket in 2013 and that you will contribute the full $17,500 for that year to a Traditional TSP. If so, you will retain the use of 25% X $17,500 = $4375 that you would have otherwise given to the Government in taxes. This is a good deal.

Traditional TSP and Traditional 401(k) plans allow your contributions to enjoy tax-deferred growth. Must you ever pay taxes on your Traditional TSP and Traditional 401(k) contributions? Yes, but you will not pay these taxes until you withdraw your contributions. When you do, you will pay ordinary federal income taxes on both the principal (what you contributed) and on the growth of that principal. Nonetheless, the date when you pay will be many years in the future. During those years, your contributions will grow, free of taxes. After a decade or two of compounding, deferring taxes on the principal that you contribute and on the growth of that principal can profoundly improve your returns.

If you are in a lower tax bracket when you eventually withdraw money from a Traditional TSP or Traditional 401(k) balance, then you will enjoy a third advantage. You will pay taxes on your withdrawals at a lower ordinary federal income tax rate, rather than at the higher ordinary federal income tax rate that you would have paid when you first earned the money.

Roth TSP and Roth 401(k) Plans

In contrast to traditional versions, Roth TSP and Roth 401(k) plans allow you to contribute dollars on which you have already paid federal income taxes. The Roth versions do not lower your taxable income. The advantage of the Roth versions is that your contributions grow tax-exempt. You will pay no more taxes on your contributions (your principal), and you will never pay taxes on the growths of your contributions, at all.

This is a fantastic deal for SMs. Many SMs will find themselves in relatively higher tax brackets, later in life. Our active duty paychecks enjoy so many tax advantages that we make healthy incomes, yet qualify for lower tax brackets. Those advantages end, once we leave the military. The Roth TSP enables SMs to pay lower taxes, today, and zero taxes, in the future. The tax-exemptions that Roth TSP and Roth 401(k) plans offer make these versions better choices for most SMs than the traditional versions. Nonetheless, personnel who are already in high income tax brackets can still make good use of Traditional TSP and Traditional 401(k) plans.

The Roth TSP is a very recent offering. For years, the Government only offered a Traditional TSP option to SMs. However, the Government began offering a Roth TSP to SMs in 2012. Unfortunately, as of the writing of this 3rd edition of "Win the Money War", the Roth TSP is not yet available to all services. Until your respective service receives the Roth TSP, continue using the Traditional TSP. Using the Traditional TSP is still an infinitely better choice than not investing, at all.

Matching Funds

Regardless of the version, if your TSP or 401(k) offers matching funds, then the benefit becomes even greater. Plans vary, but some plans match your contributions to as high as 5% of your salary. Thus, if you are making $60,000 per year and contribute $3000 to a 401(k) with a full 5% match, your employer will chip in an additional $3000 to your 401(k) for a total of $6000 for the year. That is a guaranteed 100% return on your investment. Surprisingly, of those who contribute to a TSP or 401(k), as many as 28% fail to contribute enough money to receive their employers' full matches[xiii]. These employees are forfeiting free money.

Fortunately, matching funds do not count against an employee's contribution limit. The IRS does not consider matching funds to be a part of your pay. Therefore, someone in the above scenario could annually amass a total of $17,500 contributions + $3000 matching funds = $20,500 in his or her TSP or 401(k).

Maximizing your TSP during Deployments

Returning to contribution limits, IRC Section 415(c) provides a tremendously powerful advantage to deployed SMs. For 2013, IRC Section 415(c) will enable SMs in a tax-exempt status (e.g. deployed to Iraq or Afghanistan) to contribute up to $51,000 to their TSP. This is a good deal for deployed SMs. Deployed SMs can nearly triple their yearly TSP contributions.

With various stipulations, the $51,000 limit applies to both Roth TSPs and Traditional TSPs. With respect to Roth TSPs, deployed SMs may contribute no more than $17,500 to a Roth TSP, specifically. The remaining $51,000 – $17,500 = $33,500 must go to a Traditional TSP. With respect to Traditional TSPs, SMs may contribute all $51,000 to a Traditional TSP. However, SMs may contribute no more than $17,500 of that $51,000 during months in which the SMs are still in a non-deployed (taxable) status. In almost every scenario, the Roth TSP will be the better choice for deployed SMs. Nonetheless, a few high income SMs may require the immediate tax breaks that a Traditional TSP can provide. Maximizing these tax breaks requires a bit of maneuvering.

Example: Traditional TSP contributions and deployments.

Situation

Assume that you are deploying and that you have determined that you need the immediate tax breaks that a Traditional TSP offers.

Calculations

If you knew on 31 December 2012 that you were deploying to Afghanistan on 1 July 2013, you could plan to contribute up to $2916 to your TSP each month from 1 January through 30 June 2013, while you were still at home in a taxable status. After you landed in Afghanistan on 1 July 2013, you would be able to contribute another $5583 each month from 1 July through 31 December 2013. For details on IRC Section 415(c), visit the TSP website's "Contribution Limits" section at https://www.tsp.gov/planparticipation/eligibility/contributionLimits.shtml.

Frankly, contributing these exact numbers is nearly impossible for most military families. The important point to glean is that IRC Section 415(c) enables aggressive savers in the military to contribute substantially more money to their TSP than IRC Section 402(g) permits. Making use of IRC Section 415(c), I was able to double my Traditional TSP contributions in 2006 and then again in 2007, since my Iraq deployment crossed into early 2007, as well.

You may wonder what the value was of contributing already tax-exempt dollars to a tax-deferred account. Indeed, I lost the advantage of reducing my taxable income, since my taxable income was already close to zero. What I gained was the ability to vastly increase my pot of money that was growing tax-deferred. I was able to add my tax-exempt dollars to a retirement fund – the TSP – that offers some of the lowest expenses in the mutual fund industry. The TSP funds' expense ratios for 2011 averaged a mere 0.025%[xiv]. This equates to 25 cents per year in costs for every $1000 that a SM has in TSP funds. Compare this to a typical mutual fund in the public sector with a quite good expense ratio of 0.25%. Such a fund would charge $2.50 per year for every $1000 that an investor had in the fund. Since SMs must put their tax-exempt dollars somewhere, why not put them in a fund that has 10 fold less costs and that offers tax-deferred growth?

Index Funds

The mutual funds that the Government's TSP offers are index mutual funds, or "index funds". Index funds aim to replicate, not to outperform, the returns of various market benchmarks. The "S&P 500 Index" is an example of such a benchmark. It tracks the performance of 500 large capitalization companies whose stocks are traded on the NYSE and the NASDAQ exchanges. Several investment companies offer "S&P 500 Index Funds". These index funds own the stocks of the companies that the S&P 500 Index tracks. Since index funds merely ape benchmarks, no market research by investment professionals is necessary. Not paying for market research reduces index funds' costs. Lower costs can lead to higher returns for you. The only drawback is that funds that lack market research do not seize opportunities to buy new, high quality securities or sell inappropriate securities.

Index funds maintain minimal cash reserves. This is good. Funds that maintain minimal cash reserves have more money invested in stocks. Funds that have more money invested in stocks produce better returns than funds that maintain large cash reserves. Since the indices that index funds track rarely add or drop companies from their lists, index funds rarely need to buy or sell stocks. All of an index fund's money simply remains in the stocks of the index that the fund replicates.

In contrast, some funds do hold large cash reserves. This trend is more prevalent in, but not exclusive to, managed mutual funds. Funds that maintain cash reserves do so by holding portions of the funds' dollars in easily liquidated vehicles (e.g. money market accounts). Money market accounts and other fixed income vehicles produce low rates of return. If a fund's managers keep too large of a percentage of that fund's dollars in cash reserves, the NAV of that fund's shares will drop.

Cash reserves enable fund managers to pay off fund holders who decide to liquidate their shares. Share liquidations happen more frequently in managed mutual funds. Managed mutual fund investors are more prone to move in and out of managed mutual funds in order to quickly capitalize on market trends. In contrast, index fund investors tend to be more focused on long-term gains. Index fund investors retain their index fund shares for many years.

Managers also use cash reserves to buy new stocks that the managers want to add to their funds' holdings. Such buys occur more frequently in managed mutual funds, because managed mutual fund managers attempt to quickly capitalize on new market offerings. Nonetheless, the buying and selling of underlying securities happens in index funds, as well. When indices change the securities they track, index funds must change the securities they hold.

Infrequent buying and selling of stocks minimizes turnover. Infrequent turnover is good. Every trade of a stock incurs a trading commission that all investors in a fund must cover. Additionally, every trade that enjoys a capital gain will incur a capital gains tax that all investors in a fund must cover, unless those investors are holding shares of this fund in a tax-advantaged account.

Index funds are reasonably good investment choices for SMs. Most SMs do not have large quantities of cash that they can spend on the extra fees associated with managed mutual funds. The prudent investing strategy for most SMs is to seek solid returns that exceed the rates of inflation and dollar devaluation. Analysts have written several articles stating that investors rarely succeed in consistently beating the market. Most investors will enjoy sufficient investment growth by simply matching the markets' returns.

Nonetheless, some investors may wish to pursue the potential gains that managed mutual funds offer. New markets occasionally emerge, forcing the development of new indices. New markets can contain thousands of companies around the world. Index funds that track the associated indices cannot reasonably own all of these companies' stocks. Instead, the index funds merely own representative samples of these stocks. Stocks not contained in these samples present opportunities for managed mutual funds. Managers of these funds are free to purchase such stocks; the managers are not tied to whatever stocks the associated indices hold. Due to that freedom, managed mutual fund investors can possess exposure to high quality stocks that index fund investors will not possess.

Chapter 9: Individual Retirement Accounts (IRAs)

Unlike the TSP and 401(k) plans that employers offer, IRAs are something that you establish, independently, through financial institutions. Two types of IRAs are available – Traditional IRAs and Roth IRAs. The primary difference between the two types is when you must pay taxes on your contributions.

For both the Traditional and Roth IRAs, annual contribution limits exist. For 2013, people who are less than 50 years old will be able to contribute up to $5500 per year to either type of IRA. People who are 50 years old or older will be able to contribute another $1000 for a total of $6500 per year. Contributions to IRAs must not exceed your taxable income – your "earned income". In other words, you must have earned at least as much as the amounts that you contribute. If you only earned $4000 in a year, $4000 is the most that you could contribute to an IRA for that year. However, if you are married and are filing a joint tax return, an exception to the earned income rule applies.

Your spouse can open an IRA, even if he or she has no earned income. You can cover your spouse's full $5500 contribution from your own earned income. Your spouse's IRA must be separate from your IRA, but one person can manage both accounts. Institutions that hold your family's IRAs can assist you with the paperwork necessary to make one person the manager of both IRAs. That person should probably be you.

Traditional IRAs

Similar to Traditional TSP and Traditional 401(k) contributions, Traditional IRA contributions lower your taxable income. You do not pay taxes on the money that you contribute to Traditional IRAs, or on the growth of that money, until you start withdrawing the money.

Traditional IRAs are tax-deferred investment tools. You enjoy postponing your taxes on the money that you contribute to a Traditional IRA for many years. During those years, you will enjoy compounded growth on investments that are larger than they would have been, had taxes reduced them. Nonetheless, you must pay taxes on your contributions and the growth of your contributions, someday. Those taxes will be at your ordinary federal income tax rate at the time you withdraw your money.

When investing in a Traditional IRA, you must pay a 10% penalty, on top of ordinary federal income taxes, if you withdraw your contributions or the growth of your contributions before you are 59.5 years old. On the other hand, the IRS forces you to start taking annual RMDs from a Traditional IRA, no later than 1 April of the year after you turn 70.5 years old. In that way, the IRS will finally get its taxes.

Roth IRAs

In contrast to Traditional IRAs, you do not contribute money to Roth IRAs until you have paid ordinary federal income taxes on that money. As such, Roth IRAs do not lower your taxable income. The advantage of Roth IRAs is that, upon withdrawal, you will pay no more taxes on the money that you have contributed, and you will never pay taxes on the growth of that money. Your contributions to Roth IRAs grow tax-exempt. Many years earlier, you will have paid taxes on your contributions, but you will not have paid, nor will you ever pay, taxes on the growth of your contributions. This is a decisive advantage, relative to Traditional IRAs.

A second advantage of Roth IRAs lies in how long you may leave your money in them. With respect to RMDs, Roth IRAs are not the same as the Roth TSP. No 70.5-year-old age limit exists for Roth IRAs. The IRS does not force you to take RMDs from Roth IRAs. This is another superb feature of Roth IRAs. Economic conditions may be poor when you are 70.5 years old. Being able to leave your money in your Roth IRA until that period passes will be good. You will be able to leave more money for your heirs.

A third advantage of the Roth IRA, relative to the Traditional IRA, is that you may withdraw the principal that you have contributed at any time – even before you are 59.5 years old – without a 10% penalty. This advantage applies solely to the principal, not to the growth of that principal. You may not withdraw the growth of that principal until you are 59.5 years old. Otherwise, you will suffer a 10% penalty and the requirement to pay taxes, after all.

While pulling principal from your Roth IRA is permissible, it is not advisable. Pulling money from your Roth IRA will stunt your Roth IRA's growth. Nonetheless, this advantage may prove to be a lifesaver, should you find yourself in an extreme financial crisis.

Exchange Traded Funds (ETFs)

Within IRAs, SMs have the opportunity to purchase Exchange Traded Funds (ETFs). ETFs are excellent investments. "Index" ETFs, specifically, resemble index funds. Index ETFs track one of the major indices (e.g. the S&P 500 Index). Like index funds, index ETFs hold stocks of the same companies as the index ETFs' associated indices. However, index ETFs differ from index funds due to the manner in which index ETF investors purchase shares.

For an index fund, investors buy and sell shares directly from the fund. The shares' price will equal the fund's NAV at 1600 hours, Eastern Standard Time, on the day that an investor submits his buy or sell order. The actual time that the investor submits his order is irrelevant.

In contrast, index ETF investors buy and sell index ETF shares on a stock exchange, just like individual stocks. Like the shares of an index fund, the price of an index ETF's shares will equal the aggregate value of the index ETF's underlying stock holdings. However, the index ETF investor need not wait until 1600 hours to see what that price will be. He will get the price of the index ETF's shares at very close to the moment that he submits his order. Occasionally, this timing can be crucial. I have seen my index funds' NAVs drop several points in a single day, due to some domestic or international disaster that became breaking news in the afternoon.

Each of an investor's investments in an ETF, be it a managed ETF or an index ETF, is literally a purchase of the ETF's shares on an exchange. Like individual stock purchases, ETF share purchases can incur trading costs. These trading costs can increase investors' expenses and thus lower the investors' returns. This fact is especially true for aggressive investors who trade ETF shares, throughout the day. It even hurts investors who purchase ETF shares at longer intervals, such as monthly. Until recently, these trading commissions made ETFs less cost effective than many index funds. Fortunately, more brokerages are now eliminating ETFs' trading costs. These brokerages are offering "commission free" ETF trades. As such, index ETFs from these brokerages offer cost savings that rival or even exceed index funds' cost savings.

With respect to tax efficiencies, index ETFs often exceed the cost savings of index funds. Like index funds, index ETFs already enjoy low rates of turnover. Minimal turnover results in the suffering of fewer capital gains taxes. Both index ETFs and index funds enjoy this tax advantage. However, index ETFs enjoy another tax advantage. An index ETF's structure enables investors to redeem their shares of the index ETF for the actual shares of the stocks that the index ETF holds, rather than for the face value of the shares. These "in-kind" exchanges cause no immediate capital gains tax liabilities for other shareholders. Although small-scale investors rarely, if ever, execute in-kind exchanges, large-scale investors often do execute such exchanges.

In contrast, index funds' redemptions by any of the funds' investors require immediate liquidations of the stocks that the index funds hold. These redemptions force immediate tax liabilities on all of the index funds' shareholders, regardless of whether those shareholders are redeeming any of their own shares of the index funds.

Index ETFs' low costs make them good choices for any account. Nonetheless, the tax efficiency of index ETFs makes index ETFs especially good choices for taxable accounts. To own ETFs, SMs must open brokerage accounts and agree to abide by Securities and Exchange Commission (SEC) rules. This is not a difficult process. Any brokerage will happily assist you.

Chapter 10: Social Security

Signed into law by President Roosevelt on 14 August 1935, Social Security has become a significant component of Americans' retirement calculations. Nonetheless, maintaining the viability of the Social Security system is a national challenge. The Social Security Online website explains that 159 million Americans work to pay the Social Security benefits that 55 million other Americans collect[xv]. Using these numbers, the ratio of paying Americans to benefitting Americans becomes 159 / 55 = 2.89 to 1. For every one American drawing Social Security benefits, less than three other Americans are working to generate those benefits. This ratio should make the Social Security Administration's (SSA's) candid announcement about the future of Social Security no surprise. Commissioner Michael J. Astrue issued the following warning:

> "In 2016, we will begin paying more in benefits than we collect in taxes. Without changes, by 2037, the Social Security Trust Fund will be exhausted, and there will be enough money to pay only about 76 cents for each dollar of scheduled benefits[xvi]."

In spite of this dire prediction, Social Security is unlikely to die, as some pessimists predict. The more likely result is exactly what the Commissioner said – that the Government will reduce the sizes of the benefits that future beneficiaries receive. Of course, other options exist. The Government could raise taxes on those 2.89 paying Americans, but raising taxes is rarely popular. The Government could eliminate Social Security and rely on each American to plan for his own retirement security. This option would please many high-income earners and might be the right answer for resolving many of the Government's long-term financial problems. Nonetheless, it would produce a near-term disaster for the post-World War II generations of poor to middle class Americans. These generations learned to spend. Many of them have no savings. Legions of destitute Americans camped in shanty towns outside of the Capitol is a nightmare that the Government can ill-afford to come true.

Intriguingly, the Government could enact some form of what President George W. Bush's administration proposed – privatization of a percentage of Social Security. Aside from greatly pleasing the financial industry, partial privatization of Social Security might rectify a large number of the Government's financial problems and might transition individual Americans into a future where they no longer rely on Social Security. However, given the public's evisceration of Bush's proposal, partial privatization of Social Security is unlikely to happen.

Lastly, the Government could change the current regressive FICA Social Security tax system into a flat or even progressive tax system. All employees, not simply those making less than $110,100, would pay 4.2% FICA Social Security taxes on their entire incomes. Of course, if the rate returns to 6.2%, then everyone would pay 6.2%. Since lawmakers and other well-compensated government officials benefit from our regressive FICA tax system, the implementation of a flat or progressive FICA Social Security tax is unlikely. We return to where we started – with acceptance of Commissioner Astrue's statement. We will get Social Security, but we may not get as much as we want.

Nonetheless, getting 76% of a benefit is far better than getting nothing. Though less than we desire, Social Security benefits of this size warrant analysis and planning. SMs should assume that they will, indeed, receive Social Security benefits, should realize that these benefits will comprise a significant component of their wealth, and should learn the options for maximizing these benefits. Of course, all of this "76%" stuff assumes the Government will do absolutely nothing over the next quarter century to resolve Social Security's problems. If the Government actually does do something, the size of our future Social Security benefits might be substantially larger.

Eligibility

Since SMs pay Social Security and Medicare taxes, SMs collect Social Security benefits, in addition to SMs' military pensions. Your LES lists these taxes in the "Deductions" column with "FICA" as part of the deductions' names. Once you begin drawing your Social Security benefits, the size of your monthly Social Security checks will depend on the average of your monthly earnings over the 35 years that you earned the most. This calculation encourages you to work more years than you might want. If you retire after your first 35 years of work, your 35 years might include years in which you were flipping burgers to get through college. These low-income years will bring down your average.

Additionally, you must earn at least 40 "credits" to be eligible for Social Security. You can earn up to four credits per year. As of 2013, every $1160 in wages or self-employment income that you generate will earn you one credit. After earning at least $4640 in a given year, you will get your four credits. You cannot get more credits in that year, regardless of how much more you earn. Meeting the 40-credit minimum can challenge military spouses. Frequent PCS moves limit these spouses' opportunities to work. Military families should stay abreast of where they stand with respect to this requirement. If spouses realize they are short some number of credits, they should execute part-time work and fully report the income.

I cannot tell you how large your particular Social Security checks will be. The average Social Security check at the start of 2012 was $1230 per month, or $14,760 per year[xvii]. While that is not a tremendous amount of money, the Government does index Social Security benefits to inflation. Each year, the size of your Social Security checks may increase, roughly in tandem with the Consumer Price Index (CPI).

Deciding When to Draw Your Benefits

Generally, you cannot start collecting Social Security benefits until you are at least 62 years and 1 month old. Subject to certain limitations, widows, widowers, disabled persons, and surviving parents can collect Social Security benefits, sooner. Aside from these exceptions, age 62 is the earliest age at which anyone with 40 credits can start collecting Social Security benefits. Although you are finally free to collect your Social Security benefits at age 62, you must carefully consider doing so. You have the option of waiting until your Normal Retirement Age (NRA) or later to start collecting your benefits. The longer you wait, the larger your Social Security checks will be.

All Americans have a NRA of sometime between ages 65 and 67. Your exact NRA depends on your date of birth. Those of us born after 1960 have a NRA of 67. I will use this latest NRA group for my examples, in this book. For those of you with earlier NRAs, the yearly percentages that the SSA uses to calculate your Social Security benefits will be somewhat different. However, the processes are similar.

Collecting your benefits before you reach your NRA is a costly decision. Social Security checks are considerably smaller for those who start drawing their benefits prior to their NRA. Drawing your benefits as early as age 62 will result in your receiving checks that are approximately 30% smaller than what you would have received at your NRA. Therefore, for SMs with a NRA of 67, Social Security checks will be about 6% smaller for each year before age 67 that they begin drawing their benefits.

Assuming no unique financial challenges exist, choosing to collect your Social Security benefits at your NRA is a better choice than collecting your benefits at an earlier age. Your checks will equal 100% of their stated NRA value. You will enjoy drawing these checks for many years. Collecting Social Security benefits at one's NRA is a reasonably good move that balances financial return with life expectancy.

However, postponing the receipt of your Social Security benefits until you are older than your NRA can be even more lucrative. Waiting until you are 70 years old to start collecting your Social Security benefits will result in your receiving checks that are

24% larger than the checks that you would have received at your NRA. Therefore, SMs with a NRA of 67 will receive Social Security checks that are 8% larger for each year after age 67 that they postpone drawing their benefits. Nonetheless, waiting any longer than age 70 to start collecting your Social Security benefits makes no sense. The increases stop at age 70.

[DISCLAIMER: Throughout this section on Social Security, I must individually refer to the members of a married couple. I will assume that the primary breadwinner is the husband. The purpose of these assumptions is purely to simplify the pronouns and thus improve the clarity of my points. I fully appreciate and respect the fact that many military couples' primary breadwinners will be the wives.]

Spousal Benefits

The Spousal Benefits concept recognizes homemakers' contributions to society. Homemakers receive no salaries for their work. As such, homemakers will often fail to qualify for Social Security benefits based on their work records. The Spousal Benefits rules enable homemakers to collect Social Security benefits based on percentages of their qualifying spouses' Social Security benefits. The primary stipulation is that the qualifying spouses must have already filed for their own Social Security benefits. The Spousal Benefits concept is certainly of great value to homemakers, but both members of a couple can claim Spousal Benefits. Married SMs who realize this fact can optimize their Social Security benefits.

To claim Spousal Benefits, a wife who does not qualify for Social Security benefits based on her record must wait until her husband files for his Social Security benefits. Once her husband files, the wife may claim Spousal Benefits, provided that she is at least 62 years old. Significantly, the SSA will calculate the size of the wife's Spousal Benefits based on her husband's full NRA Social Security benefits, regardless of whether her husband has already started drawing reduced benefits[xviii]. Therefore, even if the husband started collecting Social Security benefits prior to his age of 67, the amount that he started receiving will not dictate the size of the benefits that his wife will collect. Additionally, the wife's drawing Social Security benefits based on a percentage of her husband's NRA benefits will not reduce the size of the Social Security checks that her husband is receiving. The money for her checks will come from the SSA, not from her husband's checks.

The chart, below, shows what percentage of her husband's NRA benefits that the wife can draw.

Wife's Age	Spousal Benefits (% of husband's NRA benefits that wife can draw)
62	32.5
63	35.0
64	37.5
65	41.7
66	45.8
67+ (NRA)	50.0

A qualifying husband who waits until his NRA to collect his Social Security benefits wins a nice option for his non-qualifying wife and him. Provided that a qualifying husband is at least 67 years old, he can file for Social Security benefits but suspend the actual payment of those benefits. Predictably, the SSA refers to this tactic as, "Filing and suspending". A husband's Filing and Suspending enables his wife to finally start collecting Spousal Benefits, while he continues to accrue delayed retirement credits toward his own Social Security benefits.

If a wife does, indeed, qualify for Social Security benefits based on her record, her age will dictate which Social Security benefit she will receive, either the amount based on her work record or the amount based on a percentage of her husband's NRA benefit. If the wife is at least 62 years old but less than her NRA, the SSA will automatically send the wife the higher of the two amounts. If the wife is at her NRA or older, she has the power to choose. In certain scenarios, choosing the lower amount can prove more lucrative. She can choose to draw Social Security benefits based on a percentage of her husband's NRA benefit, while allowing her own Social Security benefits to sit in reserve and accrue delayed retirement credits. When she reaches 70 years old, she can revert to drawing her own benefits that are now 24% larger than what they would have been at her NRA. This option is available to both spouses, not merely the spouse who qualifies for the smaller Social Security checks.

Surviving Spouse Benefits

If you die before your NRA and before you start collecting your Social Security benefits, your spouse can collect between 71.5% and 100% of your NRA benefits. The exact percentage depends on your spouse's year of birth and the month and year that she starts drawing your benefits. If you die before you reach your NRA, your spouse cannot accrue delayed retirement credits toward your Social Security benefits. The most that she can get is 100% of your NRA benefits. Nonetheless, if you die after your NRA and you still have not drawn your benefits, your wife will collect 71.5% to 100% of whatever your enhanced benefits would have been. In this indirect way, your wife could draw more than your NRA benefits.

Surviving Spouse Benefits differ from Spousal Benefits. Spousal Benefits apply to couples in which both members are still alive. As such, the applicable percentages are smaller. Surviving Spouse Benefits apply to situations in which one member of the couple has died. As such, the applicable percentages are larger

If you have not started collecting your benefits and you die before your NRA, your spouse can qualify to collect 100% of the checks that you would have received at your NRA. However, if you start drawing your Social Security benefits early, the amount you draw will limit what your surviving spouse can draw. This is an important difference between Surviving Spouse Benefits and Spousal Benefits.

Assuming you have not started collecting your Social Security benefits, the amounts of your Social Security check that your widow can receive, after your early death, are as follows[xix]:

1. If she is at her NRA (67 for most readers), she can receive 100% of your benefits.

2. If she is at least 60 but less than her NRA, she can receive 71.5 – 99.7% of your benefits, depending on the exact year and month that she starts collecting your benefits.

3. If she is disabled and is between 50 and 59 years old, inclusive, she can receive 71.5% of your benefits.

4. If she is any age and is caring for a child who is under age 16, she can receive 75% of your benefits.

A tremendously important fact is that a surviving spouse can claim Surviving Spouse Benefits, while keeping the surviving spouse's own Social Security benefits in reserve. Those reserved benefits will not suffer any reductions and can even accrue delayed retirement credits. Therefore, if a widow qualified for Social Security benefits on her own record, she can claim Surviving Spouse Benefits as early as her own age of 60, while allowing her own Social Security benefits to sit in reserve. When the widow turns 70 years old, she will have the option to stop drawing Surviving Spouse Benefits and start drawing her own Social Security benefits. Her benefits will then be enhanced by their accrual of delayed retirement credits. By that time, her enhanced benefits might exceed the Surviving Spouse Benefits that she was drawing, based on her deceased husband's work record. This might well be the case, if the husband had started drawing his Social Security benefits prior to his NRA.

Life Expectancy

Be patient. The Government's desire has long been for you to start drawing your Social Security benefits as late as possible. Your reward for waiting as long as possible is larger Social Security checks. The Government's reward is more time for your premature death. The later you wait to collect your checks and the earlier you happen to expire, the less money the Government must pay you.

The emerging problem with this desire is that Americans are living much longer than they lived in 1935. Per the SSA's own "Life Expectancy Calculator" at http://www.socialsecurity.gov/cgi-bin/longevity.cgi, the life expectancy of a 40 year old male is roughly 81 years, and the life expectancy of a 40 year old female is roughly 84 years. These numbers are averages; roughly half of the American population will survive to even older ages. This is why the Government keeps pushing back the NRA. For example, Americans born before 1937 have a NRA of 65, while Americans born after 1960 have a NRA of 67. Americans' increasing longevity is adding trillions of dollars to the nation's overwhelming financial obligations.

This fact leads to a disturbingly enticing claim on the SSA's website. The site mentions that the total of the benefits that you receive will be roughly the same, regardless of whether you take those benefits at age 62 or at your NRA[xx]. The site bases this comment on the life expectancies for males and females and assumes that the sum of smaller checks over many years will roughly equal the sum of larger checks over fewer years. This may be true, if you die before reaching your life expectancy. However, the odds are 50/50 that you will live longer, and those are pretty decent odds. If you have already started collecting your benefits before your NRA, each year that you survive past your life expectancy will effectively reduce the yield of your Social Security benefits. Unless Social Security is all that stands between you and poverty, delay the receipt of your benefits until your NRA or even until age 70.

As already stated, choosing to accept your Social Security benefits before your NRA will limit what your surviving spouse will receive, in the event of your early death. Your spouse will only receive checks equivalent to what you chose to receive[xxi]. Had you been waiting until your NRA to start collecting your benefits, your premature death would not limit what your spouse could receive. Your spouse would receive checks equivalent to what you would have received at your NRA.

Taxation of Social Security

The Government can tax the same Social Security benefits that the Government sends to you. Fortunately, the IRS does not spring into action until your combined income reaches a certain level. Your combined income equals one-half of the Social Security benefits that you are receiving plus any other ordinary income that you are receiving. Examples of these other ordinary incomes are military pensions, interest income from fixed instruments, ordinary (unqualified) dividends, wages from post-retirement jobs, and profits from business ventures. Fortunately, the IRS continues to exclude capital gains and qualified dividends from your income.

Per the Social Security Online website, the IRS uses the following formula to determine your combined income[xxii]: Combined Income = Adjusted Gross Income + Nontaxable Interest + 1/2 of your Social Security Benefits. "Nontaxable" interest is interest received from instruments that would normally receive favorable tax treatment, such as municipal bonds. Municipal bonds are popular among retirees who are in high income tax brackets. Social Security recipients must include such interest when determining their combined incomes.

If you receive more ordinary income than simply your Social Security benefits, you must determine your combined income and then compare that result to the IRS' "base" figures. If your combined income exceeds one of the following base figures, you must pay taxes on your Social Security income:

Filing Status	If Combined Income is Between	Percent of Social Security Benefit to be Taxed	If Combined Income Exceeds	Percent of Social Security Benefit to be Taxed
Single	$25,000 - $34,000	50%	$34,001+	85%
Married Filing Jointly	$32,000 - $44,000	50%	$44,001+	85%
Married Filing Separately	Any amount	85%		

Income Cap

Know your enemy. Average Americans fear that attempts to alter Social Security are merely attempts by wealthy Americans to avoid paying Social Security taxes. To the extent that wealthy Americans would like to pay absolutely zero Social Security taxes, this fear may be valid. However, accepting that every American must pay at least some Social Security taxes, wealthy Americans are not as inclined to alter the existing Social Security system as poorer Americans might think.

Currently, the IRS cannot tax more than $110,100 of one's income for the purpose of Social Security. This cap means that wealthier Americans pay relatively less in Social Security taxes than other Americans. The majority of Americans should welcome Social Security tax reform. Extending a 4.2% or 6.2% flat FICA Social Security tax to all income levels would be an equitable solution to Social Security's problems.

Part IV

MISSION

This section of the OPORD is a single sentence that drives the entire show. All of our efforts will be in vain, if they fail to achieve the Mission. Our refined and formalized Mission statement defines the "who", "when", "what", "where", and "why" (i.e. the "5 Ws") of our operation.

Our Mission is as follows:

You (who) must immediately (when) direct your financial resources into devices (what) available through your employer and through brokerages (where) that will enable your financial resources to enjoy rates of growth that surpass the rates of inflation and dollar devaluation (why).

Part V

EXECUTION

The Situation sections enumerated the obstacles that hinder our pursuit of the Mission and the tools that are available to facilitate our pursuit of the Mission. The Mission defined what we must do, regardless of the obstacles or available tools. The Execution section will explain how we plan to overcome the obstacles and how we plan to capitalize on the tools in order to achieve our Mission.

The first four enemy forces were taxes, inflation, dollar devaluation, and the national debt. You can defer and reduce the bite of taxes by taking advantage of TSPs, 401(k) plans, and IRAs, but you cannot eliminate taxes, altogether. As for the other three enemy forces, you cannot eliminate them, at all. So, why did we discuss them? Because you must be aware of what is happening to the nation, and you must realize that you are, indeed, directly affected. You must understand the forces that are, right now, reducing your savings' purchasing power and arc, in turn, eroding your financial security. If you do not compensate for this erosion, you will add yourself to the nation's problems.

Inflation, dollar devaluation, and the national debt are synchronizing their fires to develop a crescendo of violence that threatens the economic stability of the entire nation. In 2006, Mr. Donald Trump and Mr. Robert Kiyosaki warned the nation about these threats and referred to them as "The Perfect Storm"[xxiii]. The disastrous economic events of 2008 to 2010 verified Trump and Kiyosaki's prescience. The July 2011 proposal by a Defense Business Board task force to make the current military retirement system similar to civilian retirement systems is evidence that the winds of that storm are now buffeting SMs[xxiv]. By executing the steps in this Execution section, you will position yourself and your family to survive this storm.

Chapter 11: Determine Your Household Cash Flow

Your first task is to calculate your family's monthly cash flow. Use the worksheets on the next three pages. Be conservative with your sources of income and liberal with your expenses. You must determine your total income, determine your total expenses, and subtract your total expenses from your total income. If the remainder is positive, you have excess income with which to build wealth. If the remainder is negative, you will accumulate debt. If you are accumulating debt, you must identify expenses that you can eliminate, or you must expand your income.

When listing your various incomes, use net income figures. With respect to a military salary, net income equals gross income minus deductions and allotments. As such, list your Net Pay Amount and your End of Month (EOM) Pay, not your Base Pay. When listing your expenses, list all of your expenses, not simply the ones that you are willing to cut. If you must estimate any expenses, err on the high side.

You may be paying for some items (e.g. life insurance) on a quarterly, semi-annual, or even annual basis. For the purposes of budgeting, convert these payments into monthly quantities. Do this by determining the total amount for the year that you pay for these items and then dividing that number by 12. For example, if you are paying $114 every quarter for life insurance, calculate the monthly quantity as follows: $114 X 4 quarters per year = $456 per year; $456 per year / 12 months = $38 per month.

Household Cash Flow Worksheets

INCOME:

1. Net Pay Amount (from LES): _____
2. EOM Pay (from LES): _____
3. Moonlighting net salary: _____
4. Spouse's net salary: _____
5. Home-based business profit: _____
6. Interest income (CDs, savings): _____
7. Un-reinvested stock dividends: _____
8. Rental property profit: _____
9. TDY trips: _____
10. Federal & state tax refunds: _____
11. Social Security checks: _____
12. Other: _____

Total Income: _____
(Add lines 1-12)

OBLIGATORY EXPENSES:

1. Mortgage/rent: _____
2. Property tax: _____
3. Homeowner's insurance: _____
4. Home maintenance: _____
5. PMI: _____
6. Homeowner's assoc. dues: _____
7. Garbage collection: _____
8. Basic lawn care (cut grass): _____
9. Water: _____
10. Gas: _____
11. Heating oil: _____
12. Electric: _____
13. Any taxes not withheld: _____
14. Life insurance (you): _____
15. Life insurance (spouse): _____
16. Extra dental insurance: _____
17. Drug co-payments: _____
18. Auto payments: _____

19. Auto insurance: _____
20. Auto license/registration: _____
21. Auto fuel: _____
22. Auto routine oil/lubricants: _____
23. Auto non-warranty repairs: _____
24. Tolls/parking/transit fees: _____
25. Phone (landline): _____
26. Cell phone(s): _____
27. Cable/DSL internet service: _____
28. Credit card #1 payment: _____
29. Credit card #2 payment: _____
30. STAR card payment: _____
31. Children's day care: _____
32. Children's school lunches: _____
33. Groceries: _____
34. Haircuts/cosmetics: _____
35. Clothing for work & school: _____
36. Other: _____
      Total Obligatory Expenses: _____
          (Add lines 1-36)

DISCRETIONARY EXPENSES:

1. Satellite/cable TV: _____
2. DVD/VCR rentals: _____
3. Excessive lawn care: _____
4. Lattes: _____
5. Eating out: _____
6. Charitable gifts/tithes: _____
7. Birthday gifts: _____
8. Holiday gifts: _____
9. Golf/hunting/fishing: _____
10. Typical shopping spree: _____
11. Kids' art/music lessons: _____
12. Disney Vacation or Cruise: _____
13. Tobacco: _____
14. Pets (food, medicine, vet): _____
15. Texting services: _____

16. Gadgets (e.g. iPads): _____
17. Pool/Boat/RV maintenance: _____
18. Time share dues: _____
19. Other: _____
   Total Discretionary Expenses: _____
          (Add lines 1-19)

CALCULATION OF SURPLUS OR
DEFICIT:
1. Total Income _____
2. – Total Obligatory Expenses _____
3. – Total Discretionary Expenses _____
              Surplus or Deficit: _____
          (Line 1 minus lines 2 & 3)

Eliminate Discretionary Expenses

If the subtraction of your expenses from your income
produces a deficit (i.e. your expenses are greater than your income),
then you must eliminate as many Discretionary Expenses as
possible. Being "in the red" forces you to be merciless in your cuts.
Nonetheless, not all of these cuts may be permanent. Once you are
"in the black", your new cash flow habits may permit you to safely
resume your pursuit of some of these discretionary expenses.

You can replace a few discretionary expenses with nearly
equal quality, yet far less expensive alternatives:

1. Cable/satellite TV is easy to cut and will save you $50 – $80
    per month. Antenna TV is free, and you may get nearly 20
    channels – a far cry from the 4 channels we got as kids.
    Furthermore, many channels are available on the internet,
    assuming you can afford to maintain a high-speed internet
    connection.

2. Cutting DVD and VCR rental fees should be easy. Internet
    sites such as "Hulu.com" offer hundreds of movies and even
    complete TV series that you can watch on your home

computer. With the right connection, you can even port these shows from your computer to your TV. The major broadcasting networks also offer much of their daily TV fare (e.g. soap operas) via the internet.

3. Lawn care is another easy one. When financial times are difficult, mowing is enough. Flowers and fountains are not necessary.

4. Your daily latte costs about four bucks. $4 per latte X 5 work days per week X 45 work weeks = $900 per year for fancy coffees. To arrive at 45 weeks, I subtracted 4 weeks for your annual use-or-lose leave, 2 weeks for Christmas and Thanksgiving, and 1 week for good measure. Okay, so maybe you really do only buy one latte per week, the annual cost is still roughly $180. Compare that to a 33.9 ounce container of Maxwell House coffee that costs $9.00 at the Commissary and makes 270 six ounce cups of coffee. That $9.00 will satisfy your thirst for an entire year's worth of workdays. Even if you are a "Grande" person, that 33.9-ounce container will give you nearly 68 mugs of 24-ounce coffees. If you are "in the red", this is not a nitpicky cut. You can save your family several hundred dollars and enjoy essentially the same product. Choosing not to do so is self-indulgent. I do not represent Maxwell House.

5. Eating out may be your biggest discretionary expense for which a far cheaper alternative exists. Eating out is an expensive habit. Buying groceries also costs money. However, when eating out, you are paying for the groceries that the restaurateur bought at commercial rates, not at your tax-free Commissary rates. You are paying for the labor to cook the groceries, the labor to serve the finished meals, the tips for that labor, the utilities and rent for the facility in which to eat the meals, the profit that the restaurateur tacks onto the price of those meals, and the taxes on that profit. You are also paying for the fuel and for the wear and tear on your car that you used to get to the restaurant. Eat at home and bring your lunch to work. You will save money, and

you will spend less time in traffic. You will also stand a better chance of making weight at the next fitness test.

6. Tithing is a touchy subject. If your beliefs demand it, so be it. Just remember that 10% or even 5% of your gross income is a lot of money. How about volunteering 10% of your off-duty time, instead?

7. Gifts are hard for anyone but Ebenezer Scrooge to avoid giving. Nonetheless, remember the purpose of gift giving – to show your appreciation and love, not to ensure your kids have the latest gaming consoles. As with tithing, consider giving your time. Another option is to develop a business and then give gifts from your business. This approach affords you the opportunity to give gifts purchased at wholesale (cheaper) prices. It increases your total business volume, as well.

8. My wife has shown me that a shopping spree is to a woman what a round of golf is to a man – a time for sheer joy. However, both genders must look for cheaper paths to bliss. To reduce shopping sprees' costs, use consignment shops, internet auction sites, and discount software dealers. Recent economic woes have led to an increasing market for these vendors' used goods. Many of these goods have barely a scratch on them. As for golf, forego the off-post clubs and look for reduced rate periods (e.g. Sundays after 1600 hours) at the on-post and on-base courses. Walk the course, rather than rent a cart. You will save money, and you will further improve your odds of making weight at your next fitness test.

9. Your family's annual tributes to the Big Mouse's syndicate are not necessary. The true purpose of a vacation is to reconstitute your energy and to reconnect with loved ones. These purposes are all the more imperative for SMs. The modern "staycation" fulfills these purposes with lower costs and with fewer hassles. Many posts and bases possess an MWR travel office where military families can get ideas for

and even discounts on local entertainment. A day spent at the local amusement park will amply thrill and exhaust the kids and will cost a fraction of the total cost of a trip to Orlando. My family's Disney Cruise tickets were $2500, but the total price tag for those 3 days exceeded $4000. Flights, rental cars, hotel rooms, tips, and seaside restaurants resulted in my suffering the financial equivalent of a daisy-chained IED.

You must eliminate other types of discretionary expenses, altogether.

1. Want an instant $2000 per year raise? Quit smoking. Health dangers aside, think of what a pack per day is doing to your finances. Assuming an average cost of $5.00 per pack, smoking costs you $5.00 per pack X 365 days = $1825 per year. Of course, to come up with the $1825 to give to tobacco pushers, a smoker paying 15% in taxes must earn $1825 / (100% earnings – 15% tax) = $2147. Unfortunately, pack prices are not the only costs of smoking. Higher health care costs, increased insurance premiums, job related penalties, and reduced auto and home resale values combine with pack prices to make smoking spectacularly expensive.

2. Even your dog may have to go. The www.peteducation.com website offers estimates of the costs of dog ownership. You should budget for costs of anywhere from $500 – $2000 for your first year of dog ownership, followed by annually recurring costs of $300 – $800. Possibly, a relative or friend could keep your dog, until your cash flow can handle the dog's food, medicine, fencing, and other expenses. I would give our dog, Charlie, to a new family that would love him, before I would allow my family to suffer a financial disaster. In fact, the family that previously owned Charlie made that very sacrifice.

3. Texting service is a convenience, not an imperative. It did not exist when we were kids, yet we all managed to find the parties. Drop the fees for unlimited texting, and your kids

will still communicate. At the end of the year, you will be a couple hundred dollars richer. As bonuses, your kids' fields of vision will exceed six inches, people will know your kids by their faces, not their tag lines, and your kids' spelling and syntax will improve.

4. Pools, boats, RVs, and timeshares are unnecessary drains on your resources. Sell them, or donate them and take a tax write-off. You cannot recoup the majority of what you have spent, but you can prevent further drains on your resources.

5. Sell sports cars that scratch your mid-life itch but strain your cash flow.

    a. To sell your sports car, visit the Kelly Blue Book website's "Used Cars" section at http://www.kbb.com/used-cars. From this site, you can determine an appropriate asking price for your sports car. Sell the car yourself, especially if you have kept up the car's maintenance and have clear records of that maintenance. Do not trade-in your car to a dealer. The dealer wants to resell your car. He will low-ball you in order to make room for his own profit. Use the Kelly Blue Book site to compare your car's "Trade-In Value" (what the dealer should give you for your car) with your car's "Private Party Value" (what you should get for your car when selling it, yourself). For my 2001 Honda Odyssey, the results were $3175 and $4340, respectively. In other words, I could make over one-third more money by selling the car, myself.

    b. If your spouse works and needs a vehicle to get to work, then sell the sports car and buy a Certified Pre-Owned (CPO) car with good reviews on the Car and Driver website at http://www.caranddriver.com/reviews. A CPO car will cost more than a simple used car. However, getting a manufacturer's warranty for your used car is worth the added expense. The dealer will be more likely to ensure that he sells you a reliable vehicle. Check the dealer's asking price for the car by visiting Kelly Blue Book and reviewing their section on CPO cars at http://www.kbb.com/certified-pre-owned. Alternatively, you could visit Edmunds.com's "Certified cars" section at http://www.edmunds.com/certified-cars.html to get another estimate.

c. In the unlikely event that you have already paid off your sports car and your insurance and operating costs are as low for the sports car as they are for a less sexy vehicle, then keep the sports car. Nonetheless, choosing to keep an expensive car should necessitate a resolution to drive that car "until the wheels fall off". At a minimum, you should drive a car until its annualized maintenance costs exceed the total cost of a year's worth of monthly installment payments for a new car. The Edmunds.com website's "True Cost to Own" (TCO) section at http://www.edmunds.com/tco.html is an excellent tool for determining the total price tag for owning a car.

Example: TCO comparisons (using Edmunds.com's TCO section).

2012 Ford Mustang

Observe the five-year TCO for a 2012 Ford Mustang Shelby GT500 convertible.

1. Base price = $46,229

2. Five-year TCO = $66,036

2007 Ford Mustang

Observe the five-year TCO for a 2007 Ford Mustang Shelby GT500 convertible.

1. Base price = $27,569

2. Five-year TCO = $55,085

2007 Ford Focus Sedan

Observe the five-year TCO for a 2007 Ford Focus Sedan.

1. Base price = $7769

2. Five-year TCO = $32,784

Analysis

The 2012 Ford Mustang's $66,036 TCO is $10,951 more than the 2007 Ford Mustang's $55,085 TCO. That figure equates to $2190 per year in savings, over 5 years. Depreciation costs, taxes, and financing fees are much higher for newer cars.

The $66,036 TCO for the 2012 Mustang is $33,252 more than the $32,784 TCO for the 2007 Ford Focus. The difference in the TCOs comes out to $6650 per year in savings for the person who chooses the 2007 Ford Focus. These are serious savings, especially for someone "in the red". By curbing your pride and choosing an older economy car, you can save a tremendous amount of money.

Conclusion

Do not assume that newer cars' lower maintenance costs will be enough to save you money. You must evaluate the effects of depreciation, taxes, and other costs to get a more accurate view of what a car's true cost of ownership will be.

Reduce Obligatory Expenses

By definition, you cannot eliminate your obligatory expenses. However, you may be able to reduce them. To that end, you must negotiate with your creditors. SMs grimace at the word "negotiate"; we "demand", and we "get". Unfortunately, our method will not work with civilians. Your payments will stay the same. To effectively negotiate, you must accept that your rank is irrelevant, and you must learn what leverage you truly possess.

An edge that you may have is that of being a long-time customer. Companies do value individual customers, especially given the damage they can do on today's internet blog sites. Politely reminding service providers that you have given them hundreds of dollars over the years might motivate them to provide some financial leeway. Remember that you and the service providers are both "customers". You are a customer of their products and services. They are customers of your dollars. Approach your negotiations with this fact in mind.

Playing two service providers against one another is a good way to reduce costs and to receive perks. For example, call one cell phone company, and ask for the price of their best bundle package. Then, call a second cell phone company, and ask them for the price of their best bundle package. If the second company's offer is lower, call the first company to see if they are willing to beat it. Keep going back and forth until both companies refuse to drop any further. Take the lower priced package.

Of course, one advantage that you bring to the table is the fact that you are serving your country. For truly altruistic reasons or for simply aesthetic reasons, many companies offer discounted rates to military people. Do not forget to ask. If you happen to be deploying soon, toss in that fact (without giving exact dates), and you may get a further discount.

You may wonder what you could possibly bring to any negotiating table. Remember that creditors prefer to get your payments than to watch you declare bankruptcy. Other than collecting whatever collateral you fronted, they get little from your financial failure. They no longer get your payments that were once filling their bank accounts. They must liquidate your collateral, assuming any market exists for it, to reap its financial benefits.

Convincing your creditors that you can and will make your future payments, provided that the creditors adjust their loans' terms, may motivate them to reduce your monthly payments, lengthen your allowable payment periods, or both. Of course, be careful with these adjustments, especially when dealing with credit card companies. Extensions will result in your paying more interest charges over the newly lengthened periods. Such agreements will merely push your problem forward.

Eliminate Credit Card Debt ASAP

I have listed credit card debt as an obligatory expense, even though I espouse avoiding such debt as if it were a discretionary expense. The debt is obligatory; the item that you purchased is discretionary. To illustrate, a stereo is a discretionary item, but the credit that you used to buy the stereo is an obligatory expense. You entered a binding financial contract. Whatever the definition, rid yourself of credit card debt ASAP. The high interest rates and daily compounding of those rates will annihilate your finances.

Determine which of your credit cards charges the highest interest rate. This is the credit card that you should pay off, first. Let nothing deter you. Do not wait until the end of the next billing period to fire another payment round at your balance. Since credit card interest accrues daily, you are pennies ahead with every day earlier that you pay[xxv].

Some financial authors recommend that you first pay off your credit cards that possess the smallest balances or the shortest remaining payment periods, regardless of whether your other credit cards possess higher interest charges. The concept behind this recommendation is that you will get a "morale boost" with each target that you successfully destroy, even though that target is not the High Pay-off Target. Unfortunately, this approach will cost you more money than eliminating your most expensive credit cards, first.

Do not attempt to simplify your credit card payments by falling victim to the claims of debt consolidators. Accept the administrative headaches of writing separate checks. The pain will save you money, regardless of the debt consolidators' claims. Debt consolidators add fees for their service of consolidating your monthly payments. More fees are the last things that you need.

Paying off your credit cards takes precedence over investing. If you are carrying a credit card balance, delay sending money to investment vehicles. The interest charges on your credit cards will almost certainly exceed the gains from any of your investments. Zero your savings account, suspend allotments to your retirement accounts, suspend allotments to your kids' college accounts, or sell something – anything – to free up some cash. Use that cash to pay off your credit card balances.

Pay off the credit card with the highest interest charges, first, and then work your way down the remaining cards. Do not worry that you are diminishing the base upon which your retirement accounts will grow or that you are "stealing your children's future". These concerns are secondary to your need to free your finances from the clutches of the credit card companies. Even a 15% annual return on your investments is irrelevant when bounced against your credit cards' 20% interest charges that become nearly 22% after a year of daily compounding.

Increase Income

Even after all of your cuts and reductions, the subtraction of your expenses from your income might continue to yield a negative number. If so, you must expand your income. The means for earning extra income are too varied for me to address in this book. Instead, I will offer a few recommendations for balancing your military career with any civilian job or business that you pursue.

The existence of the UCMJ's extraordinary power over your freedom should already be clear. Most SMs understand that "we defend democracy; we don't practice it". As such, you must inform your chain of command prior to "moonlighting" for extra income. Your military career takes precedence over your extracurricular employment. Ensure your civilian employers understand this fact, prior to your accepting their job offers. You must give your military leadership the opportunity to assess whether your civilian jobs present conflicts of interest with the military.

Given your status of being in the red, starting a traditional "brick and mortar" business and buying into a traditional franchise system (e.g. buying a McDonalds restaurant) are infeasible routes. Both require huge quantities of start-up capital that you do not possess. Further, banks will not loan you that capital, because you have no net worth. On the other hand, a home-based business might be possible. Everything from starting online businesses to fixing cars is available. Just be aware of your off-post housing area's zoning restrictions and on-post housing area's Command policies, before hoisting your "Jim's Garage" sign.

For an MLM operation, specifically, avoid recruiting anyone within your chain of command. Your MLM partners will develop lasting relationships with you that may conflict with your requirement as a military leader to impartially execute your duties. Selling products to those with whom you serve is somewhat less of an issue. The equal exchange of product and payment satisfies most quid-pro-quo expectations. However, demand cash payments in full. Allowing the accumulation of accounts receivable will create long-term debts that can still cause problems.

With the growth of civilian "out-sourcing" during the Global War on Terror, many SMs developed civilian contacts that could be future employers. Be careful when considering working for a contractor with whom you had contact in the desert. I can think of no instances in which accepting sideline employment with such a contractor would be acceptable while you were still on active duty. However, even in retirement, prohibitions exist. If a contractor offers you a job, seek a ruling from your local Staff Judge Advocate (SJA) before accepting the contractor's offer. Give the SJA the full history of your dealings with the contractor. The SJA will inform you whether accepting the contractor's offer is legal.

W-4 Form

One simple means for somewhat increasing your income is to adjust your allowances on your W-4 Form. Increasing your W-4 Form's allowances will reduce your paychecks' withholdings. Your monthly paychecks will be larger. You will get a smaller tax refund at the end of the year, but you will have more money to use, throughout the year.

Nonetheless, some SMs decrease their W-4 Form's allowances in order to increase their paychecks' withholdings. At the end of the year, these SMs get a sizable tax refund. Contrary to what most people think, getting a tax refund is bad. It simply means that you gave the Government an interest free loan. SMs who want tax refunds see those refunds as gifts from Uncle Sam. Unfortunately, Uncle Sam is the gift recipient. He gets to use the SMs' dollars for a year, without paying the SMs interest.

If you are a habitual saver and investor, decreasing your withholdings is good. You will retain more money for investments. You will no longer get a check from the Government. Instead, you might have to send a check to the Government. On the other hand, if you are a habitual spender, decreasing your withholdings may actually be bad. You might spend all of your savings on bass boats or diamonds. At tax time, you will have nothing in your accounts with which to pay your taxes. If you are this type of person, disregard my advice to decrease your withholdings.

You can download a copy of the W-4 Form by searching on-line for the form. Alternatively, you can get a copy of the form from your local Military Pay office. Use line 5 of the W-4 Form to change your allowances. Fill in the rest of the form's data, sign it, and give a copy of the form to your Military Pay office.

Chapter 12: Build Wealth

If the subtraction of your expenses from your income yields a surplus, you are ready to build wealth. Emulating a couple of your Great Depression and World War II era grandparents' money habits will help:

1. Save your pennies.

2. Buy what you need, not what you want.

The nation's World War II generation understood these steps. Surviving the Great Depression and World War II entailed saving pennies and delaying gratification. Embracing your grandparents' frugal habits is critical for building wealth. Nonetheless, I will add a rule with which the World War II generation might disagree. This rule is more akin to what your Baby Boomer parents would espouse:

3. Invest your saved pennies.

Boomers were willing to invest far more money in the stock market. These investments expanded Boomers' purchasing power. Unfortunately, many Boomers also developed a more optimistic view of spending and did so, prolifically. Many Boomers nullified their investment gains by purchasing luxuries. These luxuries created liabilities that reduced the Boomers' net worth.

The trick for you is to glean the best of both generations. Save your money, buy only what you need, and invest your money. Adopting these tenets will make your wealth accumulation a reality. Your money will stand the greatest chance of out-pacing inflation, dollar devaluation, and the other enemy forces that threaten your net worth.

Execute a Four-Step Process

Building wealth requires you to put money into the following areas in the order in which I have listed them:

1. Emergency Fund.

2. Roth Thrift Savings Plan (TSP).

3. Roth Individual Retirement Account (IRA).

4. Taxable Account.

This process will come as no revelation to many of you. You have heard this before, and you may already be doing it. However, you might not be doing it in the method that stands the best chance of consistently generating wealth. That method lies in the sections that follow. Executing this method will improve your odds of obtaining a large net worth.

Chapter 13: Establish an Emergency Fund

The purpose of an emergency fund is to ensure that you possess a reasonable quantity of immediately available cash. An emergency fund is a fixed income account that offers minimal interest income but enables you to immediately withdraw your money. Usually, an emergency fund takes the form of a savings account (SA) or a money market account (MMA). SAs and MMAs offer small quantities of interest income, while allowing you some limited withdrawal abilities. An emergency fund makes some of your money immediately accessible for near-term crises. The rest of your money should be in investments, generating wealth.

Certificates of deposit (CDs) are tempting alternatives to SAs and MMAs. CDs offer somewhat larger interest income rates. However, CDs tie up your money for months or even years. Money in a SA or MMA will be more liquid. An emergency fund's primary purpose is to provide quick cash. Gaining a few more fractions of a percent in interest income is a secondary concern. The interest income that you get with a SA or MMA will suffice, and the SAs or MMAs will give you the liquidity that you need.

If you tire of deploying and decide to leave the military, having money in an immediately liquid account may enable you to survive until you can establish a new income. Even if you love deploying and have no intention of getting out, automobiles die, kids need braces, and uninsured dogs get sick. These little catastrophes can cost you thousands of dollars. Not having immediately available cash to cover these unanticipated expenses will lead you to cover these expenses with credit cards. Of course, using credit cards adds consumer debt to your woes.

Determining the exact number of months' worth of expenses to park in your emergency fund requires a self-assessment. No widely accepted formula exists. Some advisors recommend that eight months' worth of your living expenses be in an emergency fund. This may be good advice for civilians. The current economy's high unemployment rate is forcing the average person to spend between two and six months searching for a new job. An eight-month emergency fund gives unemployed civilians a two-month cushion. However, maintaining an eight-month emergency fund is poor advice for SMs. Parking eight months' worth of your obligatory expenses in an emergency fund puts too much of your money in a poorly performing investment, given the relative security of your military career. If you remain in the military long enough to get a retirement, then parking eight months' worth of your obligatory expenses in the SA or MMA of an emergency fund will be especially unnecessary. Your retirement paycheck will be enough to cover most of your basic survival expenses.

Eight months' worth of your expenses is too much to park in an emergency fund, and zero months' worth is too little. We have the left and right limits but not the precise azimuth. Determining your precise azimuth necessitates reviewing your household's cash flow and anticipating as many financial traumas as possible. If no major financial traumas are likely, then you might safely keep as little as two or three months' worth of your expenses in your emergency fund. The less cash you can hold in an emergency fund, the more cash you can invest. Endeavor to hold as little cash as possible in fixed income instruments. Invest as much cash as possible in long-term growth instruments.

Choose SAs or MMAs with the highest post introductory interest income rates. High introductory rates are teasers to get you to invest your money with the institutions that offer these rates. Unfortunately, once the introductory periods end, these rates drop, precipitously. The post introductory interest rates on these accounts will be lower than what you can get from institutions that offer fixed rates. Also, avoid SAs and MMAs that charge monthly fees or demand that you maintain minimum balances. The purpose of your emergency fund is to provide a cushion for large expenses. Large expenses might well pull you under the minimum balance.

Do not blithely allow your hometown bank to hold your emergency fund. Other banks might offer higher interest rates on their SAs and MMAs. You can compare various banks' rates by visiting Bankrate.com's "High Yield Rates for MMA and Savings Account" section. This site shows the requirements for various institutions' SAs or MMAs. This site also lists all of these institutions' contact numbers. Call the institution that looks best to you, and determine how to open an account with them. If nothing else, use this institution's rates to haggle with your hometown bank.

Chapter 14: Maximize a Roth Thrift Savings Plan (TSP)

After establishing your emergency fund, contribute to the Thrift Savings Plan (TSP). For 2013, you can contribute $17,500 to a TSP account. The $17,500 can go to a Traditional TSP, a Roth TSP, or a combination of the two. Of these options, your best choice is to send all of your contributions to a Roth TSP. Since you will have already paid taxes on your contributions prior to placing them in your Roth TSP, your contributions will grow tax-exempt. Many years from now when you withdraw your dollars, you will pay no more taxes on the principal that you contributed, and you will pay no taxes on the growth of that principal, at all. Therefore, the growth of your Roth TSP contributions is utterly tax-free.

For nearly all SMs, the Roth TSP will be a better choice than the Traditional TSP. Nonetheless, a few wealthy SMs might opt for the Traditional TSP to defer large tax burdens. If so, the exact amount of taxes that they will defer will depend on their marginal tax rates at the times they contribute to their Traditional TSPs. For example, assume that such a SM is in the 28% marginal tax bracket. If he contributes $1458 to his Traditional TSP for each of the 12 months in 2013, he will defer 28% X $1458 contributions = $408 in federal income taxes, each month. Assuming he remains in the 28% marginal tax bracket all 12 months, he will defer $4896 in taxes.

Nonetheless, he must eventually pay taxes on his

contributions. That time will be when he starts withdrawing those contributions, sometime after he turns 59.5 years old. He will pay taxes on the entire amount of his contributions, to include the growth of his contributions. Those taxes will be at his ordinary income tax rate at the time he withdraws his money. Personnel who choose a Traditional TSP should invest in the following sequence:

Priority	SM	Civilian
1	Emergency Fund	Emergency Fund
2	Roth IRA	TSP (up to match)
3	TSP	Roth IRA
4		TSP

The TSP's Ten Funds

When contributing to a TSP account, be it a Traditional or Roth version, your money will go into one or more of ten funds. The Government's TSP offers five "individual" funds and five "lifecycle" funds. These funds are your only investment options. You may not fill your TSP account with funds from any other source. You are stuck with the specific basket of funds that the Government has chosen. Fortunately, the Government filled the basket with reasonably good options. The Government's TSP offers index funds that track appropriate indices, charge extremely low expenses, and charge zero loads and zero 12b-1 fees.

The TSP's Five Individual Funds

1. G Fund: The G Fund invests your contributions in non-marketable, short-term U.S. Treasury securities. The return from this fund comes solely from interest income. This fund will give you the lowest returns from your contributions, but those returns will be relatively secure. Your principal will enjoy virtually zero volatility. However, inflation will rapidly erode your principal's purchasing power. Do not leave your money in this fund for long. This fund's primary use is as a short-term staging area for dollars that you anticipate spending in the very near future.

2. F Fund: The F Fund invests your contributions in a bond index fund that tracks U.S. Government, mortgage backed, corporate, and foreign government sectors of the U.S. bond market. The return from this fund comes from interest income on the bonds that the fund holds and on the changing face values of those bonds. This fund will give you poor returns in our current and foreseeable environment of steady inflation. Historically, bonds' returns have trailed equities' returns.

3. C Fund: The C Fund invests your contributions in the stocks of the 500 large to medium sized companies that the Standard & Poor's 500 Index tracks. The appreciation of these 500 companies' stocks and the dividends from these companies will determine your returns. This fund can give you solid returns when the U.S. economy is strong. This is a good fund for your TSP account.

4. S Fund: The S Fund invests your contributions in the small to medium sized companies that the U.S. Completion Total Stock Market Index tracks. In short, these are companies that the S&P 500 Index does not track. The appreciation of these companies' stocks and the dividends from these companies will determine your returns. This fund can give you excellent returns when the corporate giants of the S&P 500 Index stagnate. During such times, small and medium sized companies' innovative methods and fresh products flourish. This is another good fund for your TSP account.

5. I Fund: The I Fund invests your contributions in the stocks of the companies that the Morgan Stanley EAFE index tracks. These are companies in the First World locations of Europe, Australia, and the Far East (primarily Japan). The appreciation of these companies' stocks and the dividends from these companies will determine your returns. This fund can give you good returns, in spite of a slowing of the U.S. economy. This fund is yet another good fund for your TSP account.

The TSP's Five Lifecycle Funds

The lifecycle funds are the L Income, L 2020, L 2030, L 2040, and L 2050 funds. The lifecycle funds are not actually separate funds. The lifecycle funds are simply systems for investing in the five individual funds that we have already discussed. The L Income Fund is the least volatile; the L 2050 Fund is the most volatile. The L Income Fund will invest a large amount of your contributions in the G Fund. The L 2050 Fund will invest the majority – but not all – of your contributions in the C, S, and I funds. Lifecycle funds automatically shift the weight of your contributions from the more volatile C, S, and I funds to the less volatile G and F funds, as the years pass. For example, by the actual year of 2050, your L 2050 Fund's holdings will resemble the L Income Fund.

The lifecycle funds will give you decent returns. However, the lifecycle funds will park too much of your money in fixed income securities and bond funds. Even the L 2050 Fund will place more than 10% of your contributions in these poorly performing investments. The lifecycle funds offer convenience but sacrifice gains. Lifecycle funds are only appropriate for SMs who are unwilling to manage their own investments.

How to Establish Your TSP

You can start your TSP in one of two ways. One way is to give a Form TSP-U-1 to your local finance office. You can download a copy of the form by visiting the TSP website's "Establishing Your TSP Account" section at https://www.tsp.gov/planparticipation/eligibility/establishingAccount.shtml#US. This is the slower way to start your TSP, but it enables you to discuss administrative questions with a military-pay professional. The critical component of this form is Section II where you designate the percentage of your monthly paycheck that you want DFAS to send to your Traditional or Roth TSP account. The faster way to start your TSP account is to access the "myPay" website at https://mypay.dfas.mil/mypay.aspx. This is the same website that you use for your LES and is where you can find a digital equivalent of Section II of Form TSP-U-1.

The percentage or dollar figure that you enter in either version of the form will tell DFAS what percentage of your paycheck to send to your new TSP account each month. Most SMs will choose a percentage that spreads their contributions over 12 months. However, you are free to contribute as much as 100% of your monthly base pay, provided that you are able to cover your deductions and allotments. Aggressive investors wishing to get their contributions working as soon as possible might select such a high percentage for the early months of a year. In such cases, the investors' TSP contributions will automatically cease, once the total of their contributions reaches the IRS' limit.

Selecting the Source of Your TSP Contributions

You have the option of contributing money to your TSP account from your Basic (Base) Pay and from any special, incentive, and bonus pays that you might be receiving. However, you should pull your contributions solely from your Base Pay. Your Base Pay is relatively constant, so you will have a good idea of what is coming out of your paycheck each month. Your spouse and you will grow accustomed to this percentage of your Base Pay's not going into your checking account. You will learn to live within your means. This lesson will make you more likely to continue your contributions. You will suffer less temptation to buy a new bass boat or a new diamond.

Determining What Percentage to Send to Your TSP

This decision requires you to review your household cash flow. Execute the following steps:

1. Verify that you possess a positive cash flow (surplus). If not, stop. Return to the expense cutting section.

2. Divide your cash flow surplus by your Base Pay on your LES.

3.   Multiply the resulting decimal by 100.

4.   Round that figure down to the nearest whole number. This is the maximum percentage of your Base Pay that you should contribute to your TSP, each month.

Examples: Determining how much you can contribute to the TSP.

Situation #1

Assume your monthly surplus is $900, and assume you are an active-duty officer with a Base Pay of $5117.

Calculations

Your calculation will become $900 / $5117 X 100 = 17.588. Round 17.588 down to 17. You can afford to put "17" in the Basic Pay text box. You will start making 17% X $5117 = $869.89 in monthly investments to your TSP. You should not run out of money. I realize that you can actually contribute another $30.11. However, the TSP will only accept whole percentages, and rounding 17.588 up to 18 would result in your contributing 18% X $5117 = $921.06. This is $21.06 more than your monthly surplus (more than you can afford).

Situation #2

If your monthly surplus equals $1459 or more, you can contribute enough money each month to achieve the 2013 annual IRS limit of $17,500. Assume you have a monthly surplus of $1490.

Calculations

Your monthly percent can be as high as $1490 / $5117 X 100 = 29.12, or 29%. If you enter "29" in the Basic Pay text box, DFAS will take 29% X $5117 = $1483.93 out of your monthly Base Pay. You will reach the IRS limit in $17,500 / $1483.93 = 11.79 months. In this case, DFAS will take out $1483.93 in each of the first 11 months of the year, thus making your total contributions equal to $16,323.23 by the end of November. In December, DFAS will automatically take out no more than $17,500 – $16,323.23 = $1176.77. DFAS will send no more contributions to your TSP for that year. DFAS will not allow you to contribute more than the IRS limit, unless you are in a deployed status.

If you desire the greatest benefit from your TSP contributions, get those contributions working for you ASAP. This means contributing as much as you can as early as you can. If you could somehow contribute the entire $17,500 to your TSP on 1 January, then you would be wise to do it. The earlier you get your money working for you, the more time it has to grow. So long as you do not exceed your LES' allowances and deductions, you can contribute as much of the $17,500 limit as you wish. On the other hand, if you distribute your TSP contributions over 12 months, you sacrifice the better part of a year's growth for half of those contributions.

Nonetheless, if you prefer easily managed investing to higher growth rates, you may have to distribute your contributions over 12 months. This is not a terrible choice. You will still get vastly better growth rates than your buddies who are not investing in the TSP. In fact, if you are prone to impulse purchases, this may be the better choice. Every month, your cash flow will be the same. This will force you to live within your budget. You will have no financial bonanza months that might tempt you to buy that bass boat or diamond.

Roth TSPs during Deployments

During deployments, a Roth TSP is still a better choice than a Traditional TSP. In both deployed and non-deployed scenarios, the growth of Roth TSP contributions is tax-exempt. However, in deployed scenarios, Roth TSP contributions will come from tax-exempt dollars. You will not have paid taxes on your $17,500 in deployed contributions – and you never will. As such, by choosing a Roth TSP while you are deployed, you will pay taxes on neither the principal – your contributions – nor the growth of that principal.

If your monthly surplus exceeds $1458 while you are deployed in 2013, you should take advantage of IRC Section 415(c) to increase your Roth TSP contributions. While deployed, you can contribute $51,000 to your TSP, rather than the normal $17,500 limit. Of that deployed $51,000, you may send as much as $17,500 to a Roth TSP, specifically. The remaining $51,000 – $17,500 = $33,500 must go to a Traditional TSP. The growth of that separately tracked $33,500 will, indeed, suffer taxes upon withdrawal. Nonetheless, the Roth TSP is a great deal for deployed SMs.

Traditional TSPs during Deployments

You might be one of those few SMs who chooses to contribute to a Traditional TSP rather than to a Roth TSP. In such a case, if your monthly surplus greatly exceeds $1458 and you are deploying to or are already deployed to a designated combat zone, you should increase your TSP contributions, differently. Again, during a year in which you are deployed, you can contribute $51,000 to your TSP. However, when contributing before-tax dollars, you may not contribute more than $17,500 of that $51,000 during months in which you are still in a taxable status.

If you will deploy later in the year, you should start contributing as much of that $17,500 as possible during the months in which you are still at home. Doing so will give you the greatest tax-advantage. If you happen to get the entire $17,500 contributed before you deploy, you must wait until you are in theater to contribute the remaining $51,000 – $17,500 = $33,500 that the IRS permits for 2013.

If you are already deployed but are confident that you will be home a few months before the end of the year, gaining tax advantages requires a bit of maneuvering. In this case, hold onto $17,500 so that you can contribute that money after you are home and are back in a taxable status. While still deployed, contribute as much of the other $51,000 – $17,500 = $33,500 as possible.

Example: Maximizing the tax benefits of a Traditional TSP.

Situation

Assume that the month is January of 2013, that you are already deployed, and that you have a $3000 per month surplus.

Calculations

You would have $3000 X 12 months = $36,000 to contribute over the course of the year. Assume that you know that you will go home at the end of June. In this case, you should contribute $36,000 – $17,500 = $18,500 during the months in which you are still deployed. Once you hit your $18,500 mark, you should enter the "myPay" website and manually stop your contributions (set your Basic Pay percentage to "0"). In late June, you should return to that website and re-set your contribution percentage to enable you to contribute $36,000 – $18,500 = $17,500 from July thru December. This approach violates the "contribute as much as possible as early as possible" concept. However, it ensures that you get the maximum tax-deferred benefits.

If you will deploy for all 12 months of the year, then you should contribute the full $51,000 as early as you can. Since you will not be home during any months of that year, you will not be able to execute the tactic, above. Regardless of your wealth, you should choose a Roth TSP for $17,500 of your $51,000 in deployed contributions.

Allocating Your TSP Contributions

Thus far, you have only told DFAS to automatically send contributions from your Base Pay to your TSP. Now, you must tell the TSP administrators where to invest those monthly contributions. You have few choices to make. The Thrift Savings Plan only offers the five individual index funds and the five lifecycle funds that we have already discussed. You can choose to distribute your contributions in various percentages to one, some, or all of the individual index funds. Alternatively, you can choose to send 100% of your contributions to the one lifecycle fund that best matches your likely retirement year. This would be your full retirement year, not simply the year that you will leave the military.

Shortly after starting your TSP, the Thrift Savings Plan will send you your TSP PIN. This number is the key that gives you access to your TSP account. Enter this PIN along with a password in the TSP login at https://www.tsp.gov/tsp/login.shtml. This action will take you to the "Account Balance" page for your TSP account. From there, select "Contribution Allocations" under "Online Transactions". Lastly, click the "Request Contribution Allocation" button at the bottom of the "Contribution Allocations: Uniformed Services" page. A digital form like the one on the next page should appear:

Investment Funds	Balance	Current %	New %
Lifecycle Funds			
L 2050	$0.00	0%	___%
L 2040	$0.00	0%	___%
L 2030	$0.00	0%	___%
L 2020	$0.00	0%	___%
L Income	$0.00	0%	___%
Individual Funds			
G Fund Government Securities	$0.00	0%	___%
F Fund Fixed Income Index	$0.00	0%	___%
C Fund Common Stock Index	$0.00	0%	___%
S Fund Small Cap Stock Index	$0.00	0%	___%
I Fund International Stock Index	$0.00	0%	___%
Total	$0.00	0%	0%

In the text boxes under the "New%" column, enter the numbers for the percentages of your contributions that you wish to go into the various TSP funds. You are free to enter any combination of numbers in any or all of the boxes on the G, F, C, S, and I fund lines, so long as the total of these numbers equals 100. Alternatively, you could simply enter "100" in the text box for one of the lifecycle funds. The final steps to review, submit, and confirm your entries will be self-explanatory.

Asset Allocation and Asset Classes

Knowing which TSP funds to select requires an understanding of what constitutes an effective asset allocation. For the most in-depth understanding of how to obtain such an allocation, read Mr. Gillette Edmunds' book, "How to Retire Early and Live Well (with Less than a Million Dollars)". Edmunds proposes allocating your dollars among 3 to 5 non-correlated asset classes. His proposal differs from the typically recommended asset allocation in which all asset classes possess close correlations. Correlated assets rise and fall together in response to changing market conditions. In contrast, non-correlated assets move in different directions. This inverse relationship of non-correlated assets is the key to obtaining effective diversification. Such diversification is necessary to give you the greatest chance of possessing at least some assets that will enjoy positive returns, regardless of which sector of the economy is doing well.

Correlated asset allocations typically distribute your dollars among U.S. stocks, U.S. bonds, and cash. Such allocations often fail to achieve the stability that they promise. For example, although stocks do better than bonds during normal inflation, high inflation hurts both assets. High inflation increases the costs of materials, labor, and manufacturing equipment. These rising costs raise a company's bottom line, thus narrowing profit margins. Narrowing profits lead to lower stock values. With respect to bonds, inflation makes the yields of older bonds less attractive than the yields of newer bonds. This lowers the face values of older bonds.

Holding cash is bad in nearly any environment. During periods in which interest income rates are inflating, the returns from cash will still be lower than the returns from equities' dividends and capital gains. During periods of deflating interest rates, cash instruments will offer ever-smaller quantities of interest income. Additionally, when the economy inevitably rebounds, being caught with a large cash position will sacrifice the large gains that equities will enjoy.

On page 51 of Edmunds' book, he lists the major asset classes in which you can invest, and he lists these assets' average returns[xxvi]. The returns he quotes are uninspiring but reliable. Edmunds' returns account for all bear and bull markets over the past century, to include the stock market crash of 1929. Over a 20 to 30-year investment horizon, basing the structure of your portfolio on his asset classes and their expected lifetime returns will provide you with a high probability of enjoying a significant and lasting growth of your investments. The asset classes and their average returns follow:

Asset Class	Expected Lifetime Return
Emerging market stocks	14%
U.S. small company stocks	12%
U.S. large company stocks	10%
Foreign company stocks	10%
U.S. real estate	10%
U.S. oil and gas	8%
Corporate bonds	7%
Foreign bonds	7%
Treasury bonds	6%
Municipal bonds	5%
Money markets and CDs	4%
Treasury bills	3%
Gold	3%

Allocation Guidelines

Edmunds recommends that you invest in three to five of these asset classes. On pages 210-213 of his book, Edmunds discusses a general structure for your investment portfolio[xxvii]. 2/3 or more of your dollars should be in the top five performing asset classes. 1/3 or less of your dollars should be in the bottom eight performing asset classes. Quite possibly, all 3/3 of your dollars could be in the top five asset classes, and zero dollars could be in the bottom eight asset classes. Nonetheless, Edmunds cautions investors to put at least something in the bottom eight asset classes. These eight asset classes respond to substantially different economic cycles than the cycles to which the top five asset classes respond.

With respect to the specific asset classes, Edmunds recommends structuring your investments in accordance with the following guidelines:

1. 1/3 of your dollars should be in foreign stocks. Foreign stocks are stocks of companies in developed foreign markets ("Foreign company stocks", above) and emerging foreign markets.

2. 1/3 of your dollars should be in U.S. stocks. U.S. stocks are stocks of both U.S. small companies and U.S. large companies.

3. The last 1/3 of your dollars can be in any of the remaining asset classes. Nonetheless, weighting the majority, if not all, of this last 1/3 in real estate may offer the best returns.

Guidelines' Rationales

Edmunds recommends that no more than one-third of your dollars be in U.S. stocks. His rationale is that the impending retirement of the Baby Boomer generation will result in large-scale U.S. stock liquidations. The majority of Baby Boomers' investments are in U.S. stocks. Unfortunately, once Boomers liquidate these stocks, the supply of these stocks will increase. Demand for these stocks will decrease. The numbers of Americans in later generations are smaller than the number of Baby Boomers. Fewer buyers of Boomers' U.S. stocks will exist; U.S. stock prices will drop[xxviii]. However, since the writing of Edmunds' book in 1999, Hispanic immigration has exponentially grown. This population increase may restore some of the demand for U.S. stocks by augmenting the number of available buyers. For now, though, this is little more than optimistic speculation.

Edmunds further recommends that up to one-third of your dollars be in foreign and emerging market stocks. This protects a healthy percentage of your portfolio from the deleterious effects of any uniquely poor U.S. market. Stocks of companies in developed foreign countries are not correlated with U.S. stocks. Stocks of companies in foreign countries with newly emerging economies are even less correlated with U.S. stocks. Though globalization and the internet (e-commerce) are chipping away at this lack of correlation, the differences between U.S. and foreign stocks are still large and thus warrant Edmunds' recommendations.

Edmunds does not recommend uniformly distributing your dollars over all 13 asset classes. This is especially true for the bottom eight asset classes. For example, bonds have their time, but that time is not in the foreseeable future. Persistent inflation and dollar devaluation will characterize the nation's coming years. For most of these years, equities will out-perform bonds. A major shift in our Government's policies that precipitates a shift of our economy from inflation to deflation and reduces the supply of U.S. dollars would make bonds attractive, but such a shift is improbable. In his book, Edmunds acknowledges that many strong portfolios may contain no bonds, at all[xxix]. The majority of your dollars should be in the top five performing asset classes.

Roth TSP Individual Fund Course of Action (COA)

To meet Edmunds' guidelines, you should only use the Roth TSP's individual funds. Do not use the Roth TSP's lifecycle funds. The individual funds will reward you with larger returns, over a lifetime of investing. Within the individual funds, you should only contribute to the C, S, and I funds, not to the F or G funds. Sending your Roth TSP dollars to the C, S, and I funds will give your tax-advantaged portfolio good exposure to three of the top five performing asset classes. This is an aggressive allocation that will complement your Roth IRA's funds that we will discuss in the next chapter. Your Roth TSP and your Roth IRA will possess funds with unique (non-correlated) investing objectives. Each fund will respond differently to various economic conditions. This will give you true diversification, as opposed to simply distributing your contributions according to some pat mix of stocks, bonds, and cash.

Initially, distribute your Roth TSP contributions as follows:

1. Send 25% of your dollars to the C Fund.

2. Send 40% of your dollars to the S Fund.

3. Send 35% of your dollars to the I Fund.

These percentages will start your Roth TSP allocation in the proper direction. Over time, changes in the values of your C, S, and I funds' values may force you to temporarily adjust these percentages. However, the goals of all of your adjustments will be the same – to bring your allocation back into alignment with the allocation guidelines.

The Roth TSP Individual Fund COA puts 100% of your Roth TSP contributions into index funds that contain equities. This COA possesses an atypically heavy weighting in international markets. Your holdings will include neither bonds nor fixed securities. This COA gives you a reasonable stake in large, well-established U.S. companies (C Fund) and an even larger stake in small to medium sized U.S. companies (S Fund). You will benefit from the small but steady growth of large U.S. companies and the large but erratic growth of smaller U.S. companies. Lastly, this COA gives you a strong stake in the growth of foreign companies in well established markets (I Fund). These companies can enjoy progress, in spite of what may be happening in the U.S. economy.

Periods in which the nation's economic growth is gradual but steady are often due to the successes of large companies. Large companies benefit from their overwhelming development capital and their strong influence over our Government. In contrast, when large companies stagnate, small companies' fresh approaches and novel products enjoy a Phoenix effect. Unfortunately, you cannot consistently predict which way the economy will go. Investing in both the C and S funds enables you to benefit from either economic environment.

When coupled with what I will recommend for your Roth IRA's holdings, the Roth TSP Individual Fund COA will equally weight your contributions between U.S. companies and foreign companies. If you are new to investing, this may concern you.

America is what you know and trust; America is where you are comfortable investing your paycheck. Nonetheless, the TSP's I Fund invests in the extremely stable foreign markets of the EAFE index. These markets are in countries that are industrially developed and have generally been aligned with the U.S. since World War II. As such, 67% of the I Fund's holdings are in Europe, and the other 33% of its holdings are in Australia and Japan. These First World foreign economies will form one portion of the international holdings in your portfolio. You will use your Roth IRA to cover the other portion of the international holdings in your portfolio. You will fill that other portion with an emerging market fund. The TSP does not currently offer exposure to emerging market economies, but such exposure is vital to the growth of your portfolio.

Investing in funds that own stocks of companies in foreign economies is a critical move for securing your financial future. The world economy is globalizing, U.S. exports are declining, U.S. debt is growing, and the value of the U.S. dollar is falling. Baby Boomers will soon add to these problems by liquidating their U.S. stocks. The supply of these liquidated U.S. stocks may exceed demand. U.S. stock values could fall. America's economic policies and generational shifts are straining America's finances. Prepare for the worst by doing your best to secure your family's financial future. Investing a large portion of your dollars in foreign economies is crucial. If the U.S. economy suffers a long period of poor growth, the values of your U.S. stock funds will shrink. In such an environment, your foreign stock funds may sustain you.

Minimize Your Exposure to the TSP's Bond Fund

The F Fund is the TSP's bond fund. If you invest in this fund, ensure that this fund represents a relatively small percentage of your portfolio. The equities of the C, S, and I funds should hold much larger percentages of your portfolio. In fact, you may wish to completely avoid the F Fund. This will be especially true in your early investing years – a time when you can more easily weather market volatility.

We will see perpetual inflation in the years ahead. Perpetual inflation will lead to constantly rising interest rates. Rising interest rates will drive down the F Fund's returns. Rising interest rates' being attached to newer bonds will mean that newer bonds will offer greater returns than older bonds. This will make newer bonds more attractive than older bonds to new investors. New investors will buy the newer bonds that cost the same as the older bonds but pay larger coupon rates. Holders of the previous years' bonds will be stuck with bond portfolios that sell for less and that pay less interest income than the interest income that buyers of newer bonds will enjoy. This pattern will adversely impact the performance of the underlying bonds in the F Fund.

A particular problem with the F Fund's bonds is that these bonds are in a *fund*. Investors who hold funds of bonds will suffer even more losses than investors who directly hold individual bonds. Individual bonds offer fixed rates of interest and fixed maturity dates. Individual bond investors know exactly when their bonds will mature, and individual bond investors know exactly how much interest they will accrue. They know these things, because they know that they, alone, decide when to liquidate their individual bonds.

Holders of individual bonds have the option of holding their bonds until maturity. Mature bonds return their full face values upon liquidation. However, holders of bonds in funds do not control the timing of when their funds' bonds are liquidated. In bond funds, fund managers decide when to sell and buy the underlying bonds. In pursuit of newer, seemingly better bonds, bond fund managers often sell older bonds prior to those bonds' maturity dates. During inflation, bonds sold prior to their maturity dates sell at discounted rates. Fund managers' selling of bonds prior to those bonds' maturity dates can lower bond funds' returns.

If deflation ever begins in earnest, the F Fund will become more useful. The F Fund's bonds will possess fixed interest income rates that will become more valuable as newer bonds with smaller fixed interest income rates hit the market. However, deflation is not likely to exist in the coming years.

Wait until Retirement to Use the TSP's G Fund

The G Fund is the TSP's fixed securities fund. Contributions to the G Fund will enjoy very little growth, especially after inflation takes its toll. Nonetheless, the time may come when the G Fund will be useful. This time will probably be just prior to your making a withdrawal from your TSP to meet your expenses in an impending retirement year. This will be a time when you may value predictability more than potential growth. At this time, you will execute an "interfund transfer" from your Roth TSP's C, S, and I funds to the TSP's G Fund.

Roth TSP Lifecycle Fund COA

This alternative COA is for those of you who want a simpler way of making your Roth TSP contributions. You do not want to monitor three funds. You do not want to periodically change your contribution percentages to maintain some sort of complicated asset allocation.

This is also the COA for those of you who believe that the Roth TSP Individual Fund COA is too volatile. You agree that the economic forecast warrants some degree of aggressive investing. You agree that a majority of your Roth TSP dollars should be in equities. However, you want a portion of your Roth TSP dollars ready for deflation. You are willing to sacrifice potential gains for this assurance.

Your following this alternative COA is certainly better than your not investing at all. However, your pursuit of investing ease and your taking counsel of your fears will result in your eventually possessing less purchasing power than SMs who execute the Roth TSP Individual Fund COA. If you insist on using this Roth TSP Lifecycle Fund COA, do the following: send 100% of your contributions to the L 2050 Fund, regardless of your projected, full retirement date. Whenever the TSP offers an even longer-term fund (e.g. L 2060), then shift 100% of your existing and future contributions to that longer-term fund. Again, disregard your projected, full retirement date. If the TSP ever offers "Strategy" funds, ditch your lifecycle funds, altogether. Shift 100% of your existing and future contributions to the most aggressive strategy fund. Later, I will discuss strategy funds.

As already stated, the lifecycle funds are not different funds. The lifecycle funds are simply predetermined plans for allocating your Roth TSP contributions to the five individual funds that we have already discussed. The lifecycle funds' allocations are at https://www.tsp.gov/investmentfunds/lfundsheet/fundPerformance_L.shtml. Use the L 2050 Fund, regardless of when you expect to fully retire.

If you start investing in the L 2050 Fund in January of 2013, the L 2050 Fund will allocate your contributions as follows:

1. 4.17% to the G Fund (U.S. fixed income instruments)

2. 8.33% to the F Fund (U.S. bonds)

3. 43.00% to the C Fund (U.S. large sized company equities)

4. 18.50% to the S Fund (U.S. small-medium sized company equities)

5. 26.00% to the I Fund (EAFE company equities)

Putting "100" in the text box on the "L 2050" line under "New%" on the TSP's "Contribution Allocations: Uniformed Services" page initiates this plan. The TSP administrators will automatically distribute your initial Roth TSP contributions in the percentages, above.

Every quarter, the L 2050 Fund will automatically adjust its contribution percentages. The goals of these adjustments will be to gradually reduce investors' exposure to volatility. Each quarter, the TSP administrators will shift progressively greater percentages of all L 2050 Fund investors' TSP contributions to the fixed income instruments of the F and G funds. Therefore, if you start investing in the L 2050 Fund in a later quarter, your initial percentages will be different than what I have shown.

This shifting of investors' assets is an automated process. It does not account for changing economic conditions, and it does not account for individual investors' changing requirements. The process assumes that all conditions and requirements are equal. Such an assumption requires no work, thus the fund's costs are low. Unfortunately, this process of quarterly liquidations and purchases is the antithesis of the "buy and hold" guideline that we will later discuss. A "buy and hold" investor establishes his allocation of assets and then stays with that allocation, possibly for decades. This is nearly the opposite of what the L 2050 Fund will do.

By the actual year of 2050, the L 2050 Fund's allocation will have transformed into the L Income Fund's allocation that follows:

1. 74% to the G Fund

2. 6% to the F Fund

3. 12% to the C Fund

4. 3% to the S Fund

5. 5% to the I Fund

Many of you will fully retire much sooner than 2050. You should still select the L 2050 Fund. Remember that this is the secondary COA; the recommended COA is the Roth TSP Individual Fund COA. This secondary COA nets you as much growth as possible, while conceding to your demand for greater simplicity and, to a lesser extent, to your desire for less volatility. For those seasoned warriors who will retire much sooner than 2050, realize that your L 2050 Fund will not look like the L Income Fund upon your full retirement year. Your L 2050 Fund will look more like the L 2040 Fund, the L 2030 Fund, or even the L 2020 Fund, depending on just how seasoned you are.

If your full retirement date is closer to 2030 or even 2020, advancing inflation and dollar devaluation remain significant enemy forces that you must overcome. The L 2050 Fund is a better choice for you than the L 2030 or L 2020 funds. The L 2050 Fund keeps the greatest percentage of your money working to significantly outpace inflation and dollar devaluation. Your pension and your emergency fund will give you sufficient stability and liquidity.

Fortunately, the TSP's lifecycle funds do not charge additional fees for their automatic rebalancing mechanisms. You pay the same 25 cents for every $1000 in contributions to the lifecycle funds that you pay for $1000 in the individual funds. This is not necessarily the case with other investing companies' comparable funds. Some of these companies charge additional fees for their own lifecycle funds' rebalancing services.

The Roth TSP Lifecycle Fund COA is not a one-for-one substitute for the Roth TSP Individual Fund COA. Resorting to this secondary COA will not give you the same returns as executing the Roth TSP Individual Fund COA. By the start of 2013, the L 2050 Fund will place over 12% of your contributions in the F and G funds' bonds and fixed securities. Over the long-term, these funds will offer lower rates of return than do the C, S, and I funds. As time passes and inflation progresses, your purchasing power will diminish.

Another drawback of this secondary COA is that the L 2050 Fund places over 61% of your contributions in U.S. companies' stocks. Over two-thirds of that 61% will be in U.S. large companies' stocks. Placing this much of your contributions in U.S. companies' stocks reduces your diversification. Reduced diversification makes you less capable of profiting during changing economic environments. Weighting your U.S. investments in favor of large companies' stocks, specifically, is an added mistake. Smaller U.S. companies' stocks will give you greater returns, over time.

The L 2050 Fund will park growing quantities of your contributions in the cash vehicles of the G Fund. While the term "cash" may sound comforting, a fund's maintaining cash reserves will lower your returns. If you disagree, consider what banks do. They do not park their (your) money in cash vehicles. They pay you a pittance for allowing them to use your money, and then they put your money to work for them in the form of loans. These loans pay the banks much higher rates of interest income than the banks are paying you. Cash vehicles are acceptable for your emergency fund but not for your growth-oriented investments. You want as much money as possible working to significantly outpace inflation and dollar devaluation.

Gradual inflation and dollar devaluation will characterize the majority of the coming years. Nonetheless, a few of these years will suffer recessions and lower rates of inflation that appear to be – but are not – deflation. During these years, having some money in the F and G funds will prevent your portfolio from sinking as deeply as it would sink if all of your dollars were in the C, S, and I funds. However, during the powerful rebounds that inevitably follow such years, your F and G funds will damage your returns. During the "bear" (declining) market of 2008, many SMs who possessed bond-heavy portfolios boasted of how the drops in their portfolios' values were not that severe. They compared their bond-heavy portfolios to equity-heavy portfolios that suffered dramatic drops in value. However, the boasting subsided during the following year's spectacular 72% market rally in equities. Most, if not all, investors should hold equity-heavy portfolios, not bond-heavy portfolios

Always remember that drops in a fund's value are not really "losses". You will still own the same number of shares. For the moment, each of those shares will simply be worth less. The odds are almost 100% that the economy will rebound. When this happens, your shares' values will return to their former sizes and will probably grow larger. In fact, if you continue contributing money to a fund with reduced share values, you will buy more shares than you would normally buy. When the rebound comes, you will benefit that much more. Invest to maximize gains, not to minimize losses. Invest in equities.

Common Rationale for the Two COAs

SMs have inflation-indexed pensions that start immediately after 20 years of military service. This is a decisive advantage, relative to what civilians possess. It changes the applicability of some of the advice that financial advisors customarily provide. Financial advisors normally recommend that clients hold "X%" equities and "Y%" bonds while incrementally decreasing their equity holdings and increasing their bond holdings as clients approach retirement. Given the low returns of bonds in an inflationary economy and the fact that our pensions immediately start, this advice is inappropriate for most SMs. We can and should invest more aggressively.

Being too conservative with your investments will make you a casualty of increasing inflation and worsening dollar devaluation. Conservatively investing your money will give you conservative returns on your investments. The returns from conservative investments stand little chance of out-pacing the perpetual rise in prices in the coming decades.

In the near future, the economy will absorb the bulk of the Baby Boomer retirees. These retirees' demands for goods and services will drive up inflation. Additionally, our government will continue to print money to cover its social obligations, internal mechanisms, and global operations. Perpetual dollar devaluation will follow.

Perpetual inflation and dollar devaluation will make your dollars worth less, each year. Your purchasing power will inexorably shrink, and your quality of life will inexorably diminish. Consider a hypothetical scenario in which a retired SM possesses a bond-heavy portfolio averaging 6% returns. If inflation averages 3.1% and his annual withdrawals are a typical 4%, his portfolio will shrink by more than 1%, every year. Of course, slight decreases in his bonds' returns, or slight increases in the rate of inflation, or slight increases in his expenses, or combinations of all three of these misfortunes could lead to far more rapid losses in his portfolio's purchasing power. Over long periods, bonds' returns offer limited margins of error.

In contrast, consider a scenario in which a SM possesses an equity-heavy portfolio averaging 10% returns. After 3.1% inflation and 4% withdrawals, the SM would still enjoy a nearly 3% growth in his purchasing power. Will he see years in which equities' greater volatility will force him to suffer less than 10% returns? Of course. However, he will also see years in which he enjoys returns that are larger than 10%. Over a lifetime of investing, equities' returns offer healthier margins of error. Embrace the volatility of equities; that volatility is the reason for equities' premium returns.

Hyper-Dollar Devaluation

While perpetual inflation and dollar devaluation are probable, hyper-dollar devaluation is improbable. Earlier, I stated that the forces that reduced the value of Germany's Reich mark following World War One were currently at work in modern America. Indeed, this has been true since at least 1971. The supply of U.S. dollars has continually grown, and the value of those dollars has continually fallen. Nonetheless, our economy has contained this tiger, more or less, for nearly 40 years. Our nation's Federal Reserve has the ability to influence interest rates. This ability gives the nation a means for slowing the pace of dollar devaluation.

As stated earlier, price inflation is averaging about 3.1% per year. This means that, on average, your investments must return better than 3.1% for you to realize true profits. Fearing the economy and seeking the security of fixed income instruments will garner the opposite of what you seek. Certificates of deposit (CDs) are popular choices. However, today's 5-year CDs are earning less than 2%, nationally, according to the Bankrate.com website at http://www.bankrate.com/funnel/cd-investments/. If CDs continue to offer such low rates of return and price inflation maintains its 3.1% average, those who "protect" their money by putting it in CDs will actually lose 3.1% inflation rate – 2% interest income = 1.1% in purchasing power, every year. Ordinary federal income taxes on the interest income and withdrawals for living expenses will increase these losses. CDs are not safe.

Bond Values

In times of declining interest rates, bonds can be good. If the U.S. economy were to show signs of entering a deflationary era, the Federal Reserve would likely take actions that lead to a lowering of the Federal Funds Rate and, in turn, the Prime Lending Rate. A lower Prime Lending Rate would encourage entrepreneurs and developers to seek more business loans. The price of investment capital is low when interest rates are low. When this is the case, more people are willing to borrow money to start businesses. In such an environment, investing in bonds is good. Bonds are loans of investment capital.

Holding bonds in eras of declining interest rates would benefit you. The bonds that you bought in the early years of a deflationary era would offer higher interest income rates than bonds offered in the subsequent years of that deflationary era. The face values of your older bonds would rise. Investors would pay more for your older bonds, because your older bonds would offer higher rates of interest income. However, this will not be the era to come. Inflation and dollar devaluation, not deflation, will be the norms.

A military person's natural tendency is to secure his financial position as he would secure his battle position. A military person wants the comfort of knowing that he has covered all of an enemy's avenues of approach. Bonds offer protection against deflation. Unfortunately, protecting your financial position against deflation is similar to protecting your mountain outpost against a tank division. Such protection wastes assets against an unlikely threat. With respect to your finances, inflation and dollar devaluation, not deflation, are more likely threats.

Inflation reduces bonds' face values. The "face value" of a bond is what an investor will pay for the bond. The "coupon rate" is the amount of interest that the investor will receive from the bond. The face value can change, but the coupon rate is fixed. When the bond's face value changes, the bond's "yield" changes. The yield is the ratio of the amount of interest that the investor gets to the price he paid for the bond.

Example: Bond Yields.

Situation

You have purchased a bond carrying a face value of $1000, offering a coupon rate of 6% annually, and possessing a maturity date of 10 years.

Return

You will get 6% X $1000 = $60, each year for ten years. At the end of the tenth year, you will also get back your $1000.

Analysis

In effect, you will have loaned someone $1000 to use for 10 years. Your compensation for letting that person use your money will be your receipt of $60 per year. This is okay, if a 6% return satisfies you, if you have no desire to sell the bond prior to its maturity date, and if a deflating economy makes your 6% return appear high.

However, what if the economy recovers several years prior to the maturity date of your bond? What if interest rates rise and newer bonds with $1000 face values start offering 10% coupon rates? Since coupon rates are fixed, the yield of your old $1000 bond paying $60 will be less than the yield of newer $1000 bonds paying $100. The only way for you to sell your bond would be for you to discount the price – the face value – of your bond to a figure that would make the bond's yield equal to 10%. The question becomes, "Of what face value does $60 equal 10%?" The answer is $60 / 10% = $600.

Rising interest rates will have lowered the face value of your bond from $1000 to $600. Of course, you could hold the bond to maturity and then redeem your full $1000, but what if interest rates continue to rise? What if they hit 12%? Would you be happy holding a bond that is earning half of what other investors' bonds are earning? Would you be comfortable knowing that price inflation is persistently reducing your bond's returns?

If you ever determine that deflation will, indeed, characterize the U.S. economy, you may wish to invest in bonds. Nonetheless, even in a deflationary economy, you should primarily invest in individual bonds, not in bond funds. You lose control of bonds that are in a fund. The bond fund's managers, not you, will determine when to buy and sell the fund's bonds.

But What if They "Civilianize" Military Retirements?

If the Government makes our retirement system more like civilians' retirement systems, then the intensity of our need for sensibly aggressive investing will increase, not decrease. If the Government approves anything like the aforementioned Defense Business Board proposal, the economic forces that affect civilians' retirement security will more equally affect SMs' retirement security. SMs will become more vulnerable to inflation and dollar devaluation. SMs' primary weapon for battling these enemy forces will no longer be relying on the Government to levy higher taxes on the American people. Our primary weapons will become our Roth TSPs and our Roth IRAs. This will be problematic for SMs who are conservative investors. Conservative investors stand little chance of outpacing inflation and dollar devaluation.

The TSP follows rules that are similar to the rules that civilians' 401(k) plans follow. Even though today's companies tout the 401(k) as a retirement plan for middle class Americans, the 401(k) is actually a savings plan for wealthy Americans. "401(k)" is simply the designation of a line in the U.S. tax codes. In 1981, the IRS ruled that employees, not just executives, could use the 401(k) code. Corporate analysts looking for ways to avoid paying life-long pensions to employees quickly used this ruling to justify the elimination of defined benefit pension plans[xxx].

Since 1981, average Americans' abilities to play the various markets have determined those Americans' financial futures. Unfortunately, most Americans lack the financial savvy to successfully do this. SMs and most civilians are employees. Employees work for paychecks. Such people value predictability over opportunity. Unfortunately, investing for near-term predictability sacrifices long-term purchasing power. Avoiding volatility forfeits the necessary growth to succeed when costs of living rise.

Corporations once paid entire crews of professional money managers to ensure the corporations' pension funds weathered economic challenges and outpaced inflation and dollar devaluation. These crews appreciated the realities of the economy and possessed the financial expertise to aggressively invest their client corporations' capital. Employees with 401(k) plans or TSPs do not possess such planning cells. To succeed, SMs and civilians must break from their employee mindsets and adopt aggressive investment strategies. If your entire financial future rests on the growth of your investments, then you should invest for growth, not for predictability. This is especially true in an era of persistent inflation and dollar devaluation.

Thus far, SMs have enjoyed a pleasant irony. SMs are not rich, but our pensions have enabled us to use the TSP in nearly the same way as wealthier Americans use the 401(k) – as a way to shelter excess income from taxes. However, our pension system may soon change. The income that we have been able to shelter might no longer be excess; it might become the core of our retirement plans. Since SMs are unlikely to develop the cash producing business ventures that wealthy Americans develop, SMs must maximize their retirement investments. With or without a defined benefit pension plan, the recommendations of this book are the same.

Chapter 15: Maximize a Roth Individual Retirement Account (IRA)

Once you have filled your Roth TSP's C, S, and I funds, establishing a Roth IRA becomes your next mission. You must establish your Roth IRA with a brokerage of your choosing. The Government does not perform this task for you. Your Roth IRA funds' expenses will likely be higher than your Roth TSP funds' expenses. However, your Roth IRA can hold any funds that the brokerage offers. Your Roth IRA will offer more investing choices than your Roth TSP will offer.

The funds that you select for your Roth IRA should complement, not copy, the funds in your Roth TSP. Your Roth IRA's funds should cover market sectors that your Roth TSP's funds do not cover. The combination of your Roth TSP's and your Roth IRA's funds will enable you to cover all economic avenues of approach.

Again, for all but wealthy SMs who need immediate tax breaks, Roth IRAs are better choices than Traditional IRAs. Roth IRAs offer tax-exempt growth, impose no deadlines by which you must start your withdrawals, and even permit penalty-free, early withdrawals of principal. Traditional IRAs offer only tax-deferred growth, will force you to start taking RMDs when you reach 70.5 years old, and permit no early withdrawals of principal. Roth IRAs' tax-exempt growth offers the chance to realize much larger gains, since current taxes are likely to be lower than future taxes.

The freedom to leave your dollars in a Roth IRA past the year that you turn 70.5 years old offers the opportunity for even more years of compounded growth. This lack of a forced deadline for taking RMDs offers the security of knowing that you can leave your dollars in your Roth IRA until an economic downturn passes. Given Fate's wicked sense of humor, choosing a Traditional IRA will all but assure that such a downturn will occur, just as you turn 70.5 years old. Note that a Roth IRA's lack of a RMD requirement differs from a Roth TSP. The Roth TSP does, indeed, require you to start taking RMDs when you turn 70.5 years old. The difference is due to the Roth TSP's being an employer-sponsored plan, whereas a Roth IRA is an individually established plan.

Being able to pull principal from your Roth IRA without suffering a 10% penalty is a nice-to-have option. Of course, this option is a double-edged sword. As already stated, the premature pulling of principal from your Roth IRA will reduce the ultimate size of your retirement nest egg. Only execute this option during severe financial emergencies.

Selecting a Brokerage

Making your own choice about which brokerage will hold your Roth IRA is not complicated. Simply open an internet search engine and look for "brokerages" or "low cost index funds and index ETFs". At the time of this writing, such brokerages as Vanguard and Fidelity appeared. Alternatively, you could entrust your IRA to a full service financial firm. Doing so will increase your expenses but will result in your finances' receiving comprehensive analyses by investing professionals. These analyses may produce gains that more than compensate you for the extra expenses.

Incidentally, you should search for brokerages from the perspective of a passive investor – one who buys and then holds his funds. Some brokerages orient their services toward active investors. Active investors frequently trade their stocks and funds. Active trading increases a portfolio's turnover. More frequent turnover leads to higher costs. Active trading is not the focus of this book.

You should determine the quality of a brokerage's funds based on at least 5 criteria:

1. Investing philosophies. The closer their alignment with your desired asset classes, the better.

2. Variety of funds. Having more choices is better

3. Operating expenses. Paying lower fees is better.

4. Investing minimums. Having lower thresholds is better.

5. Loads. Paying smaller loads is better.

Do Not Attempt to Out-Perform the Markets

The simplest way to meet all five of the criteria is to select low cost index funds or index ETFs. Low cost index funds and index ETFs will suffice for setting you on the path to wealth. Unlike actively managed mutual funds, index funds and index ETFs will never actually beat their respective markets' returns. They will merely replicate their markets' returns. Nonetheless, markets can enjoy impressive growth. Merely replicating such growth will largely meet your investing needs.

Some websites will list funds that have enjoyed spectacular returns, relative to the markets' returns. These funds' 40% to 50% returns are tempting. Unfortunately, several problems exist with choosing these funds. First, if the funds are doing well, then the prices of the funds will be high. You may be "buying high", rather than "buying low". Are you absolutely positive that these funds will continue to grow? What if you are viewing the final days of these funds' positive growth? Being able to consistently time markets is the Holy Grail of investing. Many have tried; none have consistently succeeded.

Second, funds with high returns have high returns for a reason. The reason is that these funds often invest in extremely speculative companies. This is not necessarily a bad thing, provided that such investments fit within your overall asset allocation.

However, if all of your investments are in speculative funds, you will suffer some disturbingly low returns. If these low returns occur at a time when other categories of investments are doing well, you will have sacrificed the benefits of growth in those other areas.

Third, trying to beat the markets requires you to invest in managed mutual funds. Not all managed mutual funds are bad, but some managed mutual funds carry expenses that are too high. Managed mutual funds use teams of analysts to determine which companies to buy. Occasionally, these analysts will see things in the market that you cannot see. Such insight will benefit you, provided that you are not paying too much for it. Unfortunately, the fees for managed mutual funds can be as high as 1.5%. When compared with index fund fees of 0.2% or lower, 1.5% is quite large. Are high fees worthwhile? Sometimes, but certainly not always. If you have an index fund or index ETF gaining 8% with expenses of 0.1%, your return is 7.9%. A managed mutual fund gaining 9% with expenses of 1.5% gives you a return of 7.5%.

If my assumption of a mere 9% return for the managed mutual fund seems contrived, consider Mr. Mark Hurlbert's 21 February 2009 article entitled "The Index Funds Win Again" in the New York Times. In this article, Hurlbert relayed the findings of Mr. Mark Kritzman of Windham Capital Management of Boston and Professor Russell Wermers of the University of Maryland:

> "Mr. Kritzman calculates that just to break even with the index fund, net of all expenses, the actively managed fund would have to outperform it by an average of 4.3 percentage points a year on a pre-expense basis. For the hedge fund, that margin would have to be 10 points a year. The chances of finding such funds are next to zero, said Russell Wermers, a finance professor at the University of Maryland. Consider the 452 domestic equity mutual funds in the Morningstar database that existed for the 20 years through January of this year. Morningstar reports that just 13 of those funds beat the Standard & Poor's 500-stock index by at least four percentage points a year, on average, over that period. That's less than 3 out of every 100 funds[xxxi]."

A fourth, potential drawback of managed mutual funds is that, over time, they can simply become high-priced index funds. As the managed mutual funds receive more capital from investors, the funds' managers attempt to purchase more shares of companies that fall within the managed mutual funds' respective philosophies. Every day, millions of investors use the internet to quickly scrutinize the stocks of the many companies in the markets. Competition is fierce. Finding new companies that other investors have not found is difficult. Managed mutual funds ultimately buy many of the same companies that everyone else is buying. Various indices already track many of these companies, and the corresponding index funds and index ETFs already own the stocks of these companies. For example, a managed mutual fund with the philosophy of obtaining large value companies will hold many of the same companies that an S&P 500 index fund holds. The only difference will be the higher expenses in the managed mutual fund.

Finally, economically adept committees use careful research and follow sound tenets to select the companies that their indices represent. The average analyst tucked away in a managed mutual fund's office is unlikely to consistently find companies that better represent the tenets of a given index. If an analyst does appear to consistently find new companies, then a possibility exists that his new companies will be outside of his managed mutual fund's investing philosophy. A fund that strays from its investing philosophy will compromise the structure of your asset allocation.

Roth IRA Course of Action (COA)

You should choose funds for your Roth IRA that complement, not copy, the funds that you selected for your Roth TSP. Your Roth TSP's C, S, and I funds already give you sufficient exposure to three of Edmunds' top five asset classes. The C Fund holds U.S. large company stocks, the S Fund holds U.S. small (and medium) company stocks, and the I Fund holds foreign company stocks of the EAFE Index. Your Roth IRA should hold funds that expose your portfolio to different asset classes. At a minimum, your Roth IRA should expose you to emerging markets and U.S. real estate. Emerging markets and U.S. real estate are the other two of the top five performing asset classes. You may also wish to add a sixth asset class that we will discuss in a moment. Using your Roth IRA to complement your Roth TSP will ensure that your tax-advantaged portfolio covers multiple economic avenues of approach. Your portfolio will possess good diversification.

You should determine your asset allocation prior to actually contacting the brokerage that will hold your Roth IRA. Doing so will make you more capable of properly answering the inevitable "risk tolerance" questions that the brokerage must ask you. Brokerages design these questions to reveal your ability to endure market volatility. Conservative investors fear market volatility and usually respond that preserving their principal – the amount that they initially invest – is more important than seeing their principal grow. At that point, your brokerage's salesperson or your full service firm's financial advisor will have little choice but to recommend funds that experience less volatility. Over time, such funds will lower your purchasing power.

Purchasing all of the funds in this recommended COA may not be immediately possible. One or more of the funds may exhaust your $5500 limit for the year. If so, ask your spouse to purchase for her Roth IRA the funds that are still absent from your Roth IRA. Her Roth IRA will complement your Roth IRA and your Roth TSP. Your wife and you will invest as a team, more rapidly exposing your family's tax-advantaged investments to the recommended asset classes. If you are single or your wife refuses to help, you must wait until next year to add more funds to your Roth IRA. Do not panic over such a delay. You are building a lifetime of wealth that may pass to your children or grandchildren. Taking a couple of years to properly structure it will not be disastrous.

Emerging Market Index ETF (or Emerging Market Index Fund)

Your first purchase for your Roth IRA should be an emerging market index ETF. If your brokerage does not offer an ETF in this asset class, then an emerging market index fund will suffice. Emerging market index ETFs own stock in companies that are in "Second World" or "Third World" countries. Financial analysts refer to such markets as "emerging markets". The Morgan Stanley Capital International (MSCI) Emerging Market Index tracks the performance of over 20 countries with emerging market economies. Emerging market countries have only recently started large-scale economic interaction with the traditionally capitalist countries in the EAFE index and the U.S.

Emerging market stocks sound risky. Many of us have "visited" Third World countries and would never dream of investing money in such places. However, most of the countries in the MSCI index are a far cry from Iraq or Afghanistan. If the term "emerging market" conjures images of guys hammering on tin pots in an Afghani mud hut, think again. The companies of emerging markets are actually in nations like Brazil, Russia, India, and China. Goldman Sachs refers to these countries' economies as the "BRIC" economies. These are powerful nations. They are industrially developed and possess large capital reserves. Their "Second World" and "Third World" labels merely come from the fact that their prior economic activities were not strongly aligned with the traditionally capitalist nations of the "First World". Thus, the "World" labels are more a function of Cold War era geopolitical alignments than a function of economic development.

In their 20 May 2010 issue of "BRICs Monthly", Goldman Sachs reported that the BRICs' populations have greatly increased their incomes over the past decade and that the combined BRIC economies could surpass the U.S. economy by 2018[xxxii]. Citizens of BRIC nations now have the wealth to demand higher value goods. Creating these higher value goods requires the creation of larger and more sophisticated manufacturing facilities. Emerging market funds enable you to benefit from the economic growth that this demand spurs.

Note that investing in emerging markets is an area in which managed mutual funds can be useful. Emerging market indices struggle to track the many companies that exist in these markets. Developing index funds to adequately replicate those indices is equally challenging. Within emerging markets, many opportunity-buys exist. Managed emerging market mutual funds are free to profit from these opportunities. Nonetheless, the managed emerging market mutual funds' expenses must not be so high that they negate the funds' gains. Additionally, these funds must not reserve too much cash for contingency buys and must keep their rates of turnover as low as possible. Pending your discovery of such well managed funds, emerging market index funds and index ETFs will suffice.

REIT Index ETF (or REIT Index Fund)

Your second purchase for your Roth IRA should be a REIT index ETF. Again, if your brokerage does not offer an ETF in this asset class, then a REIT index fund will suffice. REIT index ETFs invest in Real Estate Investment Trusts (REITs). REITs are companies that focus on real estate investments. REITs possess full staffs of real estate professionals. These professionals specialize in various types of properties. REITs invest in commercial properties, residential properties, or both.

By owning a REIT index ETF, you get exposure to a variety of REITs. This is good. The influence of local market conditions on real estate can make real estate performance especially difficult to predict. Will trends be local, regional, or national? Will commercial development increase? Will the homeowners' market collapse? These questions are nearly impossible to answer. Owning a REIT index ETF eliminates the need to answer these questions.

You can start a REIT index ETF with far fewer dollars than you need to purchase an actual piece of property. The 2013 contribution limit for a person's Roth IRA will be $5500. This is plenty of money for you to participate in a brokerage's REIT index ETF. Try purchasing an actual piece of commercial property for less than $5500. At best, you will have a piece of undeveloped land on which you will pay property taxes but will enjoy no income.

Yet another benefit of REIT index ETFs over actual properties is that you can "improve" your REIT holdings with almost any sum of dollars, at any time. You could add $458 per month for a year to your Roth IRA's REIT index ETF, or you could add $1375 per quarter for a year, or you could invest all $5500 on the first day of the year. Making improvements in this fashion to an actual piece of property is nearly impossible.

A major problem with owning actual real estate is that you lack liquidity. Turning a piece of real estate into cash involves many steps. These steps take time and cost money. Turning a REIT index ETF into cash merely requires calling your brokerage and placing a "sell" order. You will be able to immediately liquidate your REIT index ETF shares, and you will be able to liquidate a REIT index fund by the end of the day. You will be free to transfer your funds to whatever new instruments you wish. You will pay neither realtors nor advertising agencies. Assuming this transaction occurs within your tax-advantaged accounts, you will not even pay taxes on your gains.

Your brokerage might offer two types of REIT index ETFs. One type might track equity REITs, while the other type might track mortgage REITs. If so, choose the type that tracks equity REITs. Mortgage REITs bear a strong resemblance to bond funds. Mortgage REITs do not invest in properties. They invest in the mortgages on those properties. Mortgage REITs' returns are tied to the performance of debt instruments. Debt instruments are highly susceptible to changing interest rates. In contrast, equity REITs invest in the properties, themselves. True, the same rising interest rates that hurt older bonds can curtail real estate growth. Rising interest rates increase the costs of development loans. Nonetheless, equity REITs can enjoy the benefits of appreciation and cash flow that come with property ownership. Further, property managers can temper the effects of inflation by simply demanding higher rent payments.

Regardless of the advantages that REITs offer, you might still prefer to directly invest in real estate. However, directly investing in real estate exposes you to numerous hassles. Maintaining existing facilities, increasing marketing qualities with upgrades, evicting dead-beats, recovering from storm damages, paying property taxes, paying realtors' commissions, processing legal and administrative paperwork, and handling mid-night calls can make real estate a tremendous pain. Most career SMs have neither the time nor the inclination to fool with real estate. Nonetheless, real estate is an important diversifier for your portfolio. Since local market conditions drive real estate values, the general economy can be diving while portions of your real estate holdings are climbing. The trick is determining how to enjoy most of real estate's advantages while avoiding real estate's headaches. The solution is a REIT index ETF.

REIT index ETFs are a sensible way to quickly and effectively get into the real estate market. REIT index ETFs allow you to enjoy the benefits of owning real estate without the headaches of property management and without the risks of property ownership. These advantages are critical for SMs. With respect to mortgages and down payments, SMs will expend all rounds (dollars) on their homes. SMs who wait until they accumulate enough dollars to purchase commercial properties will miss the benefits of owning real estate for many years. Another drawback is that interest payments are usually larger on commercial real estate mortgages than they are on residential property mortgages.

We have all heard stories of SMs who bought awesome properties and raked in the dough. These stories make us worry that we are somehow missing the real estate boat. While a few of these stories are true, most are exaggerations. The average SM simply does not possess a large enough net worth to secure a sufficiently large loan for purchasing a good quality commercial property. If a SM did manage to obtain a commercial property, the property would be either too small to warrant the headaches or would be in a slum where tenants will default on their lease payments. The SM who owns a tiny commercial property or has become a slumlord will almost certainly have put most of his savings into this one asset class. Having little diversification is dangerous. What if the local government is low on cash and commissions a real estate assessor to re-appraise your property, thus raising your taxes? By itself, this rise might turn a seemingly good deal into a money pit.

Precious Metals and Mining Fund

Your third and final purchase for your Roth IRA should be a precious metals and mining fund (precious metals fund). Note that this purchase will result in your owning a sixth asset class – three in your Roth TSP and three in your Roth IRA. While this number exceeds the three to five asset classes that Edmunds recommends, recent economic conditions warrant this addition. Nonetheless, this sixth asset class should comprise little more than 10% of your portfolio. Of the six asset classes that you should own, a precious metals fund should be the last that you purchase. You should not buy a precious metals fund until you have fully funded the other five asset classes.

A precious metals fund serves as your hedge against dollar devaluation and is a reasonable bet on the rising demand for hard currency. A precious metals fund will narrow its investments to companies that find, mine, and process precious metals. Gold and silver are a couple of the precious metals that these companies seek. When demand for gold or silver rises, these companies will profit. As the value of the U.S. dollar continues to fall, the demand for precious metals will continue to rise. By owning a precious metals fund, you will benefit from the profits of these companies.

Economists often view gold as a commodity. Commodities' prices rise and fall in tandem with inflation's rises and falls. If you believe that gradual inflation will persist for many years, then you already have a pseudo rationale for investing in precious metals. However, your understanding the true rationale for investing in precious metals will ensure that you do not dump your precious metals fund at the wrong time.

In reality, the demand for gold and silver is more driven by these metals' values as hard currencies than by their values as commodities. Countries desire gold as a currency reserve against the falling dollar. Thus, the driving force behind gold and silver prices is dollar devaluation, and dollars can devaluate in both inflationary and deflationary economies.

In his August 2010 article, "Rethinking Gold: What if It Isn't a Commodity After All?", Mr. Jeff Opdyke of The Wall Street Journal reported that virtually no correlation exists between inflation and gold prices. Gold prices can rise or fall, regardless of whether inflation exists. However, he reported that a very distinct correlation does, indeed, exist between gold prices and the value of the U.S. dollar[xxxiii]. As the value of the U.S. dollar falls, the price of gold rises.

The Chairman of the Federal Reserve, Mr. Alan Greenspan, told Congress in 1999, "Gold is always accepted and is the ultimate means of payment and is perceived to be an element of stability in the currency and in the ultimate value of the currency, and that, historically, has always been the reason why governments hold gold[xxxiv]." Analyzing the price of gold over our nation's history reveals the truth of Greenspan's words.

Prior to 1971, the U.S. Government participated with other countries in a monetary system that fixed national currencies to a specific weight of gold. This made dollars "hard", since holders of U.S. dollars could literally exchange these dollars for precise quantities of a precious metal. This arrangement increased other countries' faith in the value of the U.S. dollar. As such, the U.S. dollar and the price of gold generally moved in tandem from 1792 until 1971. The price of gold in 1792 was $19.39 per ounce and did not reach $44.60 per ounce until late 1971, a mere 2.3 fold increase in 179 years[xxxv]. However, in late 1971, President Nixon took us off the Gold Standard. By August of 2012, the price of gold was an astounding $1617.00 per ounce. In only 41 more years, the price of gold experienced a 36.3 fold increase. That rise has been particularly steep since 2001, in the wake of the U.S. Government's reactions to the 9-11 terrorist attacks.

The 3% average return for the gold asset class that appears in the Asset Allocation Chart may lead you to question the wisdom of purchasing a precious metals fund. However, you must consider the recent history of gold. Between 1792 and 1971, the price of gold raised an average of 14 cents per ounce, per year. Since 1971 and 2012, the price of gold raised an average of $38.35 per ounce, per year. By owning a precious metals fund, you will position yourself to benefit from an economic trend that has permeated the last half-century.

Knowing that gold's value is inversely proportional to the value of the U.S. dollar will enable you to question someone who recommends that you dump your precious metals fund, prior to an impending deflation. Ask that person whether he believes the U.S. Government will continue printing money to cover its debts. If his answer is, "Yes", keep your precious metals fund. If his answer is, "No", ask him why gold prices soared over the last few years, in spite of the fact that the rate of inflation decreased from over 6% in late 1990 to less than 2% between 2010 and 2011[xxxvi]. A reduction in the rate of inflation is not actually deflation. Nonetheless, this period's trend gives you a reasonable standard by which to analyze the relative persistence of rising gold prices.

As our Government's financial problems persist and grow, the negative effects of dollar devaluation will persist and grow. You will profit by investing in funds that invest in a more tangible currency than paper. Understanding that dollar devaluation, not inflation, influences the prices of precious metals will keep you from making a financial mistake. If I am wrong about impending inflation and we actually do suffer a considerable amount of deflation, you might decide to liquidate your precious metals fund. Unfortunately, that would be the wrong response. Regardless of deflation's existence, the U.S. Government will continue to print money to pay for the Government's overwhelming financial obligations. The value of the U.S. dollar will continue to drop. The demand for hard currency in the forms of gold and silver will continue to grow. Keep your precious metals fund.

Purchasing a precious metals fund is an area in which you might not be able to follow the recommendation to purchase index ETFs or index funds. You might only be able to find managed mutual fund versions of precious metals funds. Nonetheless, some brokerages offer precious metals funds with no loads and with expenses that are well below 1%.

Precious metals funds can be quite volatile. You will experience impressive value increases and sobering value decreases. When purchasing a precious metals fund, you are using a small portion of your money to "go for long yardage". Just as in football, though, a properly timed long-bomb that rationally analyzes the score, clock, and field position can be a sensible play.

Do not directly invest in gold or silver bricks. Invest in a precious metals fund that focuses on the mining and processing of these precious metals. Directly investing in gold or silver bricks necessitates your paying for storage, sales fees, administrative fees, insurance, and research. Additionally, converting gold or silver bricks into cash is a slower means of getting your money than simply selling shares of a precious metals fund.

How about an Energy Fund?

At some point, you might consider purchasing an energy fund. Rising fuel prices make such funds attractive. Energy funds invest in the production and shipping of existing oil and gas and offer the promise of profiting from this trade. For the foreseeable future, oil and gas prices will remain high. The Government may be giving more support to the development of alternative energy sources, but costs are still too high for companies to fully embrace the production of alternative energy without substantial government subsidies[xxxvii]. This may be a compelling point for energy funds, but you should resist the temptation to buy them.

Energy funds often contain the stocks of companies that your index ETFs and index funds already possess. Exxon Mobil Corporation is an example of a major holding in some energy funds that is also a major holding in S&P 500 index ETFs and index funds. Funds with overlapping holdings directly correlate. This correlation will reduce your portfolio's diversification.

Energy funds will almost certainly be managed mutual funds. Managed mutual funds have higher expenses than index ETFs or index funds. Yet, as we just discussed, energy funds can hold some of the same stocks that your index ETFs and index funds hold. You are paying more for exposure to a stock in an energy fund than you are paying for exposure to the same stock in an index ETF or index fund. Why pay more for the same stock exposure?

A final problem with energy funds is that their minimum investments are usually quite large. A minimum starting investment might be as large as $25,000. Obviously, this amount greatly exceeds your annual IRA contribution limit. Fulfilling the minimum requirements for an energy fund might take several years and might exhaust the dollars you need for the more recommended funds.

Spouse's Roth IRA

As mentioned in Chapter 9, your spouse can open a Roth IRA account of her own. Your spouse's Roth IRA eligibility might be due to her own job history. Alternatively, her eligibility could be due to the fact that she is married to you. In this latter case, she is taking advantage of a "Spousal" IRA. Spousal IRA rules permit married homemakers to open IRAs and fund their IRAs with money from their working spouses' incomes. Her account will be separate from yours and can receive its own annual contribution of $5500 in 2013. In effect, your family will have $11,000 to invest in Roth IRA funds.

You should use your spouse's Roth IRA to hold funds that complement, not duplicate, the funds in your Roth IRA. You cannot add her Roth IRA contributions to your Roth IRA account, but your spouse can purchase funds that complete your household's combined portfolio. Essentially, you and your spouse should invest as if you are one person. Indeed, this is how I structured my wife's and my investments. Rather than holding identical Roth IRAs, her Roth IRA contains funds that my Roth IRA does not. The benefit of this approach is that we more quickly purchased the recommended Roth IRA funds.

If you choose to do the same, you should be confident that your marriage will last. If you follow this COA but later discover that your confidence was misplaced, consult an attorney and an accountant for the effects on your Roth IRA. Divorce settlements can, indeed, transfer Roth IRA assets from one spouse to another. If you are unsure of your marriage's future, follow my recommended COA for your Roth IRA, and encourage your spouse to duplicate your tax-advantaged investments. This latter approach will not necessarily protect your Roth IRA from your ex-spouse's clutches. However, it may simplify the division process, such that the general structure of your portfolio will remain intact.

Servicing Fees

Note that some of a brokerage's funds might charge "servicing" fees. Such funds allow you to enter with relatively small initial investments but charge you servicing fees until your total holdings in the funds meet or exceed certain thresholds. For example, a fund may allow you to enter for as little as $3000. However, the fund might charge you an annual $20 servicing fee until your total holdings in the fund meet or exceed $10,000. These fees compensate brokerages for managing small accounts. While annoying, servicing fees are not valid reasons to avoid funds that properly complement your portfolio.

To illustrate the effect of servicing fees, consider a yearly Roth IRA contribution. The 2013 maximum Roth IRA contribution will be $5500 per person. For the $10,000 fund above, your $5500 would exceed the $3000 minimum initial investment but would fall short of the threshold for avoiding the $20 servicing fee. Nonetheless, that $20 fee is only 0.36% of $5500. A 10% growth in such a fund would net you a respectable 10% – 0.36% = 9.64% return. In the next year, that 9.64% return coupled with another $5500 infusion should eliminate the fee.

Investment Minimums and Additional Contributions

You may be unable to immediately purchase all of the Roth IRA funds that I have recommended. Brokerages will demand that you meet various investment thresholds before you can purchase certain funds. Typical thresholds are not less than $3000, or $10,000, or even $25,000. Funds demanding more than $5500 will obviously necessitate your waiting a few years before you will be able to purchase them.

Fortunately, after meeting a given fund's threshold, your future contributions to the fund can be in far smaller quantities. Brokerages will often accept additional contributions to their funds in quantities as small as $100. This is a nice convenience of all mutual funds, relative to purchasing and managing individual stocks.

As for ETFs, brokerages do not require that you meet minimum investment thresholds. Your only requirement is to purchase whole shares. You may not purchase fractional shares, as you may in mutual funds.

Gathering Money for Your Fund Purchases

When gathering money to purchase funds for your Roth IRA, you may have to temporarily use fixed income instruments. These fixed income instruments can and should be in your Roth IRA. Though the returns will be small, the returns will be tax-exempt. Eventually, you will accumulate enough money in your

Roth IRA account to purchase the recommended index ETFs or index funds. Later, we will discuss your taxable account. The process for gathering funds in your taxable account will be the same as for your Roth IRA.

Using savings accounts (SAs) or money market accounts (MMAs) to temporarily hold your accumulating Roth IRA dollars is the easiest COA. Simply ask your brokerage about opening one of these accounts in your Roth IRA. Toss your excess dollars into this account. Once you have accumulated enough money to purchase a fund, the brokerage can immediately use your SA or MMA money to do so. Dollars in a SA or MMA will retain their current value plus whatever miniscule interest income rate your account offers. Of course, the rates of inflation and dollar devaluation will surpass this rate, resulting in your eventually losing purchasing power. Placing money in a SA or MMA should be a temporary COA.

Using CDs is a bit more lucrative, but much less liquid COA. You can purchase 6-month and 12-month CDs for as little as a couple hundred dollars. CDs offer better interest income rates than SAs or MMAs. As the holding periods increase, the interest rates increase. The drawback is that CDs lock-up your money for these 6-month to 12-month periods.

Do not use bonds to accumulate money in your Roth IRA. Bonds possess maturity dates that are too long to meet your liquidity needs. Further, while bonds' coupon rates are predictable (fixed), bonds' face values are not. The face values of bonds fall in inflationary economies, making older bonds less valuable than newer bonds. In such economies, you will suffer a loss when selling your older bonds prior to their maturities. We will be in an inflationary economy for quite some time.

Chapter 16: Maintain Investing Temperance

Following the preceding recommendations for your investments will give you the best chance of achieving the returns listed in the Asset Class chart. However, do not expect to enjoy these returns every year of your investing career. The chart's returns are average returns that were calculated from nearly a century's worth of annual returns. Many of these years' returns were higher and some of these years' returns were lower. Expect to see such ebbs and flows.

Trust that your battle-plan (your asset allocation) is sound and that your troops (your investments) know what they are doing in their respective skirmishes and negotiations. Do not jump into your up-armored HUMV and race to the front at the first hint of a problem. Do not sell a core fund within your asset allocation, simply because it suffers an occasional drop in value. Allow your investments to run their courses during both good and bad times. If you show this level of calm under fire, you will enjoy a lifetime of returns that approximate those listed in the Asset Class chart.

On the next page is an example of the probable performance of a hypothetical portfolio. The example should illustrate how to calculate your own returns for various quantities that you might invest. Note that this example deals only with the Roth TSP and the Roth IRA. It does not consider what you might be investing in a taxable account.

Example: Projected returns for a reasonable asset allocation.

Situation

A SM has attempted to follow the recommended asset allocation. She has just retired from the military. The SM and her husband have the following investments:

1. $20,000 in the C Fund (Roth TSP)

2. $37,000 in the S Fund (Roth TSP)

3. $35,000 in the I Fund (Roth TSP)

4. $27,000 in an emerging market index ETF (Roth IRA)

5. $16,000 in a precious metals fund (Roth IRA)

6. $30,000 in a REIT index ETF (husband's Roth IRA)

Calculations

The total of the SM and her husband's tax-advantaged investments is $165,000. Dividing each of their six investments by $165,000 yields the "Own Percents Invested" percentages in the table on the next page. Multiplying the "Own Percents Invested" percentages by the "Expected Lifetime Returns" percentages from the Asset Class chart yields the "Own Returns" percentages. Adding the "Own Returns" percentages yields the "Total" return figure.

Asset Class	Own Percents Invested		Expected Lifetime Returns		Own Returns
U.S. large company stocks	12.1%	X	10%	=	1.2%
U.S. small company stocks [Note *]	22.4%	X	12%	=	2.7%
Foreign company stocks	21.2%	X	10%	=	2.1%
Emerging market stocks	16.4%	X	14%	=	2.3%
Gold	9.7%	X	3%	=	0.3%
U.S. real estate	18.2%	X	10%	=	1.8%
			Total	=	10.4%

Analysis

The SM's current allocation generally aligns with the recommended allocation. The SM's total return stands a good chance of averaging 10.4% per year, over a lifetime of investing. At least two thirds of her investments are in the top five asset classes. Approximately one third of her investments is in U.S. stocks (i.e. 12.1% + 22.4% = 34.5%). Not greatly more than one third of her investments is in foreign stocks (i.e. 21.2% + 16.4% = 37.6%). Two thirds of the final one third of her investments are in real estate, and one third of that final one third of her investments is in a precious metals fund.

The SM's precious metals fund is one of the bottom eight asset classes. The bottom eight asset classes should hold no more than one third of her investments. Specifically, a precious metals fund should comprise about 10% of her investments. Her 9.7% investment in a precious metals fund essentially meets that guidance. Her precious metals fund is her only investment in the bottom eight asset classes. This is acceptable. If she wished to increase her total return, she could redistribute her gold investment between her other five investments. However, this 9.7% of her investments is a reasonably sized hedge against the enemy force of dollar devaluation.

The SM's allocation includes her husband's Roth IRA. Her husband's Roth IRA could be due to his own earnings or to his use of a Spousal IRA. Given the IRS' contribution limits for IRAs and the TSP, familial collaboration enables the faster attainment of the recommended asset allocation. The REIT index ETF in her husband's Roth IRA satisfies the family's need for real estate exposure. Nonetheless, in "How to Retire Early", Edmunds makes the point that the utmost diversification that an investor can derive from real estate comes from owning actual commercial properties. Unfortunately, the average SM possesses too little capital to invest in good quality commercial properties. Owning REITs is an effective and feasible alternative for SMs.

Maintaining Her Allocations

Our SM's allocation of dollars among the asset classes roughly meets the guidelines. Over time, changes in her funds' values may change her allocation. These changes may result in her holding too much or too little of a given asset class. When this occurs, she must adjust the percentages and quantities of her future Roth TSP contributions or Roth IRA investments. These adjustments should aim to realign her allocation with the guidelines. However, our SM should not adjust her future contributions in anticipation of any particular market conditions. That would be market timing. She should build her allocation to meet the guidelines and then "let it ride".

Note *: S Fund versus a Pure Small Cap Index

In Edmunds' Asset Allocation chart, the anticipated return of 12% applies to small capitalization U.S. company stocks, only. The 12% figure does not actually apply to the combination of small and medium capitalization U.S. company stocks that exists in the S Fund. Unfortunately, the TSP does not offer a fund that exclusively focuses on small capitalization U.S. company stocks. This may be due to the varying definitions of what constitutes a small capitalization stock. Floors of anywhere from $100 million to $500 million and ceilings of anywhere from $1 billion to $2 billion exist, depending on who is defining the term. A further complication is that inflation and dollar devaluation eventually antiquate all definitions. A figure that once defined a large capitalization stock might now define a small capitalization stock.

Whatever the definition, the performance of the S Fund from 2001 through 2010 showed its potential for greater returns than the C Fund. For 7 of these 10 years, the S Fund enjoyed returns that were 2.9% to 14.4% higher than the C Fund's returns. For the 3 years in which the C Fund beat the S Fund, all of the differences were less than 1.3%. Until the TSP offers a solely small capitalization stock index fund, the current S Fund should suffice. The S Fund will give SMs reasonably good exposure to the rapid growth of newer companies.

Improving Your Returns

Regardless of the preceding sections' recommendations, you may decide that you want an even greater total return. The obvious means for doing this is to put 100% of your Roth TSP dollars into the U.S. small to medium sized company stocks of the S Fund that earn nearly 12% and to put 100% of your Roth IRA dollars into emerging market funds that earn 14%. However, these moves are risky. You will lack adequate diversification.

You will have more than one third of your dollars in U.S. stocks, and all of that one third will be in small to medium sized companies. You will lack exposure to the steady growth of large U.S. companies.

All of your foreign company holdings will be in the BRICs. You will have nothing poised to benefit from the steady growth of companies in Europe, Australia, and Japan. These cultures rapidly and powerfully recovered from the utter devastation of World War II. Exposure to such cultures will benefit your portfolio.

You will possess no real estate exposure. You will not have the opportunity to benefit from local market conditions. Only national and global economic conditions will determine your portfolio's value.

Lastly, you will possess no protection against dollar devaluation. While the stronger total returns might offset that loss of protection, no guarantee of this effect exists. Choosing to possess no exposure to precious metals is akin to leaving your ships at anchor while knowing that the Japanese fleet is approaching. You know that the U.S. Government will retain its debt problems, and you know that this retained debt will cause the Government to print more money. The value of the U.S. dollar will continue to fall.

Chapter 17: Establish a Taxable Account

If you have spare dollars after eliminating your bad debt, after establishing your emergency fund, and after contributing the maximum amounts to your Roth TSP and to your Roth IRA, then the time has come to start investing in a taxable account. Where you establish your taxable account is up to you. Using the same brokerage that holds your Roth IRA is reasonable. The brokerage will keep your taxable account separate from your Roth IRA and will send you year-end statements for your taxable account. Dealing with a single brokerage or single financial advisor simplifies your personal accounting efforts and might even lead to your receipt of a few perks.

Once again, you should purchase funds that minimize loads, 12b-1 fees, and management expenses. For taxable accounts, managed mutual funds are particularly costly, relative to index ETFs and index funds. Managed mutual funds' more frequent turnover of their stock holdings will lead to fees for trading commissions and to the realization of capital gains. Fees for trading commissions lower investors' returns in both tax-advantaged and taxable accounts. However, realizing capital gains is an added danger for taxable accounts. When a fund's managers sell stocks to buy new stocks or to pay investors that are selling their own shares of the fund, the IRS will tax any capital gains that these liquidated stocks possess. If you are holding such a fund in your taxable account, you will be liable for a portion of these taxes, even though you are not the person selling shares. This is a drawback of all mutual funds in taxable accounts, but managed mutual funds' more frequent turnover worsens this drawback.

If a managed mutual fund enjoys a history of strong performance and low costs due to good management, then its returns might offset its higher expenses. Pending your discovery of such a high quality managed mutual fund, holding index ETFs and index funds in your taxable account will keep your expenses low. As explained in Chapter 9, index ETFs and index funds enjoy extremely low rates of turnover. Index ETFs, specifically, suffer fewer capital gains tax hits and offer more control over what prices investors will get for the shares that they buy or sell.

Taxable Account Advantages

You may wonder what point exists in investing money in a taxable account, given all the good tax sheltering that you have done with your Roth TSP and Roth IRA. The answer lies in three advantages that a taxable account offers.

First, no IRS-mandated limits exist on your annual taxable account contributions. If you inherit a large sum of money, you can invest it all, less any inheritance taxes.

Second, a taxable account's holdings are almost immediately liquid. Dollars in a taxable account are dollars on which you have already paid ordinary income taxes. These dollars are "after-tax" dollars. Dollars that you send to a Roth TSP or a Roth IRA are also after-tax dollars, but the growths of these dollars are locked-up until you are 59.5 years old. In contrast, you may withdraw all of the money from your taxable account whenever you wish. Actually, some restrictions on these withdrawals may apply, depending on which investment vehicles you choose. For example, a 12-month minimum holding period may apply to a mutual fund. To avoid added brokerage fees, you would have to hold the fund for at least 12 months before you could liquidate it. Such restrictions aside, money in a taxable account is more accessible (liquid) than money in a tax-advantaged account.

The third advantage of a taxable account is that your withdrawals are taxed at the capital gains tax rate. You will only pay capital gains taxes on the growth, not on the principal, of your investments. As of the writing of this book, the capital gains tax rate enjoys a ceiling of 15%. In late December 2010, Congress voted to extend the 15% rate for two more years. In 2013, the rate is slated to return to 20%, pending further legislation. The bottom rate will increase from its current 0% to 10%, for those investors in low tax brackets.

Enjoying a low 15% or even 20% tax rate on only the capital gains of your withdrawals from a taxable account significantly improves the purchasing power of those withdrawals. By withdrawing a combination of modestly taxed capital gains and untaxed principal, you can create substantial income without suffering the pain of larger ordinary income taxes. In contrast, dollars that you might contribute to a Traditional TSP account would be before-tax dollars. When you finally withdrew such dollars, you would pay ordinary federal income taxes on both the principal and the capital gains. The Traditional TSP dollars that you withdrew would increase your taxable income, possibly even placing you in a higher marginal tax bracket. Note that my discussion of a Traditional TSP is only for the purpose of comparison. I still recommend that you choose a Roth TSP.

Eliminating your bad debt, establishing your emergency fund, and contributing dollars to your Roth TSP and to your Roth IRA are still your most pressing missions. That said, saving whatever dollars you have left in a taxable account is a wise move. It is certainly a wiser move than blowing those excess dollars on a celebratory cruise.

Long-term Growth COA

Recommending specific investments for your taxable account is difficult. While the use of tax-advantaged accounts is clearly for retirement, investors can use taxable accounts for any purpose. You could use a taxable account to pay for a short-term goal, such as the impending purchase of a home. In this case, you might want very conservative investments, possibly even fixed income instruments. Preserving your existing purchasing power would be your foremost requirement. Alternatively, you could use a taxable account to augment your retirement savings. In such a case, you would invest for long-term growth. I do not know your goals, so my recommendation will focus on this second goal.

The Long-term Growth COA requires purchasing investments for your taxable account that largely mirror the investments in your tax-advantaged accounts. For your taxable account, you should purchase index ETFs that follow nearly the same indices as your Roth TSP's index funds and your Roth IRA's index ETFs. Do not purchase normal index funds for your taxable account. Index funds are good funds, but index ETFs are better for your taxable account.

Mirroring your Roth IRA is simple. Call your brokerage. Explain your wish to start a taxable account containing the following funds:

1. Emerging market index ETF

2. REIT index ETF

3. Precious metals fund (if inexpensive)

Note that the precious metals fund possesses a qualifier. A precious metals fund is a good holding for 10% of your tax-advantaged accounts. Whether it is a good holding for 10% of your taxable account depends on its expenses and its rate of turnover. Precious metals funds are likely to be managed mutual funds. Managed mutual funds charge higher expenses than index ETFs or index funds. Additionally, managed mutual funds experience higher rates of turnover. Higher rates of turnover are particularly detrimental in taxable accounts due to the realization of capital gains. For a precious metals fund to make sense in your taxable account, it must charge low expenses, charge zero or minimal loads, and infrequently turnover.

Mirroring your Roth TSP is a tad more complex than mirroring your Roth IRA. Inform your brokerage that you wish to buy three more index ETFs for your taxable account that track the following indices:

1. Standard & Poors (S&P) 500 Index.

2. Morgan Stanley Capital International (MSCI) EAFE Index.

3. MSCI U.S. Small Capitalization 1750 Index.

Index ETFs that track the S&P 500 and the EAFE indices will very closely mirror the returns of the TSP's C and I funds. However, an index ETF that tracks the U.S. Small Capitalization 1750 Index will enjoy somewhat different returns than the TSP's S Fund. This is exactly what you want. An index ETF that tracks the U.S. Small Capitalization 1750 Index will contain the stocks of purely small capitalization companies. It will not hold the stocks of medium capitalization companies that the TSP's S Fund holds.

A solely small capitalization company focused index ETF will enjoy larger gains than the gains that a fund that owns both small and medium sized companies' stocks will enjoy. The small company focused index ETF will be more volatile. As such, it will more consistently meet the 12% anticipated return from the Asset Allocation chart. Since you are now purchasing index ETFs for your taxable account, you are free to purchase whichever funds you wish. You should seize the opportunity to invest in asset classes that precisely match those of the Asset Allocation chart.

If your brokerage does not offer these index ETFs, you can substitute normal index funds. However, you will have less control over when you suffer capital gains taxes. One solution might be opening the missing index ETF(s) with a different brokerage. You will lose a few perks and you will somewhat complicate your tracking processes, but these drawbacks will be minor losses. They will not outweigh the advantage of owning index ETFs that properly diversify your investments.

Allocate dollars to your taxable account's ETFs using guidelines that are similar to those that you used for allocating dollars to your Roth TSP and to your Roth IRA.

1. One third of your dollars should be in foreign stocks.

2. One third of your dollars should be in U.S. stocks.

3. The last one third of your dollars can be in any of the remaining asset classes. Again, weighting the majority, if not all, of this last one third in real estate may offer the best returns.

Example: Allocation of taxable account dollars.

Situation

You are investing $100,000 in a taxable account. You wish to meet all of the allocation guidelines. You want to survive a variety of economic conditions. You were unable to find an inexpensive precious metals fund with minimal turnover.

Possible Allocation

1. $13,000 = Standard & Poors 500 index ETF.

2. $20,000 = MSCI U.S. Small Capitalization 1750 index ETF.

3. $17,000 = MSCI EAFE index ETF.

4. $17,000 = Emerging market index ETF.

5. $33,000 = REIT index ETF.

Analysis

Using the same calculations that we used in the earlier "Projected Returns" example, we find that the total projected return for this allocation would be 11.08%. This return is not terribly exciting, but it soundly and reliably overcomes our enemy forces.

33% of your dollars would be in U.S. stock funds. This example puts most of that 33% in U.S. small companies. Weighting even more of that 33% toward U.S. small companies could increase your overall returns but would reduce your ability to benefit from periods when the economy sees steady but modest growth.

34% of your dollars would be in international stock funds. Half of that 34% would be in the BRIC economies of the emerging markets. Weighting even more of that 34% toward emerging markets could increase your overall returns but would expose your portfolio to greater volatility. The stocks of companies in the powerful BRIC nations are not the only stocks that emerging market funds hold. These funds also hold stocks of companies in far less stable nations.

33% of your dollars would be in a REIT index ETF. Therefore, you would enjoy the gains in real estate that can come from burgeoning local markets.

Strategy Funds

Also called "Life Strategy Funds" by some brokerages, strategy funds resemble target retirement and lifecycle funds. Like target retirement and lifecycle funds, strategy funds are "funds of funds" – they are funds that contain several other funds. Strategy funds differ from target retirement and lifecycle funds in that strategy funds do not rebalance to reduce volatility. Strategy funds rebalance to maintain volatility. For example, an aggressive strategy fund might aim to hold 80% equities and 20% bonds. If the value of this fund's equities grew to the extent that the equities comprised 90% of the fund's total value, the fund would automatically sell enough of those equities and purchase enough new bonds to bring the fund's ratio back to its targeted 80/20 mix. The fund would maintain its 80/20 mix, regardless of the year or your age.

Strategy funds' ease of use may tempt you to purchase them for your taxable account or for your Roth IRA. Unfortunately, doing so will lower your returns. Even the more aggressive strategy funds maintain sizable bond and cash holdings. Holding bonds and fixed income instruments will lower your returns. If investing ease is your primary goal, then strategy funds and their lifecycle fund cousins may work for you. However, purchasing and managing the five or six funds that this book recommends will require only marginally greater efforts. The greater returns that purchasing these five or six funds will produce should adequately compensate you for the extra work.

The "Rule of 72"

The 10% and 11% total returns in the preceding tax-advantaged and taxable account examples may be unimpressive. You may have hoped to learn how to create far larger returns. Indeed, years will pass when you see larger returns. Nonetheless, the goal of this book is to show you how to obtain consistent returns that are large enough to permit sizable growth, after inflation and dollar devaluation take their bites.

10% total returns might be more impressive if you apply them to the "Rule of 72". This rule is a shorthand method for determining how many years must pass before your investments double in value. Simply divide 72 by the rate of return that you expect to average. The result is the number of years before your investment doubles.

To illustrate the Rule of 72, return to the example in which our SM had $165,000 in tax advantaged accounts and enjoyed a 10% total return. Her $165,000 investment will double to $330,000 in approximately 72 years / 10% = 7.2 years. In another 7.2 years, her investment will double to $660,000. In yet another 7.2 years, her investment will double to $1.3 million. In less than 22 years, our SM could be a millionaire. 22 years is roughly the time between a SM's age at the time of her 20-year military retirement and her age when she becomes eligible for full Social Security benefits.

Chapter 18: Follow Investing Guidelines

Reinvest Your Dividends

Tell your brokerage to reinvest all of your dividends in both your tax-advantaged and your taxable accounts. Reinvesting your dividends is critical for growing your investments. Reinvested dividends will purchase more shares of the fund that produced the dividends. These added shares will grow in the same manner that your original shares are growing. Much later in life, you may decide to receive your dividends as income. For now, reinvest them.

The return of an asset is the sum of the asset's capital gains and the income that the asset produces. For a stock or fund, the capital gain is the increase over the original purchase price, and the income is the dividends. The formula for determining your total return on a stock or fund becomes:

Total Return = Capital Gains + Dividends

The returns quoted in the Asset Class chart assume that investors are reinvesting their dividends. Of course, you are free to ignore this advice and take your dividends as income. In the near-term, you will gain a few dollars to spend, minus ordinary federal income taxes. However, over the long-term, failing to reinvest your dividends will profoundly reduce your returns.

What Are Dividends?

Companies distribute profits to shareholders in the form of dividend payments. Dividends encourage investors to purchase more shares of those companies' stocks. However, the paying of dividends is not guaranteed. A company's board of directors will determine if their current profits, their expansion plans, and trends in the economy will permit the paying of dividends to shareholders. Assuming they vote to distribute dividends, they will send the dividends to shareholders at some regular interval (e.g. quarterly or semi-annually).

If you directly own stock in these companies, the companies will send the dividends to you. If you own shares of a mutual fund that owns stock in these companies, the mutual fund managers will receive the dividends. Since different companies pay dividends at different times, the mutual fund will not immediately relay the underlying companies' dividends to you. The mutual fund will simply accumulate the various dividends. The mutual fund will later distribute its own dividend that reflects the accumulated value of the underlying companies' dividends. Mutual funds typically distribute their own dividends quarterly or semi-annually.

In taxable accounts, the receipt of dividends is a taxable event. Whether you took those dividends as checks or reinvested those dividends does not matter to the IRS. What does matter to the IRS is the date when you purchased the corresponding stocks or mutual funds and the length of time that you held those stocks or mutual funds. These factors will determine whether the IRS will tax your dividends at the full ordinary income rate or at the lower capital gains rate. In practice, qualifying for the capital gains rate will not be a problem for SMs. Most SMs will hold their mutual funds for many years.

Sometime between 1 January and 14 April, you should receive a Form 1099-DIV from your brokerage for each of your funds that received dividend distributions in taxable accounts. Box 1a of the form is "Ordinary Dividends". Box 1b of the form is "Qualified Dividends". Box 1a shows the number of dividends that you received. Box 1b shows the number of those dividends that qualify for the capital gains tax rate. For most SMs, the numbers in these two boxes will be nearly equal.

Of course, choosing to receive your dividends as income in your tax-advantaged accounts would be particularly bad. If you were less than 59.5 years old and your brokerage actually did send dividend checks from your tax-advantaged accounts, ordinary income taxes and a 10% early withdrawal penalty would apply. A more likely temptation, though, might be for you to instruct your brokerage to park your dividends in a MMA within your Roth IRA. Neither penalties nor taxes would apply to this MMA, but parking money in fixed income instruments dramatically reduces your returns. Reinvest your dividends.

Reduce Your Bond Fund Exposure

Among other objectives, the recommended COAs for your tax-advantaged and taxable accounts aim to minimize your bond fund exposure. A personal example may illustrate the reason for this aim.

Prior to February of 2011, The TSP's L 2040 Fund was putting about 9% of investors' starting dollars in bond funds. During the 12 months leading up to that month, my C, S, and I funds enjoyed average returns of 23.72%, relative to the L 2040 Fund's 19.32% returns. My own TSP Individual Fund COA performed 4.4% better than a TSP Lifecycle Fund COA would have performed. This represented a nearly 23% increase over the return of the L 2040 Fund. Over several years, repeating such a difference will produce a decisive victory.

In his book, "The New Financial Advisor", Mr. Nick Murray sternly advises investors to avoid bonds and bond funds. Murray recommends possessing portfolios comprised of 100% equities. He supports his recommendation by comparing the returns of equities and bonds, net of inflation, over the 75 years since the Great Depression and the writing of his book in 2001. Murray shows that equities' average annual returns were three times the returns of bonds[xxxviii]. Murray warns readers that, given this trend, investing in bonds jeopardizes an investor's long-term purchasing power.

Acting on Murray's premise will expose your portfolio to considerable volatility. Volatility is not actually bad, especially not for younger investors with far investing horizons. In fact, enduring volatility is the price investors pay for the premium returns from equities. Nonetheless, some investors may not have the flexibility to weather market volatility that extends for several months. Such investors may be unable to fully pursue Murray's advice.

Maintain Your Allocation

Do not chase performance. Referring to the previous section's anecdote, over the 12 months preceding February 2011, I poured 100% of my principal into the I Fund. During that time, the I Fund suffered the lowest return of the three funds. Had I been pouring some or all of my money into the C and S funds, I might have done better than 23.72%. However, my current return was not my focus. I was bringing my asset allocation back into line with the same percentages that I have recommended for you. This necessitated my temporarily changing my contribution percentages for the C, S, and I funds. Over the years, changes in the values of your funds will force you to make similar changes.

I do not lament the fact that I missed an opportunity to enjoy a higher return. During this period in which I was sending 100% of my contributions to the I Fund, the I Fund's shares were cheaper, relative to periods in which the I Fund is hot. These lower prices enabled me to buy more shares of the I Fund than I normally would have been able to buy. When the I Fund rebounds, I will benefit by having an even greater number of I Fund shares. This was a fortunate example of "buying low". I held the funds that were doing well, while I bought more of a fund that was not.

This example of "buying low" was due to pure luck. Much as my ego would enjoy claiming otherwise, I had absolutely no idea that EAFE companies would lag U.S. companies. I had no such "intel". I simply knew that my asset allocation had drifted from the recommended percentages. The returns that I will enjoy when the I Fund rebounds will be fortunate, though unintentional, derivatives of my having followed the asset allocation guidelines. Frankly, if I had invested per some hunch about the prevailing economic conditions in Europe and Japan, I would have been guilty of timing the market. As I have already said, market timing is bad. You will occasionally get it right, but you will frequently get it wrong.

By following the recommended allocation percentages, you will be able to profit from whichever way the fickle economic winds blow. As the saying goes, "Chance favors the prepared man".

Buy and Hold

Once you purchase the index ETFs and index funds that this book recommends, stop. Hold onto your purchases. As earlier prescribed, let your purchases ride. Do not sell your purchases in response to changing market conditions. In the end, your returns will be better.

Before every looming market upheaval, many investors consider selling their index ETFs and index funds. As the media's predictions of economic Armageddon gain intensity, such investors concoct schemes in which they will secure their gains by temporarily converting their shares into cash. These investors' plans are to return to equities when the market hits bottom and equity prices are low. If investors could consistently succeed in such "flipping" schemes, then such schemes might be okay. Unfortunately, nobody can consistently predict which way the markets will go. Additionally, these schemes ignore the damage of failing to receive dividends during periods in which the investors no longer hold shares of their liquidated funds.

Consistently timing the markets has been impossible for even the most brilliant investors. Warren Buffett is a billionaire because he identifies good companies and then purchases their stocks at fair prices, not because he has some innate sense of when stocks' values will rise or fall. If his chosen companies are good, the companies' stock prices may fluctuate but will inevitably reflect the high qualities of the companies. Over many years, the values of his investments in these companies grow due to reinvested dividends and capital gains. Buffett understands that to receive dividends, he must hold his companies' stocks at the times when these companies send their dividends. This requirement is just as well, since Buffett also knows that no sooner than he prepares for Armageddon, the markets will soar.

Index ETFs and index funds hold stocks of the same companies that the market indices track. The index committees have thoroughly researched these companies. Essentially, the index committees have already done the "Buffett-work" for you. Buy the recommended index ETFs and index funds and hold onto them. Do not miss the distribution of dividends that will improve your long-term returns. Do not chase price changes that you have no way of accurately predicting.

Lump-sum-invest Rather than Dollar-cost-average

In the early days of your investing, "dollar-cost-averaging" is the technique that you will probably use to get your dollars into your Roth TSP, Roth IRA, and taxable account. However, when your savings permit, execute "lump-sum-investing". Lump-sum-investing is simply the process of dumping into your accounts as much as you can, as early as you can, regardless of whether the markets are up or down. If you are a habitual saver and can discipline yourself to fill your investments before buying luxuries, then lump-sum-investing will be the more lucrative system. More of your money will have more time to grow.

In contrast to lump-sum-investing, dollar-cost-averaging evenly spreads your contributions over the course of a year. Each month, the same quantity of dollars will come out of your checking or savings account and will go into your investments. Investment firms will eagerly assist you with establishing such a system; it will assure the firms of getting your money. For habitual spenders, dollar-cost-averaging may be a necessary evil. Your money will go straight from DFAS to your bank account and will then jump to your investing accounts. You will never touch the money, so you will never get the chance to waste it on those bass boats or diamonds. The problem with dollar-cost-averaging is that it will actually reduce your returns. Half of your contributions will miss half a year's worth of growth.

Many people claim that dollar-cost-averaging provides a better chance of achieving "average" purchase costs, over the course of a year. They claim that by contributing the same amount each month to your funds, you will probably see as many months in which you "buy low" as those in which you "buy high". They will extol dollar-cost-averaging's supposed virtue of being a means for evading the potentially disastrous effects of attempting to time the markets. Indeed, the unpredictability of the markets makes consistently timing them impossible. Whether dollar-cost-averaging mitigates the damage from this unpredictability is questionable.

Over many years, the growth rates listed in the earlier Asset Class chart are reliable. However, from month-to-month, nobody knows what rates will prevail. Assume you are waiting until the NAVs of a bullish fund drop before you buy into the fund. You refuse to "buy high". You are timing the market. How can you be sure that many months will not pass before you see a drop? What about the fund's dividends that you missed during those months when your money was parked in a low interest bearing SA or MMA? All too often, this is the adverse consequence of market timing – you simply forfeit gains.

Unfortunately, dollar-cost-averaging does not eliminate this consequence. If you use dollar-cost-averaging to purchase a fund that ultimately rises from January through December, half of your contributions will miss half of this growth. You will suffer smaller gains. True, the opposite could happen. The fund might suffer consistent drops in value for 12 months. In this case, dollar-cost-averaging would benefit you. Unfortunately, following an investment strategy that aims to protect you from a few months in which funds' values might decline is shortsighted.

Your strategy should focus on the benefits of investing over many years. Over periods of several months, consistent drops in value are common. However, over periods of many years, consistent drops in value are rare. Market histories show that the odds are well in your favor of enjoying considerably more positive years than negative years. Lump-sum-investing on the first day of each year is like conducting annual dollar-cost-averaging. Yet, in this case, dollar-cost-averaging benefits you due to the yearly trend. In effect, you are already dollar-cost-averaging. The size of your military salary and the IRS' restrictions force you to invest on an annual basis. You should not compound any negative effects of this restriction by further dollar-cost-averaging on a monthly basis.

No tax advantage exists to spreading your contributions over 12 months. When reporting your income to the IRS, your total income for the year is what matters. If you paid less than the IRS requires, you will write a check for the difference. If you paid more than the IRS requires, you will get a refund.

Unfortunately, the rules for receiving matching funds in the TSP force government civilians to dollar-cost-average their TSP contributions. Government civilians should spread their TSP contributions over the course of a year. Otherwise, they will forfeit a portion of their matching funds. Matching funds are guaranteed 100% returns on TSP investments. As good as lump-sum-investing is, it stands little chance of producing returns that surpass 100%. Nonetheless, lump-sum-investing is still the better choice for SMs. SMs do not receive matching funds in TSP accounts. SMs should invest as much as they can, as early as they can.

Example: Dollar-cost-averaging versus lump-sum-investing.

Situation

Assume that you have $5000 to invest. You have the opportunity to invest in a fund that ultimately enjoys monthly gains of 0.8% for a total of 9.6% gains for the year. On 1 January, you could start investing $5000 / 12 months = $416.67 per month (dollar-cost-averaging), or you could simply invest the entire $5000 (lump-sum-investing). You wish to know which approach will provide a larger return.

Comparison

The chart on the next page shows the results of dollar-cost-averaging versus lump-sum-investing. Note that the monthly returns are rounded to the nearest whole dollar:

	Dollar-Cost-Averaging	Lump-Sum-Investing
Jan 0.8%	$420	$5,040
Feb 0.8%	$843	$5,080
Mar 0.8%	$1,270	$5,121
Apr 0.8%	$1,700	$5,162
May 0.8%	$2,134	$5,203
Jun 0.8%	$2,571	$5,245
Jul 0.8%	$3,012	$5,287
Aug 0.8%	$3,456	$5,329
Sep 0.8%	$3,903	$5,372
Oct 0.8%	$4,355	$5,415
Nov 0.8%	$4,809	$5,458
Dec 0.8%	$5,268	$5,502

Analysis

Your gain with the dollar-cost-averaging choice would be
$5268 – $5000 = $268. Your gain with the lump-sum-investing
choice would be $5502 – $5000 = $502. Therefore, your investment
return with the lump-sum-investing choice would be ($5502 –
$5268)/268 * 100% = 87% larger than it would be with the dollar-
cost-averaging choice. While such a perfectly geometric rise of 0.8%
per month would probably never happen, a total return of 9.6% for
the year is quite reasonable, especially for the top five asset classes.
The point should be clear that lump-sum-investing as early as
possible can dramatically increase your returns, relative to the oft-
touted method of dollar-cost-averaging.

Chapter 19: Properly Sequence Your Liquidations

Eventually, the day will come for you to liquidate funds in your taxable account, Roth TSP, and Roth IRA. You may even have a Traditional TSP, if you started a TSP before the Roth version became available. Determining how much to withdraw is a function of your needs and your income. If you need a house and you want the lowest possible mortgage rate, you may need to liquidate substantial portions of your accounts, all at once. However, if you simply need money to supplement your retirement income, then you might need relatively small portions of your accounts, each year.

Determining how much to withdraw for annual retirement dollars involves returning to the section on identifying your expenses and income. You should calculate which expenses your military retirement income and your Social Security checks will fail to cover. This amount is the amount that you should withdraw from your investments. If your retirement income and your Social Security payments will cover all of your expenses, then you should not withdraw dollars from your investments. You do not want to generate taxable income for no particular reason. Additionally, you do not want to sacrifice further growth in your investments by suddenly parking those investments in a checking or savings account. Of course, if you still have a TSP balance and you are 70.5 years old, then you must take your RMDs, regardless of whether you need them. If that TSP balance is in a Traditional TSP account, the RMD will increase your taxable income.

If you truly must withdraw money from your investments, then knowing the best sequence in which to draw down those investments becomes important. Your goals should be to avoid penalties and to reduce taxes. If you are less than 59.5 years old, the choice is simple. You should liquidate funds in your taxable account. Liquidating funds in your tax-advantaged accounts would force penalties and unnecessary taxes upon you. These taxes would be at the ordinary income tax rate. On the other hand, liquidations of your taxable account will not suffer the 10% penalty, and the taxes you pay will be at the lower capital gains tax rate.

If your age is equal to or greater than 59.5 years old, you may choose to liquidate funds in any of your accounts without fear of the 10% penalty. Nonetheless, you should once again choose to first liquidate funds in your taxable account. Delay the withdrawal of your tax-advantaged dollars as long as possible. These dollars will enjoy more years of tax deferrals and tax exemptions.

If you are equal to or greater than 70.5 years old and you possess a Traditional TSP, a Roth TSP, or both, you should first take your RMDs from those accounts. You must take RMDs no later than 1 April of the year after you turn 70.5 years old. If you have both types of TSPs, the combined balances of your Traditional TSP and your Roth TSP will determine the size of the RMDs that you must take. However, if in a prior year, you rolled your Roth TSP balance over to a Roth IRA, only the size of your Traditional TSP balance will determine the size of the RMDs that you must take.

Finally, withdraw dollars from Roth IRAs. These accounts are last in the sequence, because these accounts offer the opportunity for unlimited growth. No RMD requirements exist. You do not have to withdraw portions of these dollars when you turn 70.5 years old. If you can live without money from your Roth IRA accounts, then you can leave your Roth IRA accounts to your children and grandchildren.

Liquidate Principal Rather than Growth

Returning to the advice of Mr. Gillette Edmunds, to reduce your tax liabilities, you should liquidate principal, not just capital gains[xxxix]. This advice pertains to withdrawals from your taxable account; it does not pertain to withdrawals from a Traditional TSP, a Roth TSP, or a Roth IRA. Withdrawals from your Traditional TSP are fully taxed. You have yet to pay taxes on either the principal or the gains, so differentiating between them will not matter. Differentiating between principal and gains in your Roth TSP and Roth IRA is equally unnecessary. Withdrawals of both principal and gains from your Roth accounts are fully tax-free.

Nonetheless, when dealing with your taxable account, a big difference exists between withdrawing principal and withdrawing capital gains. You have already paid the taxes on your principal. You need not pay any more taxes on your principal. However, you must pay taxes on your capital gains. Your principal and, hence, your "tax basis" equal your original investment plus any reinvested dividends. Your capital gains equal the subtraction of your tax basis from the current value of your shares in a given fund. This difference is what the IRS will tax. Fortunately, the IRS will tax this difference at the capital gains tax rate, assuming that you have held your fund long enough to meet the qualification standards.

When working with taxable accounts, investors often shoot themselves in the foot by attempting to preserve their principal. They withdraw only the amount by which a fund's value exceeds its tax basis. By selling only the "golden eggs", these investors hope to preserve the goose that lays the eggs. Unfortunately, this method kills the goose. Spending only capital gains increases your taxes. On the other hand, spending principal reduces your taxes. You can invest your tax savings to replenish your goose. In the end, you will be ahead of the game.

Example: Liquidation of Principal in a Taxable Account.

Situation

Assume you need $10,000 to supplement your military retirement income and your Social Security benefits. You paid $9500 for each of five funds in a taxable account. Your total investment was 5 funds X $9500 purchase price = $47,500.

Investment Results

Each of these five funds enjoys a $2500 gain. $500 of each fund's $2500 gain is due to reinvested dividends. The remaining $2000 of each fund's gain is due to capital gains. Your principal in each fund becomes $9500 purchase price + $500 reinvested dividends = $10,000. This is the new tax basis for each of your five funds. Each fund's new value becomes $10,000 principal + $2000 capital gain = $12,000. The value of each fund minus each fund's tax basis yields the amount on which you must pay capital gains taxes. For each of your five funds, your taxable capital gains equal $12,000 value – $10,000 tax basis (principal) = $2000.

Liquidation of Capital Gains

You might be tempted to liquidate each fund's capital gains, while preserving each fund's principal. If you did so, you would produce $2000 capital gains X 5 funds = $10,000 in capital gains. Your taxes would be $10,000 capital gains X 15% capital gains tax rate = $1500. You would net $10,000 capital gains – $1500 tax liability = $8500. In this case, you would pay more taxes than are necessary, and you would fail to produce your requisite $10,000.

Liquidation of Principal

A better move would be liquidating one entire fund and not touching the other four funds. You would produce $12,000 value X 1 fund = $12,000 in personal revenue. Since $10,000 of this revenue would be principal, your capital gains taxes would only apply to $12,000 value – $10,000 tax basis (principal) = $2000. Your tax liability would drop to $2000 capital gains X 15% capital gains tax rate = $300. You would net $12,000 value – $300 tax liability = $11,700. In this case, you would meet your $10,000 requirement, and you would pay a five-fold smaller tax. In fact, you would actually have $1700 to reinvest.

A final point about liquidating funds deals with calendar dates. Your brokerage can tell you when your index ETFs and index funds will distribute dividends. This can be valuable information. If you liquidate a fund, do so after the most recent distribution of dividends, not before. Receiving these dividends will further increase your tax basis, thus reducing the capital gains that the IRS can tax. A good time to liquidate a fund is often in early January. Many funds distribute year-end dividends in the final week of December.

Staging Your Impending TSP Withdrawals

When you start making regular withdrawals from your TSP, you may finally want to use the TSP's G Fund. This is the TSP's fixed securities fund. Money that you shift into the G Fund will enjoy very little growth, especially after accounting for inflation and dollar devaluation. Nonetheless, money in the G Fund will retain most of its value in the near-term. This will be important, if covering your next year's living expenses depends on a precise quantity's coming from your TSP. Investments in the G Fund will not suffer the same sudden drops in value that investments in the C, S, and I funds can suffer. Nonetheless, if you must use the G Fund, shift no more money from your C, S, and I funds than is absolutely necessary. Transfer just enough money to cover your next year's living expenses.

Interfund Transfers

Use the TSP's "Interfund Transfer" tool to get money from your C, S, and I funds into the G Fund. Interfund transfers only affect your existing TSP contributions – the dollars that you have already contributed. Interfund transfers do not change the allocation of your future contributions.

To execute your interfund transfer, login to your TSP account. Click on "Interfund Transfers". Click the "Request Interfund Transfer" button. You will see a digital form that is identical to the digital form for allocating your TSP contributions. Use money from all three of your C, S, and I funds to make up the money that you need in your G Fund. Do not simply transfer all of the money from a single fund. Transferring amounts from each of your C, S, and I funds will enable you to maintain your asset allocation.

Example: Interfund transfer.

Situation

You must transfer $15,000 to your new G Fund to cover expenses in your first full retirement year. Your TSP starts with the balances listed in the "Current %" column in the digital interfund transfer form, below:

Investment Funds	Balance	Current %	New %
Individual Funds			
G Fund Government Securities	$0.00	0%	%
F Fund Fixed Income Index	$0.00	0%	%
C Fund Common Stock Index	$51,000.00	22.57%	%
S Fund Small Cap Stock Index	$65,000.00	28.76%	%
I Fund International Stock Index	$110,000.00	48.67%	%
Total	$226,000.00	100.00%	0%

Calculations

To make up the $15,000 that you wish to transfer to the G Fund, you should transfer the following amounts from each of your C, S, and I funds:

1. C Fund: $15,000.00 X 22.57% = $3385.50

2. S Fund: $15,000.00 X 28.76% = $4314.00

3. I Fund: $15,000.00 X 48.67% = $7300.50

Conclusion

Contributing money from the C, S, and I funds in these percentages preserves your current allocation. It avoids unduly stressing a single account and thus knocking your allocation out of balance.

Chapter 20: Choose an Affordable Home

In the Situation paragraph, we discussed the factors that impact your housing. Now, we will use that data to develop a reasonable plan of action. In reality, I cannot develop a "Best COA" that fits every situation. Local market conditions affect home prices, and local market conditions vary. Nonetheless, arming you with a list of questions to ask yourself, prior to purchasing a home, is possible.

Accepting on-post (or on-base) housing is generally a SM's best COA. In comparison to buying a home, accepting on-post housing avoids gambling on changing home equities and expensive maintenance costs. More critically, accepting on-post housing avoids being saddled with a mortgage on a home that you cannot sell when your PCS orders arrive.

In comparison to renting, accepting on-post housing avoids contracts that may not be SM-friendly. Accepting on-post housing offers other advantages, relative to living off-post. Minimal commute times lead to less wear and tear on your vehicles and less money spent on $3 and $4 per gallon fuel prices. On-post utility costs are likely to be less expensive than off-post utility costs. Living in a gated community with frequent patrolling and like-minded neighbors offers inestimable value. By itself, hassle-free and expense-free maintenance may clinch the deal. Free lawn care – my favorite – adds more benefits.

If no on-post housing is available, renting is probably a SM's next best COA. Most SMs will PCS in approximately three years.

Leaving a rental is easier than leaving a home. Provided that your rental contract permits sudden terminations, you can leave a rental with few more expenses than your final month's rent. Since the 2008 bursting of the housing bubble, a buyers' market has existed in much of the nation. The supply of homes is greater than the demand for these homes. Record numbers of foreclosures exacerbate this problem. The laws of supply and demand are driving down home prices. Renting avoids this financial quagmire.

Buying a home is the least favored COA for SMs who will PCS in three years. Three years is too brief to expect substantial increases in a home's value. After closing costs, maintenance costs, and mortgage interest costs, a strong possibility exists that SMs who sell homes after only three years of ownership will take losses – possibly large ones. However, if you are on your last assignment, buying a home may finally make sense. You will possess the time to allow a home to appreciate to a level that exceeds its costs. You may even possess the time to completely retire your mortgage. When considering purchasing a home, you should be able to answer, "Yes" to several questions:

1. Do you plan to retire in this community and remain in your house for many years?

2. If you start a second career, are you confident that it will be in this community?

3. Is your marriage solid?

4. Is the home's value likely to appreciate, every year?

5. Is your home new and did a high quality builder construct it?

6. Have independent sources verified the builder's quality?

7. Regardless of your home's age or the builder's references, has a licensed inspector (independent of the builder) recently and thoroughly inspected the home and declared that no major deficiencies exist?

8. Are you fully aware of what the property taxes will be, and can you afford to pay these taxes for the rest of your life?

9. Have you verified that the local government has no plans to build any nearby schools or other governmental projects that could increase your property taxes?

10. Can you get a low interest rate on a mortgage?

11. Can you make a 20% down payment, in addition to your closing costs?

12. If you are still accumulating the money to make a 20% down payment plus closing costs, are you steadfastly resisting the temptation to raid your tax-advantaged retirement accounts?

13. Will your monthly outflow for PITI equal no more than 25% of your gross monthly income?

14. Rather than risking your future by gambling on an Adjustable Rate Mortgage (ARM), are you prudently planning to use a fixed rate mortgage?

15. Can you afford the monthly payments on a 15-year mortgage?

16. If you cannot handle a 15-year mortgage, are you aware of and comfortable with the much larger quantity of interest that you will pay with a 30-year mortgage?

17. Will the terms on your mortgage permit you to make additional payments that go directly toward your home's equity (principal)?

18. Will the terms on your mortgage permit you to re-amortize your loan, in the event that you are able to make a sudden

large payment (e.g. from an inheritance) toward your principal?

19. Will your mortgage interest plus other tax deductible expenses exceed the standard deduction?

When determining how much house you can afford, you should use the same figures that lenders use. Your monthly PITI should not exceed 25% of your monthly gross income. Your total monthly debt load (PITI plus all other debts) should not exceed 36% of your monthly gross income[xl].

Do not even consider Adjustable Rate Mortgages. Fixed rate mortgages are far safer choices. Relative to fixed rate mortgages, ARMs offer lower mortgage interest rates for 3 to 5 years. After these periods, the ARMs' interest rates jump to rates that are actually higher than the rates offered by fixed rate mortgages. Over time, the cumulative interest that a borrower pays with an ARM will exceed the cumulative interest paid with a fixed rate mortgage.

ARMs can be very tempting. SMs know that they will PCS in about three years. Unfortunately, what SMs do not know is whether they will be able to sell their homes before their ARMs adjust to higher rates. Take the devil that you know; stick with fixed rate mortgages.

Property Taxes Never Die

Paying mortgage premiums is painful. However, mortgage premiums eventually die. Property taxes do not. In fact, property taxes may increase to levels that force you to leave your home.

Property taxes vary across the nation, and the states that charge the highest rates may surprise you. Many SMs at Ft. Hood take the opportunity to proudly proclaim their Texan allegiance. However, these income-tax refugees must be careful when buying a home in Texas. With respect to property taxes, Texans can pay some of the highest rates in the U.S. In certain Texan counties, property taxes are nearly 2.5% of a home's assessed value. That equates to nearly $4200 in annual property taxes for a home with an assessed value of less than $170,000[xli]. Can you afford to pay $4200 / 12 months = $350 in property taxes every month until the day you die, regardless of whether you eventually amortize (kill) your mortgage? In fact, can you afford to pay more than $350 per month, if your taxes increase? True, property taxes are income tax deductible, but, as always, deductions only reduce a fraction of a given tax bill. You are still money-out-of-pocket.

Just because a state does not charge income tax does not mean that that state is a great place for SMs to retire. SMs must evaluate that state's total tax burden, as well as that state's cost of living. All state governments must pay their operating expenses. To do so, state governments will tax you in one way or another. Identify all of a state's taxes and determine whether you can legally avoid or reduce any of these taxes. If so, then that state may be a good choice for you, even if that state does levy income taxes.

Zero-Money-Down Loans are Costly

Avoid zero-money-down loans, even those offered by the VA. Do your best to make a 20% down payment. For conventional loans, twenty percent is the magic number that enables you to avoid PMI payments. Frankly, given the 2008 bursting of the housing bubble and the subsequent tightening of lending standards, SMs will be lucky to find non-VA lenders who will accept anything less than a 20% down payment. Lenders know that a buyer's starting with a 20% stake in her home's equity makes her less likely to default on her mortgage.

Besides avoiding PMI, possessing 20% or more equity in a home makes a homeowner less likely to be underwater. Underwater homeowners owe more than their homes are worth. Being underwater is particularly bad when a SM is forced to sell her home in a buyers' market.

Example: Comparing losses for 20% and 0% down payments.

Situation

    A SM plans to purchase a home for $100,000. The SM possesses enough money to make a 20% down payment. The SM is considering the use of a conventional loan. However, the SM wonders if going with a zero-money-down VA loan would be better.

    If the SM uses a conventional loan, she plans to make a 20% down payment. If the SM uses a VA loan, she plans to put zero money down. The mortgage interest rate will be 3.875% with the conventional loan. The mortgage interest rate will be 4.0% with the VA loan. The SM will choose a 15-year term in both scenarios.

    PMI will be 0 in the zero-money-down scenario, because the SM will use a VA loan. The VA Funding Fee in the zero-money-down scenario will be 2.15%, because the SM is a first time VA loan user and is making less than a 5% down payment.

    The SM fears that the local housing market may suffer a roughly 3% annual value loss for each of the 3 years immediately following the SM's purchase of the home. The SM assumes that the total loss could equal $10,000.

    This example does not include taxes, insurance, and the buyer's closing costs. These figures will be roughly equal in both scenarios.

Comparisons

    The next page shows the calculations for each of the COAs that the SM is considering. What should be evident is that failing to possess any starting equity in a home magnifies one's losses, upon the sale of that home. This effect is all the more true, given active SMs' short tenures as homeowners.

COA 1: Make a 20% down payment; borrow the remaining 80%.

Item	Amount	Explanation
Price of home	$100,000	
20% down payment	$20,000	
Mortgage	$80,000	
Monthly mortgage (Princ. + Int.)	$587	Bankrate.com calculator
Starting equity	$20,000	20% down payment
Equity from 3 years of payments	$12,516	Bankrate.com calculator
Total Equity:	$32,516	
Mortgage after 3 years	$67,484	Bankrate.com calculator
Sale price after $10,000 loss	$90,000	
Revenue from sale	$22,516	$90,000 minus $67,484
Lost equity	$10,000	$22,516 minus $32,516
3 years of mortgage interest	$8,607	Bankrate.com calculator
Total Losses:	$18,607	

COA 2: Put zero money down; borrow 100% of the home's price.

Item	Amount	Explanation
Price of home	$100,000	
0% down payment	0	
Mortgage	$102,150	VA Funding Fee added
Monthly mortgage (Princ. + Int.)	$756	Bankrate.com calculator
Starting equity	0	
Equity from 3 years of payments	$15,848	Bankrate.com calculator
Total Equity:	$15,848	
Mortgage after 3 years	$86,301	Bankrate.com calculator
Sale price after $10,000 loss	$90,000	
Revenue from sale	$3,699	$90,000 minus $86,301
Lost equity	$12,149	$3,699 minus $15,848
3 years of mortgage interest	$11,353	Bankrate.com calculator
Total Losses:	$23,502	

Analysis

Failing to make a 20% down payment will add $23,502 – $18,607 = $4895 to the SM's losses, after a mere three years. This represents a 26% increase in her total losses. The culprits are the slightly higher interest rate and the substantially larger mortgage. Note that the total equity and interest losses include the VA Funding Fee and the interest on that fee, since it was rolled into the loan.

Conventional loans with 20% down payments offer lower interest rates than VA loans with zero money down. In this case, failing to invest 20% in the home's equity added ((102,150 – 80,000) / 80,000) X 100% = 27.7% to the size of the SM's mortgage. Applying slightly higher interest rates to substantially larger mortgages leads to significantly greater losses.

Conclusion

A VA loan can be useful. However, SMs should remember that a VA loan's primary purpose is to quickly get veterans into homes. Saving SMs money is not the focus of the VA Loan Program. SMs who can afford to make 20% down payments should consider using conventional loans.

A 20% Down Payment is Sufficient

Making a 20% down payment is sensible, but putting down more than 20% can hurt you. When using a conventional loan, 20% is the magic number that enables you to avoid paying for PMI. When using a VA loan, putting down 20% is not required but will also benefit you. Starting with 20% equity in your home reduces your overall interest charges and even reduces the size of your VA Funding Fee. Actually, making a mere 5% down payment can lower – but not eliminate – your VA Funding Fee.

Regardless of the loan type, 20% is plenty. After putting down 20%, further down payments suffer diminishing returns. True, your monthly mortgage payments will be smaller, and you will pay less interest, overall. However, you will sacrifice the more lucrative returns offered by other investments. You will have put too many of your investment dollars in a single asset class. After putting down 20% on your home, invest any more money that you have in equities.

Currently, mortgage interest rates are lower than they have been for many years. Rates of less than 5% are common. In today's housing market, the cost of money is low. No reason exists to frantically pursue retiring your mortgage debts. Additionally, returns on home equity have been flat and even negative.

The days of guaranteed home value increases are gone. This fact makes investing in a home's equity even less of a financial imperative. In contrast to the depressed housing market, the stock market is doing quite well. You can still expect a properly allocated investment portfolio to average a 10% return over 15 years and, even more so, over 30 years. The 2008 – 2009 Recession did not change this fact. The subsequent 2009 – 2010 Recovery nullified losses and generated profits. This recede-then-recover pattern has been the case for every market tumble since the Great Depression.

Prior to the 2008 housing crash, homes may have appreciated roughly 5% per year, but that is no longer the case. Put 20% down on your home, and then invest any additional cash in the market. If your tax-advantaged accounts are already full, place your extra cash in a taxable account. Use the allocation recommendations in this book.

If you do find a gem of a locale in which homes enjoy constant increases in value, you should still resist the temptation to invest more than 20% in your home's starting equity. Again, you would have too many dollars in a single asset class. Investing your excess cash in the market would better diversify you. Using the Financial Calculators at www.dinkytown.net, we can see why this is true, on the next page:

Example: 100% down payment versus 20% down payment.

Situation

Assume you have $100,800 in cash that you could use to pay for a house. You are considering purchasing the $100,000 house in the previous example. You wish to know whether paying for the house in full or making a mere 20% down payment is the more lucrative COA.

100% Down Payment COA

After adding closing costs of about $800, your total outlay will be $100,800. You will have no dollars remaining for investments. The $800 burnt on administration will not help you, but the $100,000 invested in your home's equity will. After 15 years of consistent 5% increases in value, your $100,000 home will be worth $207,893. This is a gain and total return of $107,893. For this example, I am ignoring insurance costs, maintenance costs, and realtors' fees.

20% Down Payment COA

Alternatively, you can simply put down $21,600. This amount equals your 20% down payment plus your closing costs. Closing costs are larger due to the greater complexity of the purchase. Once again, the $1600 burnt on administration will not help you, but the $20,000 invested in your home's equity will. After 15 years of consistent 5% increases in value, your $100,000 home will be worth $207,893. Again, this is a gain of $107,893. After subtracting your $25,615 in total interest payments due to your 3.875% interest rate on your $80,000 mortgage, your actual gain from your home will be $82,278. I am ignoring the effects of tax deductions. Given the size of this home's mortgage, the annual interest payments will be too small to warrant itemization, unless you have substantial deductions in other areas that you can include.

You started this process with $100,800, in cash. Therefore, you should have $100,800 starting cash – $21,600 down payment & closing costs = $79,200 to invest in the market. After 15 years of compounded 8% growth, that $79,200 could grow to $251,236. If none of that gain is due to reinvested dividends, the capital gains will be $251,236 – $79,200 = $172,036. 15% capital gains taxes will reduce this figure to (100% earnings – 15% capital gains tax) X $172,036 = $146,231. Your total return will be $146,231 investment growth + $82,278 home appreciation = $228,509.

Conclusion

The 20% Down Payment COA gives you a return on investment that is over twice as large as the 100% Down Payment COA's return. The 100% Down Payment COA places too much of your money in a single asset class – a residential property.

Another problem exists with the 100% Down Payment COA. This example assumes your home will enjoy consistent 5% rates of growth for 15 years, but such an assumption is optimistic. Inventory is flooding the current housing market, and this flood will exist for years. The unemployment rate is high. Americans have no incomes with which to pay their mortgage loans. Many of these Americans' homes are going into foreclosure, thus increasing the inventory of homes. Of those Americans who are still employed, many are accepting lower wages and fewer raises. As such, these still-employed Americans are attempting to reduce their mortgage payments by selling their medium-sized homes and either renting or moving into smaller homes. Again, this process is increasing the supply of homes.

Lastly, Baby Boomers are starting to retire. Their retirements will hit a crescendo as we enter the latter half of this decade. Boomers' kids will be gone, and Boomers' requirements to stay in place for their jobs will no longer exist. In efforts to augment retirement incomes or simply to reduce maintenance chores, Boomers will downsize, rent, or completely dispense with homeownership. Even more homes will flood the housing market.

Choose a 15-year Mortgage Term

The 15-year mortgage term is generally a better choice than the 30-year mortgage term. Your monthly payments will be larger, but your total interest paid will be smaller. Recommending higher monthly payments may seem contradictory, given my preceding recommendation that you put down no more than 20%. Admittedly, with smaller monthly payments, you would have more money to invest in the market. This larger cash in-flow might facilitate your making more money, overall. However, with respect to home mortgages, some degree of caution is necessary.

Most SMs will purchase their first long-term homes, shortly after retirement from the military. Most SMs will retire in their mid to late forties. Most SMs will start a second career that will generate more years of steady income. Most SMs will not fully retire until they are 67 years old. This is enough time to pay off a 15-year mortgage.

Paying off a mortgage before fully retiring is important. Upon full retirement, a SM's income may take a substantial cut. This will be a bad time to have 10 or more years of mortgage payments remaining, as could happen with a 30-year mortgage term. The persistent cash out-flows will consume a much greater fraction of the SM's reduced income. This may force him back to work at a time when his body and mind can no longer handle it. Amortizing his mortgage payments before the end of his productive years will remove a substantial amount of financial pressure.

Ensure that your mortgage agreement permits you to make extra payments that go directly toward your principal. Making extra payments will more quickly retire your mortgage and will result in your paying less interest, overall. You might never make use of this mortgage provision, but you should ensure it exists. Given our current economy, making extra principal payments is not really your best financial move. Making extra principal payments is on par with putting more than 20% down on your home. You will suffer diminishing returns. Nonetheless, 15 years is a long time. Much can change. If the economy takes a radical shift in which housing values skyrocket and stock market returns plummet, you may want the ability to more rapidly pay off your mortgage. Such a scenario is unlikely, but keeping your options open is wise.

Mortgage versus Standard Deduction

When added to your other deductions, your home's mortgage interest deduction might exceed the standard deduction. By itself, this fact should not automatically lead you to buy a home. As with any tax-deductible expense, spending $80,000 to save $20,000 is unwise. As shown in the Situation section's example, the standard deduction can often provide greater tax savings than a home's mortgage interest deduction. Nonetheless, if you have answered, "Yes" to all of the other questions pertaining to buying a home, a "Yes" for this last question means that you may enjoy a benefit that was previously unavailable. That benefit is the ability to capitalize on all of your other deductions.

By themselves, these other deductions may not have been large enough to warrant itemizing your deductions. The standard deduction was still larger. As such, you were losing the ability to claim these other deductions. Now, the addition of your home's mortgage interest deduction might enable you to finally itemize your deductions. Since you must live somewhere, this new ability is a nice bonus for buying a home.

Chapter 21: Invest for Retirement before Investing for College

Whether you pay for your kids' college or allow your kids to pay their own way through college is a decision that society no longer permits you to make. Contemporary society browbeats parents into paying their kids' college costs. Unfortunately, the cost of going to college is astronomically high. These costs lure parents into sacrificing their retirements. Do not allow this to happen to you.

The Savingforcollege.com website provides the following statistics for 4 years of tuition and fees (these figures do not include room, board, or books):

Type of Institution	2010 Enrollment	2028 Enrollment
Private College	$119,400	$340,800
Public University (in-state resident)	$33,300	$95,000
½ Community College + ½ Private College	$68,800	$196,300

These statistics assume a 6% annual increase in college costs. The Savingforcollege.com website lists the average increase from 2010 to 2011 as being 4.5% for private colleges and 7.9% for public universities. These rates of increase exceeded the rate of price inflation and exceeded the rate of increases in personal income[xlii].

Whether your kid should even go to college is a good question. In their articles on the SmartMoney.com website, Mr. Jack Hough and Ms. Liz Weston address this question. Hough makes an intriguing argument that simply investing a kid's college savings can prove more lucrative than actually spending those savings on college[xliii]. In contrast, Weston's article concedes that college may be necessary but warns against spending tuition costs for colleges that are anything less than Harvard, Yale, or Princeton[xliv]. Studies of the sizes of the lesser known colleges' graduates' earnings indicate that the graduates' parents could have received more bang for their bucks by sending their kids to less expensive institutions.

Regardless of these observations, you will probably choose to send your kids to college. If so, you must be sure that you can cover the costs. The rules dictating the repayment of college loans put loan sharks' practices to shame. College loans are a debt of which bankruptcy cannot absolve you. Like a conspiring leg-breaker, the U.S. Government will garnish your wages to force your repayment of outstanding college loans.

You must be confident that you can cover your kids' college loans with non-retirement dollars. Planning to fall back on your retirement funds is unacceptable. The maxim that nearly all financial writers espouse is that you must save for your retirement before you save for your kids' college. Loans, grants, and scholarships exist for college; no such help exists for retirement. Parents who violate this maxim jeopardize their retirements. Compromised retirements eventually force financial burdens on all but the most ungrateful kids. Make the hard choices, now. Refuse to send your kids to colleges that you cannot afford. Your kids are likely to do as well with inexpensive degrees as they will do with expensive degrees. Someday, when you are secure in your retirement and are no burden to your kids, your kids will thank you.

Post 9-11 G.I. Bill

The Government's allowing SMs to convert the Montgomery G.I. Bill into the "Post 9-11 G.I. Bill" is tantamount to making nearly every parental SM a lottery winner. For at least one of your kids, you need not worry about most college costs. The Veterans Affairs website at http://www.gibill.va.gov/post-911/post-911-gi-bill-summary/transfer-of-benefits.html lists the requirements a SM must meet to transfer her benefits to her spouse or to her children.

If a SM was on active duty as of 1 August 2009 and is still on active duty, she can transfer at least some of her benefits to her spouse or children. Her spouse and children must already be enrolled in the Defense Eligibility Enrollment Reporting System (DEERS). She must complete this transfer before she leaves the military. Her beneficiaries must use these benefits at one of the "Institutions of Higher Learning" (IHLs) that the Government has approved for G.I. Bill benefits. Programs at these IHLs can include graduate, undergraduate, and even vocational and technical training.

Salient components of the Post 9-11 G.I. Bill benefit follow:

1. The Government may pay up to 36 months of tuition and fees at the level of the SM's highest in-state undergraduate IHL. These 36 months of payments can go to the SM for her education or to her chosen beneficiaries (spouse and children).

2. The SM or her beneficiaries (children) may receive an additional $1000 for books and supplies. The spouse, specifically, may not use this $1000 stipend while the SM is still on active duty.

3. The SM or her beneficiaries (children) may receive a monthly housing allowance equal to the "E-5 with dependents" BAH rate for her chosen IHL's location. The full rate is available for resident instruction. Distance learning (non-resident) students will receive one-half of the national average BAH rate. The spouse, specifically, may not use this housing stipend while the SM is still on active duty.

4. The SM can split these 36 months among her DEERS enrolled spouse and kids in any numbers that she wishes. She allocates these 36 months to her beneficiaries when she registers at https://www.dmdc.osd.mil/milconnect/.

Again, she must register and declare her intent to transfer her benefits to her beneficiaries before she leaves the military. After she leaves the military, she cannot add more beneficiaries. She can only adjust her allocation among the beneficiaries that she has already named.

Whether you use your Post 9-11 G.I. Bill for yourself or for your family members is your decision. Either way, you should execute the transfer process. You should add all of your kids and your spouse to your list of beneficiaries. Initially, simply split the 36 months among them all. If one of your kids gets a full ride, you can later reallocate that kid's months to your other kids, to your spouse, or back to yourself.

Beware that a valid argument exists for using your G.I. Bill benefits, yourself. You could use the benefits to obtain a higher degree that increases your income. You could use your expanded income to fund your kids' college costs. After their college stints were complete, you would continue to benefit from your increased income. If you are absolutely sure of such an outcome, then using the benefits for your own education may be a wise move. Of course, your prediction could be wrong. You might lack the resolve to complete your higher degree program. Even if you do complete your program, the higher paying job that your potential employer promised might evaporate. You will have exhausted your G.I. Bill, yet your kids will still need your financial support for their own college costs.

529 College Savings Plans

529 plans are tax advantaged savings vehicles, solely for the use of paying higher education costs. 529 plans are extremely popular, especially for civilians who have no access to the Post 9-11 G.I. Bill. Parents and even grandparents can open savings accounts within the various 529 plans in order to pay for their kids' or grandkids' college costs.

Savings accounts within 529 plans function similarly to Roth accounts. Owners of 529 plan savings accounts contribute after-tax dollars. Subject to the 529 plans' withdrawal rules, no taxes are due when the owners later withdraw the contributions, and no taxes are ever due on the contributions' earnings. The foremost withdrawal rule is that the owners of the money may only use the money to pay for education. Using the money for any other purpose will incur a 10% penalty and the requirement to pay ordinary federal income taxes, after all. The penalty and the taxes apply to the earnings, not to the principal that you contributed. Nonetheless, these two hits could dramatically reduce the returns on your investment.

529 plans differ from Roth accounts in some positive ways. No 59.5-year-old age requirement exists on savings accounts within 529 plans. Subject to the stipulations of a given 529 plan, owners may withdraw their contributions and earnings whenever they wish. Contribution limits are quite generous. Each year, each parent of a marriage may contribute up to five years' worth of tax excludable gifts to a 529 account. For 2013, a single tax excludable gift will be $14,000. No income cap exists, either. Wealthy Americans may contribute to savings accounts within 529 plans.

The parents, not their children, own dollars in 529 plans. This is another positive point for these plans. Federal financial aid eligibility formulas consider no more than 5.64% of parental assets. In contrast, such formulas consider 20% of assets that are in the children's names. However, a downside does exist. In her article entitled "How to Take Money Out of 529 Plans", Ms. Jaime Pessin quotes Mr. John Hurley as explaining that some colleges view dollars that come directly from savings accounts in 529 plans as being similar to scholarships. Students who receive these 529 "scholarship" dollars might get less financial aid from colleges that maintain such a viewpoint[xlv]. Parents should realize that schools are free to establish their own methods for determining who needs the schools' internal financial aid packages, regardless of whomever the Government offers financial aid.

529 plans differ from Roth accounts in some negative ways. Individual taxpayers are free to open Roth IRAs with any brokerage. Individuals can purchase any funds that these brokerages offer. In contrast, Section 529 of the Internal Revenue Code, the section after which 529 plans are named, enables state governments – not individuals – to establish 529 College Savings plans. Individuals can only open savings accounts within the states' various offerings. All 50 states offer at least one 529 plan, but not all

of these plans are good. 529 plans offer predetermined baskets of mutual funds and other investment vehicles. The choices within these baskets are limited and can come with high expenses.

As already stated, the most significant aspect of 529 plans is that they restrict your withdrawals to those for qualified post-secondary education expenses. Such expenses are tuition, fees, educational supplies, and education related lodging. 529 plans permanently bind your contributions to these qualified expenses. Withdrawing 529 contributions for any other purpose subjects those unqualified contributions' earnings to a 10% penalty and forfeits their federal tax exemption. If your kids do not ultimately need the money that you contribute to a 529 plan, you can use the money for your own education, or you can transfer the money to a different member of your family for their education. However, you cannot add those contributions to your retirement nest egg.

Individuals can choose 529 plans in any state, regardless of the individuals' current states of residence. However, choosing an out-of-state 529 plan nearly always forfeits tax incentives that one's own state might offer for choosing one of that state's 529 plans. If your state of residence levies no income tax, this is not an issue. Choose whichever 529 plan charges the lowest expenses and offers the best investments, regardless of which state offers the plan. The Savingforcollege.com website offers detailed performance comparisons of all states' 529 plans at http://www.savingforcollege.com/compare_529_plans/.

Do 529 Plans Really Make Sense?

Our fear of taxes fuels the allure of 529 plans. We anticipate a nightmare in which our neighbor gleefully covers his kids' college costs with a vast sum of money, while we struggle to do the same with less money. We worry that we will kick ourselves for disregarding prevailing advice. Nonetheless, we must determine whether this advice is truly wise. At a minimum, SMs who have yet to maximize contributions to tax-advantaged retirement accounts should avoid 529 plans. Financial aid is available for college; no such aid is available for retirement.

Deciding whether to contribute to a 529 plan requires an evaluation of taxes' true effects. To be sure, legally reducing your tax liabilities is a good move. However, you must be sure that the medicine does not kill the patient. Avoiding taxes accomplishes little, if you lose your investment. Effectively, this is what will happen, if neither you nor your kids need your 529 contributions. Rather than blindly binding your savings to a specific purpose, consider the value of keeping your options open. Consider investing your savings in instruments that offer less highly touted tax advantages but offer 100% flexibility and are still lucrative.

Example: Determining Whether to Invest in a Typical 529 Plan.

Situation

You are easily covering your expenses. At the end of each month, you possess approximately $250 in spare cash. You are driving a CPO Ford Focus for which you paid cash in full. You are carrying no consumer debt. You have an emergency fund. You are maximizing your annual Roth TSP and Roth IRA contributions. You predict that the combination of your military pension, Social Security benefits, and withdrawals from your retirement investments will easily cover your expenses throughout your full retirement. You qualify to consider investing in a 529 plan.

Your first child will likely use all 36 months of your Post 9-11 G.I. Bill. Your second child is 4 years old and is a good student but is unlikely to qualify for any educational or athletic scholarships. Further, your many deployments have dissuaded her from participating in ROTC. You assume that she will go straight from high school to college in 14 years and that she will need your financial support. You are neither rich nor poor. The size of your donations will curry no favor; the depth of your poverty will engender no sympathy.

Your state offers zero tax incentives for participating in its 529 plans. Further, its plans are not among the top rated plans on any of the popular rating sites. You decide to look for a 529 plan outside of your state. You discover that Utah's plan is often among the rating sites' top recommendations and that Utah's plan permits non-residents' participation. You go to the "Utah Educational Savings Plan (UESP)" website at http://www.uesp.org/ to analyze this plan.

You focus your analyses on UESP's investment options that charge no loads, have minimal expense ratios, hold minimal cash reserves, have minimal turnover, and hold no bond funds. As such, you eliminate UESP's five "Age-Based" options, since these five options will gradually shift your contributions into bond funds. With only 14 years to invest and impending inflation and dollar devaluation, you want the highest possible returns. You also eliminate UESP's "Public Trust Investment Fund (PTIF)" and "FDIC Insured Savings Account", since these options invest in fixed income instruments. You concentrate on UESP's 6 "Static" options that will maintain their allocations throughout your 14 years of investing. You focus on UESP's "Equities – 30% Developed International" option. This option holds no bond funds and places the highest percentage of your contributions in international markets.

COA #1 – Investing in UESP's 529 Plan.

By 31 July 2012, UESP's Equities – 30% Developed International option's "Since Inception" performance was 6.58%[xlvi]. By the same date, UESP's Equities – 10% Total International option enjoyed a higher return of 8.71%. After considering both of these options' rates of return, you decide to rule out the second option. You want to follow the investing guidelines as closely as possible. Given the shaky state of the U.S. economy and the bright futures of many foreign economies, you want the greater exposure to international markets that UESP's Equities – 30% Developed International option provides. You believe that this option will ultimately enjoy average returns of 8% or more, over 14 years of investing. You believe that the Equities – 10% Total International option's returns will average less than 8%.

Your monthly contribution to UESP's Equities – 30% Developed International option will be $250. After 14 years of 8% returns, your $250 per month will grow to $75,756. If you use this money for your daughter's education, you will suffer no 10%

penalties and no income taxes on your withdrawals. Indeed, you will have all of $75,756 to use for your daughter's education.

However, a chance exists that neither your daughter nor anyone else will use this $75,756 for qualified post-secondary education expenses. If not, you might choose to withdraw the money to pay for something else. If so, you will end up with much less than $75,756. The IRS will tax the earnings portion of your $75,756 as ordinary income, and the IRS will slap your earnings with a 10% penalty. Your total principal will be $3000 annual principal contributions X 14 years = $42,000. Your capital gains will be $75,756 value – $42,000 principal = $33,756. If you are just inside the 25% marginal tax bracket, all of this $33,756 in capital gains will fall within that 25% bracket. You will suffer a 25% income tax X $33,756 capital gains = $8439 tax liability. Additionally, you will suffer a 10% penalty X $33,756 capital gains = $3376 penalty. Your earnings will drop to $33,756 capital gains – ($8439 tax liability + $3376 penalty) = $21,941. Ultimately, you will have $21,941 adjusted earnings + $42,000 principal = $63,941 to use for another purpose.

COA #2 – Investing in a Taxable Account that Enjoys 10% Annual Returns.

Rather than binding your contributions to qualified post-secondary education expenses, you could simply invest your monthly $250 savings in a normal taxable account. If you already possess a taxable account that you structured to earn 10%, you could add your monthly $250 to that account. After 14 years of 10% returns, these monthly $250 additions will add another $88,405 to the other dollars in your taxable account. Your capital gains will be $88,405 value – $42,000 principal = $46,405. If we assume that 14 years from now the capital gains tax rate will return to 20%, your after tax earnings will be (100% earnings – 20% capital gains tax) X $46,405 capital gains = $37,124. Ultimately, you will have $37,124 adjusted earnings + $42,000 principal = $79,124 to use for whatever purpose you desire. In this COA, you will have $79,124 (Investing Option) – $75,756 (529 Plan) = $3368 more to spend on your daughter's education, or whatever else you wish, than you would have had with UESP's 529 Plan.

COA #3 – Investing in a Taxable Account that Only Enjoys 8% Annual Returns.

If you are skeptical, you could simply assume that your own investments will do no better than 8%. Your monthly $250 infusions will add another $75,756 to your taxable account. Your capital gains will be $75,756 value – $42,000 principal = $33,756. After capital gains taxes, you will have (100% earnings – 20% capital gains tax) X $33,756 capital gains = $27,005. Ultimately, you will have $27,005 adjusted earnings + $42,000 principal = $69,005 adjusted total to use for whatever purpose you desire. In this COA, you will have $75,756 total (529 Plan) – $69,005 (Investing Option) = $6751 less to spend on your daughter's education. On the other hand, you will have $69,005 (Investing Option) – $63,941 penalized & taxed withdrawals (529 Plan) = $5064 more to spend on something else.

Coverdell Education Savings Account (ESA)

Coverdell ESAs function in much the same way as 529 plans. However, Coverdell ESAs impose restrictions that 529 plans do not. Unless you anticipate needing to pay for elementary or high school level education, you might as well go with a 529 plan.

After-tax contributions to ESAs grow tax-deferred, and withdrawals for qualified education expenses are tax-exempt. The earnings portions of improper withdrawals incur ordinary federal income taxes and a 10% penalty. Coverdell ESAs are assets of the account owner (parent), not the beneficiary (child). Coverdell ESAs offer baskets of investments. As implied above, Coverdell ESAs permit you to use your contributions for elementary or high school level education. 529 plans do not permit such lower-level-education uses.

However, ESAs possess drawbacks. Account owners cannot save more than $2000 per year per beneficiary. The account owners' increasing incomes can further reduce this $2000 cap. Account owners can no longer contribute money to Coverdell ESAs, once the beneficiaries turn 18 years old. The beneficiaries must use the contributions by the time the beneficiaries turn 30 years old.

Otherwise, the IRS assesses a 10% penalty and levies ordinary federal income taxes on the withdrawals' earnings.

Roth IRA

You can, in fact, use your Roth IRA to fund your kids' college education. Provided that your withdrawals are for qualified education expenses, the IRS waives the 59.5-year-old age requirement.

Though using your Roth IRA is permissible, it is not advisable. You should not damage your retirement nest egg. True, $5500 per year can grow to a healthy sum, after 18 years of compounding at a 10% annual rate of return. Nonetheless, using those quarter million dollars for your kids' college costs could leave you nothing for your retirement.

UTMA

The new Uniform Transfers to Minors Act (UTMA) is a more flexible version of the old Uniform Gifts to Minors Act (UGMA). Most states simply use the newer UTMA. Whatever the acronym, these vehicles are poor college savings choices. Few, if any SMs will enjoy significant benefits when using UTMAs.

The detailed rules for the states' various UTMAs differ, but the UTMAs' basic components are the same. UTMAs enable adults with money (donors) to transfer some of that money to young people (beneficiaries). UTMAs do not exist for the sole purpose of saving for college. The purpose of UTMAs is to enable those with money to gradually "gift" modest chunks of that money to loved ones. This stops the Government from seizing that money via estate taxes upon the deaths of the donors. In this way, UTMAs are similar to trusts. However, trusts' higher management expenses make trusts more appropriate for much larger sums of money. UTMAs are quicker, easier, and cheaper. UTMAs lack the fine-tuning and safety features that trusts offer.

The beneficiary of the money in an UTMA owns the UTMA. Commonly, that beneficiary is a child. As such, the child's lower tax bracket, not the higher tax bracket of the donor, determines the income tax rate that applies to withdrawals. This beneficial tax structure is only valid up to a very low limit. Unearned income over $1900 reverts to the donor's income tax rate. This low size limit eliminates much of an UTMA's tax benefits. Adding insult to injury, this money's being in the name of the child will lead to the receipt of less financial aid.

An UTMA is the sole property of the recipient. That recipient is usually a child, and that child can spend the money in any way that he wishes. He might invest that money in his education, or he might spend that money on a new Ford Mustang. The donor has absolutely no legal recourse for preventing the beneficiary's frivolous use of UTMA dollars. Further, the donor cannot retrieve dollars that the donor has already contributed to an UTMA. The gift is irrevocable.

Chapter 22: Maximize Your Social Security Benefits

In the Situation paragraph, we explained the Social Security program. Now, we will discuss the means for capitalizing on what that program offers. As you approach age 62, you must determine whether you will take early and reduced Social Security benefits, will wait until your NRA to collect normal Social Security benefits, or will wait until age 70 to collect enhanced Social Security benefits.

Your Social Security benefits at age 62 will be about 30% less than your normal benefits at your NRA. Your enhanced Social Security benefits at age 70 will be about 24% more than your NRA benefits. For those whose NRA is age 67, that 24% increase equates to a guaranteed 8% gain per year for three years. That is a good deal. Over many years, index ETFs and index funds will return more than 8% per year. However, over spans as short as three years, even the best index ETFs and index funds cannot guarantee consistent 8% returns. Given this fact and our increasing life spans, your best financial move is to wait until you are 70 years old to start drawing your Social Security benefits. At a minimum, you should wait until your NRA.

Married Personnel

When both members of a marriage amass the requisite 40 credits to qualify for Social Security benefits, several COAs exist for capitalizing on those benefits. Two such COAs follow:

COA 1: The "62/70 Split"

Many advisors recommend this tactic. This COA is for couples in which both members qualify for Social Security benefits. This COA puts at least some Social Security money in the hands of these couples, immediately, while preserving enhanced Social Security benefits for the future widow or widower.

Assume that a husband and wife are the same age and that the husband qualifies for Social Security benefits that are larger than the benefits for which his wife qualifies. When the wife is at least 62 year old, she immediately draws her early and reduced Social Security benefits. The husband waits. He will not collect his Social Security benefits until he is 70 years old. However, when the husband reaches his NRA of 67, he temporarily draws Spousal Benefits equal to 50% of his wife's NRA benefits. The fact that his wife is already drawing her reduced Social Security benefits does not matter. The husband will draw 50% of whatever his wife's NRA benefits would have been. His own benefits will stay in reserve, accruing delayed retirement credits.

When the husband reaches age 70, he reverts to his own enhanced benefits. When the husband eventually dies, his widow will stop drawing her own reduced benefits and will claim Survivor's Benefits. Since she will already be past her NRA, she will start drawing 100% of her deceased husband's enhanced benefits.

Example: The "62/70 Split".

Situation

A husband and his wife are ages 62 and 60, respectively. They are wondering when they should draw their Social Security benefits. If the husband waits until his NRA of 67 to draw his Social Security benefits, he will draw $2200 per month. In spite of their frequent PCS moves, his wife managed to obtain the minimum 40 credits to qualify for Social Security benefits of her own. If she waits until her NRA of 67 to draw her benefits, she will draw $1600 per month.

Since the husband is 62 years old, he could start drawing Social Security benefits, immediately. If he did so, the SSA would reduce his benefits by roughly 30%. He would collect 70% X $2200 = $1540 per month ($18,480 per year). In two years, his wife could start drawing her Social Security benefits. If she did so, she would draw 70% X $1600 = $1120 per month ($13,440 per year).

Wife's 70% Social Security Benefits

The husband will wait until he is 70 years old to collect his benefits. On the other hand, his wife will collect her reduced benefits as soon as she turns 62 years old. Therefore, from the husband's ages of 64 to 66, the couple's sole Social Security income will be the wife's $13,440 per year. In this case, the SSA will not bother to compare the wife's benefits on her record to the Spousal Benefits on her husband's record. This is because her husband will not yet have filed for his Social Security benefits. The wife will simply collect her reduced benefits based on her record.

Husband's 50% Spousal Benefits

When the husband turns 67, he will claim 50% Spousal Benefits. He will be able to do this, because his wife will have already filed for her benefits. The husband will allow his own benefits to accrue delayed retirement credits. From ages 67 through 69, the husband will collect 50% X $1600 NRA Social Security (hers) = $800 per month ($9600 per year). Again, the 50% multiplier applies to the wife's full NRA Social Security benefits, even though she has already started collecting reduced benefits. From the husband's ages of 67 through 69, the couple's Social Security income will equal $13,440 Social Security (hers) + $9600 Spousal Benefits = $23,040.

Husband's 124% Social Security Benefits

When the husband turns 70, he will drop his Spousal Benefits and revert to his own enhanced Social Security benefits. He will begin drawing 124% X $2200 = $2728 per month ($32,736 per year). From that time forward, the couple's Social Security income will equal $13,440 Social Security (hers) + $32,736 Social Security (his) = $46,176.

Wife's Survivor's Benefits

After her husband's death, the widow will claim Survivor's Benefits. She will no longer draw the benefits that were due to her record. If she is at her NRA or older, she will start receiving 100% of what her deceased husband was receiving. In this case, she will get 100% of $2728 per month. For the rest of her life, the widow's total Social Security income will be $32,736 per year. This amount is more than half of what she and her husband were receiving, when her husband was still alive. She will qualify for this amount, because her husband survived until he was at least 70 years old, and he did not draw his benefits until after he achieved that age.

Conclusion

The 62/70 Split gives a married couple some quantity of Social Security income every year from age 62 until death. Simultaneously, the 62/70 Split preserves the growth of what will ultimately be the larger source of Social Security income for whichever member of the couple dies second. This gives peace of mind to a couple's primary breadwinner. He knows that, upon his death, his widow will stop collecting reduced Social Security benefits and will start collecting more substantial Survivor's Benefits. If she is at her NRA, she will start collecting 100% of his benefits. That will be true, even if those benefits were enhanced due to his having survived past his NRA and his having waited to collect his benefits.

COA 2: Both Members of the Couple Wait until Age 70

This second COA is good for couples in which both members anticipate very long lives, both members are eligible for Social Security benefits, and both members are close in age. In this COA, neither member of the couple files for early and reduced Social Security benefits at age 62. When both members of the couple reach their NRAs, they "file and suspend". Then, they each claim 50% Spousal Benefits while accruing delayed retirement credits toward their own Social Security benefits. When each member of the couple reaches age 70, he or she reverts to drawing his or her own 124% NRA benefits. Contact the SSA at 1-800-772-1213 to learn more about all of your options.

Chapter 23: Purchase Life Insurance

Purchasing life insurance is a complicated process. You will need an agent to successfully negotiate the many options. Nonetheless, sufficiently educating yourself to ask a few intelligent questions will increase your odds of getting what you want. For the most part, that education involves understanding the differences between term life insurance policies and cash value life insurance policies.

Understanding the two major types of insurance becomes imperative, if you have been relying on Soldiers' Group Life Insurance (SGLI) to cover your family. 120 days after your military retirement date, your SGLI will terminate. Assuming you opted for the maximum SGLI benefit, you will lose $400,000 in coverage. You should replace that coverage. You do not want your sudden death's forcing your family to prematurely liquidate long-term investments.

Term Life Insurance

No later than your late 30s, you should purchase a level term life insurance policy, not a cash value life insurance policy. Level term life insurance policies will offer fixed premiums that are vastly lower than cash value life insurance policies' premiums. Nonetheless, level term life insurance policies can provide substantial death benefits to the policies' beneficiaries. While you are relatively young, insurance companies will readily sell you term life insurance policies. Your youth means that little risk exists that the companies will ever pay the policies' benefits.

Term life insurance policies provide a set amount of money to your beneficiaries, provided that you die within a specific time span. These spans can be anywhere from 1 to 30 years. A typical term life insurance policy might provide a $500,000 lump sum to your beneficiaries, if you die within 20 years of purchasing the policy. That $500,000 lump sum will be tax-free for your beneficiaries. They will receive the entire $500,000. If you bought a level term life insurance policy prior to your 40th birthday, your premiums might be fixed at about $120 every quarter. Thus, you would pay a total of about $480 per year, each of those 20 years, and this amount would never increase. This is reasonably inexpensive coverage. Waiting until your 40s or 50s to purchase such a policy will result in your paying much larger premiums.

The other type of term life insurance that you might purchase is "annual renewable". Annual renewable term life insurance will provide the same $500,000 coverage for the same 20-year span, but the premiums will change, each year. Annual renewable term life insurance is tempting. The early years' premiums are lower than what you will pay with level term life insurance. Nonetheless, after a few years, annual renewable insurance premiums will exceed level term life insurance premiums. The pitfalls of annual renewable term life insurance are similar to those of Adjustable Rate Mortgages (ARMs).

Cash Value Life Insurance

As you pass 60 years old, term life insurance policies become exponentially more expensive. Some insurance companies might not even sell you term life insurance policies when you are in your 60s. Cash value life insurance policies may be your only options. Like term life insurance policies, cash value policies offer tax-free proceeds to the policies' beneficiaries. Cash value policies are substantially more expensive than term life insurance policies, but the time-spans over which cash value policies' benefits are available are longer than term life insurance policies' time-spans. A cash value policy might cover you until you are 120 years old –

essentially, forever.

Since the span of your coverage is much longer and the odds of the insurance company's having to pay the benefit are much greater, the premiums for a cash value policy are much larger. If you purchase a $500,000 policy while you are in your early 40s, the premiums might be more than $400 per month ($4800 per year). Waiting until your 60s to purchase such a policy could result in your paying over $1000 per month ($12,000 per year).

A portion of each of your cash value policy's premiums secures the face value – the "death benefit" – of the policy for your policy's beneficiaries. The other portion of each premium goes toward an investment component. This investment component invests in growth instruments that grow tax-deferred. After many years of paying your premiums, the investment component of your cash value policy may possess a sizable cash value. The cash value of a policy's investment component is a tangible asset of the policyholder. The policyholder can cancel his policy and recoup the money in this investment component, or he can keep the policy while taking loans against the investment component's cash value. Nonetheless, a cash value policy's beneficiaries will not receive the investment component as an *addition* to the policy's stated death benefit. The beneficiaries will only receive the face value of the policy. For example, if a policyholder dies after amassing a $50,000 cash value in a policy with a face value of $500,000, his beneficiaries will only receive a death benefit of $500,000, not $550,000.

While the inclusion of an investment component may be enticing, understand the limitations of these investments. These investments can be in fixed income instruments. As we have already seen, fixed income instruments offer low rates of return. These fixed income instruments will likely offer some minimal interest income rate that the insurance company guarantees. 3% is a common offering. The company might also offer a slightly higher but adjustable rate. So long as the insurance company is profitable, the company may continue to offer you this slightly higher rate, possibly 2% more. Unfortunately, after 3% price inflation and whatever a policy's management expenses might be, a 5% interest income rate yields less than a 2% rate of return.

Alternatively, the investment component's investments could be in mutual funds. This might result in the investment component's achieving a larger cash value than it would achieve with fixed income instruments. In fact, a policy's use of mutual funds offers the opportunity to produce a death benefit that actually exceeds the policy's stated face value. Unfortunately, cash value policies tie you to specific mutual funds. These funds might not be the types of funds that you would have chosen. You will pay the management expenses inherent in the funds, in addition to the management expenses that you will pay for the insurance policy, itself. In all, your expenses may be higher and your investment component's performance may be poorer than what you would have enjoyed with index ETFs in a normal, taxable account.

Ask your insurance agent to explain which funds the investment component uses and to explain the fees associated with these funds. Realize that your agent will tout the investment component as being a good savings vehicle. The agent will highlight the fact that the cash value policy's investment component will enjoy tax-deferred growth. Indeed, this is true. However, if you use the investment component for yourself, rather than leave it for your beneficiaries, you will lose the tax advantage and must pay the taxes, after all. In this case, you would be cancelling your policy, so you would also pay "surrender charges". These added charges would further reduce the value of what you recoup from the investment component.

On the other hand, if you keep the policy but merely take a loan against the investment component's cash value, you retain your tax advantage. Nonetheless, you must pay interest charges on the amount that you use. Effectively, you would be paying interest charges for the right to use your own money. If you die before your repay the loan, the insurance company will subtract the remaining balance of your loan and any unpaid interest charges from the death benefit that your policy's beneficiaries receive.

Ultimately, you should compare the projected performance of the agent's cash value life insurance policy's investment component to the performance of a properly allocated group of index ETFs in a normal, taxable account. Calculate the effects of surrender charges, interest charges, and policy fees. If the cash value life insurance policy's performance easily exceeds the combined costs of the charges and fees, then the cash value life insurance policy may be a good purchase

Deciding Whether to Buy Insurance

While you are young (in your late 30s or younger), you should buy a level term insurance policy that covers your spouse until you are at least 60 years old. The premiums will be inexpensive, and the benefits will be large.

Obtaining coverage for your later years requires more careful consideration. Circumstances may force you to purchase a cash value life insurance policy. Alternatively, you may determine that no more life insurance is necessary. You must ask yourself several questions:

1. Do you have anyone for whom you wish to care, after your death? If not, you may have no reason to purchase life insurance, at all.

2. Will the level term life insurance policy that you are considering last until your spouse is at least 60 years old? If yes, insurance benefits will cover your widow(er) until the time when she or he can collect a percentage of your Social Security checks.

3. Will your spouse have any other sources of income, such as investments, his or her own pension, rental properties, business residuals, inheritances, or the Survivor Benefit Plan (SBP)? If yes, you may be able to put your money into something other than life insurance premiums.

These are only some of the questions you should ask yourself, prior to binding yourself to an expensive insurance plan. Your goal in whatever questions you ask is to determine how much insurance you truly need. Some people are over-insured, with respect to life insurance. Being over-insured unnecessarily reduces your ability to profit in other areas.

Chapter 24: Participate in the Survivor Benefit Plan (SBP)

As SMs approach retirement, they must determine whether to participate in the SBP. The SBP's mechanics are different than those of typical insurance products, but the SBP's promise is nearly the same – to give your family long-term security, following your death. Assuming your family stays within the SBP's eligibility criteria, the SBP will send your family inflation-indexed checks equivalent to as much as 55% of your retired pay, every month following your death.

Mechanics of the SBP

The Office of the SECDEF's "Military Compensation" website explains the SBP at http://militarypay.defense.gov/survivor/sbp/index.html. The website's major points concerning the SBP follow:

1. Your monthly premiums go directly from your retired pay to the SBP. Therefore, SBP premiums are before-tax dollars. Your SBP premiums will reduce your taxable income in much the same way as Traditional TSP contributions. This effectively lowers the cost of your premiums.

2. The SBP applies yearly Cost of Living Adjustments (COLAs) to the SBP payouts that your beneficiaries will receive. This is another positive point for the SBP. Inflation and dollar devaluation will have fewer negative impacts on the purchasing power of your beneficiaries' benefits.

3. Determining the size of the payout that your beneficiaries will receive requires you to select a "base amount". The base amount can be as little as $300 or as much as your full retired pay. Do not get confused. The base amount is not what your beneficiaries will receive. The SBP administrators will apply a 55% multiplier to the base amount that you select. This product is what your beneficiaries will receive.

Example: Determining what your SBP beneficiaries will receive.

Situation

Assume you will retire in 2013 as an E-8 with 20 years of service. Per the "High-3" retirement calculator at the same Office of the SECDEF website, your retired pay will be $2235 per month.

Calculation

If you want your beneficiaries to get the maximum SBP benefit, you will make your base amount equal to your full retired pay of $2235. Your beneficiaries will receive 55% X $2235 = $1229 per month.

---

4. SBP premiums will equal the lesser of the following two formulas:

    a. Premium = 6.5% X base amount

    b. Premium = 10% X (base amount – $747 threshold) + 2.5% X $747 threshold

For base amounts lower than $1600, the second calculation can benefit the SM by producing a lower premium. The $747 figure is simply a threshold that the SBP uses, as of 2012. In tandem with annual active duty pay raises, this $747 threshold will rise. As it does, the $1600 break-even point will rise.

Example: Comparing the two SBP formulas.

Situation 1

If our E-8 makes his base amount equal to his full retired pay, the first formula will apply.

Calculation

His monthly premium with the first formula will be 6.5% X $2235 = $145.28. His monthly premium with the second formula would be 10% X ($2235 – $747) + 2.5% X $747 = $167.48. The first formula produces the lower premium, so the first formula applies.

Situation 2

Alternatively, the E-8 could choose to make his base amount equal to some amount less than his full retired pay.

Calculation

If he chooses a base amount of $1500, the second formula will apply. His monthly premium with the second formula will be 10% X ($1500 – $747) + 2.5% X $747 = $93.98. His monthly premium with the first formula would be 6.5% X $1500 = $97.50.

---

5. You start paying SBP premiums immediately upon your retirement from the military. You continue paying SBP premiums until you die. The SECDEF's website is clear that participating in the SBP is a nearly "irrevocable decision". Exiting the SBP contract is only possible in very specific situations.

6. Although your SBP premiums reduce your taxable retired income, the IRS will tax the SBP benefits that your beneficiary receives. These taxes will be at your beneficiary's ordinary federal income tax rate. Nonetheless, the website points out that your beneficiary may be in a lower tax bracket, by the time you die.

7. If your beneficiary dies before you die, you can stop paying SBP premiums. However, you do not get any payouts of your own. No reciprocal arrangement exists.

8. Fortunately, when SBP participants reach 70 years old, they can stop paying SBP premiums. The SBP system considers such senior participants to be "paid up". Although premium payments cease, full benefits continue to be available to the participants' designated beneficiaries.

Should You Participate in the SBP?

For most SMs, the answer is, "Yes". The SBP offers financial security for your widow(er) that is difficult to match. Relying on your investments and various insurance products to cover a lifetime of your widow(er)'s expenses is risky. If your widow(er) lacks your investing savvy and frugality, he or she might quickly become insolvent. The burden of supporting him or her will fall to your children. This is not the legacy that most parents want. Avoiding an extended warranty on a stereo system is one thing; avoiding insurance for a lifetime of your family's survival expenses is another thing, entirely.

The SBP is especially good for SMs with health issues. The size of your retirement check, not your health, determines the size of your SBP premiums. Your premiums will be the same, even if you are an unrepentant chain smoker, heavy drinker, fast-food junkie, or couch potato. Your genetics will not increase your premiums. In spite of the lengths of your ancestors' lives, your SBP premiums will stay the same. In contrast, your health plays a substantial role when determining the size of your premiums for typical insurance products. Poor health habits or an unfortunate health history can increase your typical insurance products' premiums to prohibitive sizes.

If you do, in fact, have good health habits and strong genetics, avoiding the SBP may be tempting. When looking for reasons to avoid paying SBP premiums, you will probably notice that the SBP's blindness with respect to one's health history works against healthy SMs. Such SMs are likely to spend many years paying into a system that never pays them back. Effectively, healthy SMs who participate in the SBP will transfer their wealth to unhealthy SMs' beneficiaries. You might conclude that the performance of your properly structured investments and the existence of other forms of long-term income will make your participation in the SBP unnecessary. However, if any doubt about your future widow(er)'s financial stability exists and you can handle the reduced cash flow, participate in the SBP.

The example that follows analyzes the necessity of the SBP. This example is vastly larger than any of the previous examples. Evaluating the necessity of paying a lifetime of SBP premiums required analyzing many of the financial topics that "Win the Money War" discusses. Therefore, the following example will provide the added benefit of illustrating how this book's recommendations will function as a whole. This example will serve as the book's capstone event.

Example: Determining the necessity of the SBP.

Situation

Our E-8 purchases a 20-year level term life insurance policy, just prior to his 40th birthday. The E-8's annual policy premiums are $480. The policy provides $500,000 in coverage until the E-8 turns 60 years old.

The E-8 retires from the military on his 44th birthday. The E-8's annual military pension is $2235 per month X 12 months = $26,820. Additionally, the E-8 starts a second career that he will pursue until he fully retires at his NRA of 67 years old. The annual income from his second career is $50,000 before taxes. His wife focuses on being a homemaker. The couple's taxable income will be $26,820 military pension + $50,000 second career income = $76,820. His second career offers meager pay increases. The couple's income never increases enough to move the couple out of the 15% marginal tax bracket.

The E-8's second career enables him to contribute more money to his tax-advantaged accounts. His employer offers a Traditional 401(k) with a 3% match. The E-8 contributes enough to his 401(k) to receive his employer's full match. This amount equals 3% match X $50,000 = $1500. Beyond the $1500 that the E-8 contributes to his employer's 401(k), the E-8 can only afford to invest another $1500 per year in other accounts. He chooses to split this $1500 between his wife's and his Roth IRAs. Therefore, the couple's total tax-advantaged account contributions will be $1500 Traditional 401(k) contribution + $1500 Traditional 401(k) employer's match + $1500 Roth IRA contributions = $4500 per year. The E-8 lump-sum-invests his $4500 on 1 January of each year. 1 January happens to be his birthday and, coincidentally, his wife's birthday.

After retiring from the military, the E-8 chooses to leave his contributions in his Roth TSP. The TSP permits this choice, unlike many civilian 401(k) plans. The E-8 knows that the TSP's investment choices are reasonably good and that the TSP's expenses are extremely low.

The couple maintains an emergency fund of roughly $10,000 that earns negligible interest income. Prior to retiring from the military, the couple managed to invest a total of $50,000 in their Roth IRAs, $50,000 in the E-8's Roth TSP, and $20,000 in a taxable account. The E-8 structured all of these accounts to produce annual returns of 10%. However, we will conservatively assume that the investments average no more than 8% returns, per year.

The E-8's Social Security benefits at his NRA of 67 will be $2200 per month. His wife's Social Security benefits at her NRA of 67 will be $1600 per month. We will use the Social Security Administration's average life expectancy predictions for both males and females. The E-8 and his wife are non-smokers who remain physically active and eat reasonably well. Given his family members' survival records, the E-8 stands a good chance of living until he is 81 years old. His wife is two years younger than he and stands a good chance of living until she is 84 years old.

Objective

The E-8 will determine how much money will be available to his wife, without SBP benefits, in any year that he passes away, after he retires from the military. He will use this information to decide whether his widow will require SBP benefits to survive.

Investment Growth

The table on the following page shows the annual growth and total value of the couple's investments. The products and sums within the table are what the couple stands a fair chance of possessing on the E-8's respective 1 January birthdays.

The table uses 8% returns and adds $1500 to the "Roth IRAs" column and $3000 to the "Traditional 401(k)" column, each year. Upon retirement from the military, the E-8 adds nothing more to either the "Roth TSP" or the "Taxable Account" columns.

Once the E-8 reaches age 67, his $4500 worth of contributions to his retirement accounts will stop, altogether. At that time, he will shift from saving for retirement to living in retirement. All future growth in the couple's accounts will come from capital gains and reinvested dividends. The accounts will receive no more additions of principal.

E-8's Age	Roth IRAs	Roth TSP	Traditional 401(k)	Taxable Account	Emergency Fund	Total Investments
44	$50,000	$50,000	$0	$20,000	$10,000	$130,000
45	$55,620	$54,000	$3,240	$21,600	$10,000	$144,460
46	$61,690	$58,320	$6,739	$23,328	$10,000	$160,077
47	$68,245	$62,986	$10,518	$25,194	$10,000	$176,943
48	$75,324	$68,024	$14,600	$27,210	$10,000	$195,158
49	$82,970	$73,466	$19,008	$29,387	$10,000	$214,831
50	$91,228	$79,344	$23,768	$31,737	$10,000	$236,078
51	$100,146	$85,691	$28,910	$34,276	$10,000	$259,024
52	$109,778	$92,547	$34,463	$37,019	$10,000	$283,806
53	$120,180	$99,950	$40,460	$39,980	$10,000	$310,570
54	$131,414	$107,946	$46,936	$43,178	$10,000	$339,476
55	$143,548	$116,582	$53,931	$46,633	$10,000	$370,694
56	$156,651	$125,909	$61,486	$50,363	$10,000	$404,409
57	$170,804	$135,981	$69,645	$54,392	$10,000	$440,822
58	$186,088	$146,860	$78,456	$58,744	$10,000	$480,148
59	$202,595	$158,608	$87,973	$63,443	$10,000	$522,620
60	$220,422	$171,297	$98,251	$68,519	$10,000	$568,489
61	$239,676	$185,001	$109,351	$74,000	$10,000	$618,028
62	$260,470	$199,801	$121,339	$79,920	$10,000	$671,530
63	$282,928	$215,785	$134,286	$86,314	$10,000	$729,313
64	$307,182	$233,048	$148,269	$93,219	$10,000	$791,718
65	$333,377	$251,692	$163,370	$100,677	$10,000	$859,116
66	$361,667	$271,827	$179,680	$108,731	$10,000	$931,905
67	$392,220	$293,573	$197,294	$117,429	$10,000	$1,010,516
68	$423,598	$317,059	$213,078	$126,824	$10,000	$1,090,559
69	$457,486	$342,424	$230,124	$136,970	$10,000	$1,177,004
70	$494,085	$369,818	$248,534	$147,927	$10,000	$1,270,364
71	$533,611	$399,403	$268,417	$159,761	$10,000	$1,371,192
72	$576,300	$431,355	$289,890	$172,542	$10,000	$1,480,087

We will assume that the E-8 made his wife the sole beneficiary of his Roth IRA, Roth TSP, and Traditional 401(k) balances. Upon his premature death, his widow will be able to immediately withdraw money from these accounts. She must pay ordinary federal income taxes on the Traditional 401(k) withdrawals, but even if she is younger than 59.5 years old, she will not have to pay the usual 10% penalty. The IRS also waives the 10% penalty on withdrawals from her deceased husband's Roth IRA and Roth TSP accounts.

Since the E-8 already paid taxes on his contributions to his Roth TSP and Roth IRA, his wife will not have to pay taxes on her withdrawals. However, if the E-8 had owned his Roth accounts for less than five years, his widow would have to pay taxes on any capital gains. Of course, the widow will be free to withdraw the principal – but not the growth – from her own Roth IRA account. As always, a person can withdraw principal from a Roth IRA at any time, free of penalties.

Lastly, the E-8's widow could withdraw money from the couple's emergency fund and taxable account. She must pay taxes on the capital gains of the dollars in the taxable account, but these taxes will be at the capital gains tax rate. If the tax bases of the couple's taxable account's funds are high, the capital gains taxes might be reasonably small.

Note that many 401(k) plans operate differently than the TSP with respect to beneficiaries. A strong chance exists that the E-8's employer who offered the Traditional 401(k) plan will force the E-8's widow to immediately take her deceased husband's entire Traditional 401(k) balance out of the account. Employers do not wish to incur account management costs for employees that are no longer working. The employer may demand that the widow accept the balance in a lump sum. She will not be able to simply leave the money in that plan. This requirement will force the widow to immediately pay ordinary federal income taxes on the entire balance. Fortunately, the widow can avoid paying immediate taxes on the entire balance of her deceased husband's Traditional 401(k) by simply transferring his Traditional 401(k) balance into a Rollover IRA.

In contrast to such 401(k) plans, the TSP will allow the widow to leave her deceased husband's money in the TSP. The widow will be free to withdraw only what she needs. This permits the further tax-advantaged growth of the remainder.

Investment Income

We must analyze how long the amounts in the "Total Investments" column on the previous page's chart could sustain the E-8's wife at any age that the E-8 might pass away. For this purpose, we can use the "How long will my retirement savings last?" calculator on the Dinkytown website at http://www.dinkytown.net/java/RetirementDistribution.html. We can experiment with various rates of inflation, rates of return, and annual quantities that the widow might wish to withdraw.

If the widow annually withdraws the estimates under the "Allowable Withdrawals" column in the table on the next page, her Total Assets will last until she is 100 years old. The estimates are rounded to the nearest hundred. Age 100 is a reasonable target. The widow already has a 50/50 chance of exceeding age 84, and four decades of medical advances will transpire. The inputs for the calculator were a 3.4% annual price inflation rate and a 4% rate of return on the remaining balance.

To account for the possibility that the widow might suffer some degree of greater inflation, I added a few tenths of a percent to the common 3.1% inflation estimate. The 4% rate of return that I used exceeds the average inflation rate by less than 1%. While a properly invested portfolio should be more than capable of enjoying a greater rate of return, the widow may lack the financial education or simply the inclination to monitor a variety of investments. This possibility necessitated the assumption of an extremely conservative rate of return.

The next page's table shows the couple's investing and life insurance assets that will be available to the widow after the death of her husband. Until the widow is 58 years old, her husband's term life insurance policy will be available. The proceeds from that policy will be tax-free. Following the policy's termination, the widow will suffer a reduction in potential assets for approximately 6 years. Should her husband die within those 6 years, the widow must greatly reduce the sizes of her withdrawals. This reduction will enable her savings to last until she is 100 years old. Nonetheless, by the 7th year, the compounded growth of the couple's investments should enable the widow to withdraw quantities that meet or exceed what she would have been able to withdraw when the couple's term life insurance policy was still active.

Widow's Age	Total Investments	Life Insurance	Total Assets	Years Assets Must Last	Allowable Withdrawals
42	$130,000	$500,000	$630,000	58	$12,700
43	$144,460	$500,000	$644,460	57	$13,200
44	$160,077	$500,000	$660,077	56	$13,800
45	$176,943	$500,000	$676,943	55	$14,300
46	$195,158	$500,000	$695,158	54	$15,000
47	$214,831	$500,000	$714,831	53	$15,600
48	$236,078	$500,000	$736,078	52	$16,400
49	$259,024	$500,000	$759,024	51	$17,200
50	$283,806	$500,000	$783,806	50	$18,000
51	$310,570	$500,000	$810,570	49	$19,000
52	$339,476	$500,000	$839,476	48	$20,000
53	$370,694	$500,000	$870,694	47	$21,100
54	$404,409	$500,000	$904,409	46	$22,400
55	$440,822	$500,000	$940,822	45	$23,700
56	$480,148	$500,000	$980,148	44	$25,200
57	$522,620	$500,000	$1,022,620	43	$26,900
58	$568,489	0	$568,489	42	$15,200
59	$618,028	0	$618,028	41	$16,900
60	$671,530	0	$671,530	40	$18,800
61	$729,313	0	$729,313	39	$20,900
62	$791,718	0	$791,718	38	$23,200
63	$859,116	0	$859,116	37	$25,800
64	$931,905	0	$931,905	36	$28,700
65	$1,010,516	0	$1,010,516	35	$31,900
66	$1,090,559	0	$1,090,559	34	$35,400
67	$1,177,004	0	$1,177,004	33	$39,200
68	$1,270,364	0	$1,270,364	32	$43,500
69	$1,371,192	0	$1,371,192	31	$48,400
70	$1,480,087	0	$1,480,087	30	$53,800

Social Security Income

If the E-8 happens to die immediately after he turns 60 years old, his wife will face two challenges. As already stated, her husband's $500,000 term life insurance policy will no longer be available. Additionally, his Social Security checks will not yet be available; the widow will only be 58 years old. She will only have the couple's investments to sustain her. This challenge will exist for two years. Once she turns 60, she can claim Surviving Spouse Benefits to draw a reduced percentage of her deceased husband's Social Security benefits. She will be able to draw 71.5% standard reduction X $2200 NRA benefits (his) = $1573 per month ($18,876 per year). From her ages of 60 years to 66 years and 11 months, that 71.5% will gradually increase to 99.7%, depending on how many months she can postpone taking benefits.

When the widow reaches her NRA of 67 years old, she will be able to draw a full 100% of her deceased husband's Social Security benefits. Alternatively, the widow could stop drawing Surviving Spouse Benefits and start drawing 100% of her own Social Security benefits. Remember that claiming Surviving Spouse Benefits does not eliminate nor reduce any Social Security benefits for which you qualify on your own record. In fact, the widow could immediately start drawing Surviving Spouse Benefits when she turns 60 years old. She could draw those benefits until she reaches age 70. Once she turns 70 years old, she could revert to her own enhanced Social Security benefits. In this case, 124% of the widow's Social Security benefits would be less than 100% of her deceased husband's NRA benefits. Nonetheless, our widow's executing such an option would immediately provide her with income at age 60 while preserving a sizable increase in Social Security income for the year she reaches age 70.

The following chart shows the benefits that the widow would receive at various ages. The chart assumes that her husband dies at or before his NRA and has not yet filed for his benefits. Note that the size of her Surviving Spouse Benefits caps at $26,400 – her deceased husband's NRA benefits. This is because survivors do not earn delayed retirement credits toward their deceased spouses' Social Security benefits.

Widow's Age	Survivor Benefits	Social Security (hers)
59 or less	0	0
60	$18,876	0
61	$19,958	0
62	$21,014	$13,440
63	$22,097	$14,400
64	$23,179	$15,360
65	$24,262	$16,646
66	$25,318	$17,914
67	$26,400	$19,200
68	$26,400	$20,736
69	$26,400	$22,272
70 & older	$26,400	$23,808

Potential Income without Participating in the SBP

The following chart shows the income that the E-8's widow might receive from a combination of the couple's investments, insurance proceeds, and largest possible Social Security benefits:

Widow's Age	Allowable Withdrawals	Social Security (his)	Total Income
42	$12,700	0	$12,700
43	$13,200	0	$13,200
44	$13,800	0	$13,800
45	$14,300	0	$14,300
46	$15,000	0	$15,000
47	$15,600	0	$15,600
48	$16,400	0	$16,400
49	$17,200	0	$17,200
50	$18,000	0	$18,000
51	$19,000	0	$19,000
52	$20,000	0	$20,000
53	$21,100	0	$21,100
54	$22,400	0	$22,400
55	$23,700	0	$23,700
56	$25,200	0	$25,200
57	$26,900	0	$26,900
58	$15,200	0	$15,200
59	$16,900	0	$16,900
60	$18,800	$18,876	$37,676
61	$20,900	$19,958	$40,858
62	$23,200	$21,014	$44,214
63	$25,800	$22,097	$47,897
64	$28,700	$23,179	$51,879
65	$31,900	$24,262	$56,162
66	$35,400	$25,318	$60,718
67	$39,200	$26,400	$65,600
68	$43,500	$26,400	$69,900
69	$48,400	$26,400	$74,800
70	$53,800	$26,400	$80,200

Taxes

Of course, the widow will pay taxes on portions of the "Total Income" amounts, above. Fortunately, these taxes will not severely reduce the Total Income that the widow enjoys. Only those portions of the widow's "Allowable Withdrawals" that come from the Traditional 401(k) plan will increase the widow's taxable income. In contrast, withdrawals from the widow's taxable account will enjoy capital gains tax rates. By liquidating principal in that taxable account, the widow could further reduce her capital gains taxes. By taking withdrawals from Roth accounts, she might avoid even more taxes. Lastly, only half of the widow's Social Security income will increase her taxable income.

SBP Income

If the E-8 elects to participate in the SBP, his monthly SBP premiums will be 6.5% X $2235 = $145.28. His annual premiums will be 12 months X $145.28 = $1743.36. The E-8 will start paying his SBP premiums immediately after he retires from the military. These premiums will reduce the quantity of his income that is subject to federal income taxes. The E-8 and his wife's MAGI places them in the 15% marginal tax bracket. Thus, the effective cost of the E-8's SBP premiums will be (100% tax – 15% marginal tax) X $1743.36 = $1482 per year (rounded to the nearest whole dollar). Without a sizable increase in the couple's income, the couple will remain in the 15% tax bracket.

The couple can afford to invest no more than $3000 per year, with another $1500 coming from the E-8's employer's Traditional 401(k) match. If the E-8 participates in the SBP, $1482 will no longer be available for investing. The couple will only be able to contribute $1518 to their retirement accounts. Once the E-8 is a civilian, the prioritization of his investments will differ from what they were when he was a SM. His new first priority will be to obtain the 100% return on investment offered by the 3% match in his civilian employer's Traditional 401(k) plan. Meeting the 3% figure will consume $1500 of the money that he has available to invest. He will only be able to contribute $18 per year to his Roth IRA.

Adding only $18 per year to the $50,000 starting balance in the couple's Roth IRAs will reduce the growth of these IRAs to $171,887 by the time the E-8 is 60 years old. This represents a sacrifice of $220,422 – $171,887 = $48,535 in potential earnings. By the time the E-8 is 72 years old, the sacrifice will be $576,300 – $433,095 = $143,205 in potential earnings. Note that the $18 per year infusions stop when the E-8 hits 67.

The gain for this sacrifice will be his widow's receiving SBP benefits of 55% X $2235 base amount = $1229 per month ($14,748 per year). The widow will receive these benefits, regardless of when her husband dies. The IRS will tax the widow's SBP benefits, using the widow's ordinary federal income tax rate. Unlike life insurance death benefits, SBP benefits are fully taxable. Fortunately, the widow's ordinary federal income tax rate should be quite low.

Observations

If the E-8 dies long before his widow turns 60 years old, she will appreciate her husband's participation in the SBP. The couple will suffer a negative cash flow for a small number of years, while the widow enjoys a more positive cash flow for a large number of years. If the E-8 expects an early death, he should participate in the SBP.

If the E-8 believes he will survive until his wife is close to 60 years old, seeing the necessity of participating in the SBP is more difficult. Participating in the SBP will effectively cost the couple $1482 per year. Choosing not to participate in the SBP will give the couple the option of investing this $1482 or simply adding this $1482 to the couple's household cash flow. If the couple invests the $1482, the couple's savings could be $48,535 larger by the E-8's 60th birthday. By the E-8's 72nd birthday, the couple's savings could be $143,205 larger.

$48,535 and $143,205 are nice sums of money. However, relying on these sums to sustain the E-8's widow is risky. The E-8 could die soon after reaching age 60. If so, the $48,535 figure will produce less than $5000 per year, even with a healthy 10% rate of return. If the E-8 survives until he is 72, the $143,205 figure will provide $14,321, assuming the same healthy 10% rate of return. Both figures are less than the $14,748 income that the SBP would provide. Neither figure is guaranteed, nor does either figure receive a guaranteed inflation adjustment. Again, the E-8 should participate in the SBP.

However, if the E-8 and his wife survive until their life expectancies, his participation in the SBP will not be profitable. If the E-8 dies on his 81st birthday, he will have paid $1482 SBP premiums X 26 years (age 44 through and including age 69) = $38,532 in total SBP premiums. Note that his premium payments cease, once he turns 70 years old; he will be "paid up". If his wife dies on her 84th birthday, she will collect $14,748 SBP benefits (before taxes) X 5 years = $73,740. $73,740 is more than $38,532, but the difference will not be large enough to warrant the E-8's having paid into the SBP system and having reduced the couple's quality of life for all of those years.

Lastly, we should consider the couple's cash flow. For many military families, $1482 is a lot of money. Paying today's bills might appear to be a more pressing priority than insuring the income of a future widow(er). If the E-8 and his wife anticipate difficulties covering their expenses while both members of the couple are still alive, they might conclude that participating in the SBP is unwise.

Conclusion

This example shows that participating in the SBP is not absolutely necessary for the widow to survive. Provided that the E-8 lives a long life, his widow will possess sufficient funds to pay her bills. Additionally, the couple will enjoy stronger cash flows during all of the years that the E-8 is still alive. The couple's quality of life will be better.

Nonetheless, what if the E-8 dies, early? What if he has good health habits and strong genetics but winds up in a car wreck? What if that wreck occurs the day after he retires from the military? If such a premature death occurs and he is not participating in the SBP, his widow will be in financial trouble. That trouble could be severe for 20 years or more. Due to their frequent PCS moves, she may have very limited work experience. If she can obtain any work at all, that work might only be part time and might only reward her with minimum wages.

Eventually, the couple's grown children – assuming any exist – may have to support their mother. The burden of supporting their mother may come at a time when the mother's grown children are already struggling with their own children's college debts. Due to supporting their mother, the grown children might no longer be able to cover their own children's education. This situation may force the widow's grandchildren to pursue college loans that will place the grandchildren in debt for many years. By failing to protect his future widow's income, the E-8 might well precipitate a financial disaster that passes to several generations.

How likely to occur is this nightmare? After all, most of us know very few families whose primary breadwinners have died in car wrecks. Thus, the odds of dying in car wrecks appear to be quite low. Further, the odds of living past our life expectancies appear to be quite high. A 50% probability exists that the E-8 will live more than 81 years. His odds of simply surviving into his 70s are even better. By his 70s, his enhanced Social Security benefits might easily sustain his widow. These facts make participating in the SBP appear to be a poor bet.

Indeed, betting on such odds in Las Vegas would be unwise. However, we are not discussing how to quickly turn $10 into $100, nor are we discussing whether to insure a simple stereo system that costs a couple hundred bucks. We are discussing how to protect our family's livelihood. The SBP protects the source of that livelihood, and that source is easily worth six to seven figures. Paying a few thousand dollars per year to protect an asset of such magnitude may not be a good bet, but it is still a wise move.

Ultimately, the question of whether to participate in the SBP is similar to the question of whether to insure your home. Catastrophic fires and floods are rare. Homeowner's insurance premiums pay for protection against unlikely threats. Avoiding these premiums would save money. However, what if a fire does completely destroy your home? What if this happens when you no longer have homeowner's insurance and you have not amassed the resources to purchase a new home? Of course, the answer is that you would be in tremendous financial trouble. For this reason, we insure our homes. For a similar reason, we should participate in the SBP. Some losses are so catastrophic that we simply cannot risk being forced to cover these losses with our own assets.

Participating in the SBP insures your family's income against an unlikely but devastating threat. Relying on your investments to protect your family's income is risky. Your death may come long before your investments have matured. Frankly, if your investments grow to such a size that they can easily support your family, why should a few thousand dollars in annual SBP premiums matter? Participate in the SBP. If money is tight, improve your cash flow.

Part VI

SERVICE SUPPORT

This section of the OPORD discusses resources that may assist you in the execution of your mission.

Chapter 25: Books

The following books provide more depth on some of the topics that this OPORD covered. They appear in the sequence in which you should read them. The first book will give you the reasons why you must take aggressive action, with respect to your finances. The second book will give you techniques for cutting costs and generating savings that you can invest. The third book will explain the investments that you should use.

"Why We Want You to be Rich" by Donald Trump and Robert Kiyosaki (Rich Press, 2006)

Trump and Kiyosaki warn us about the economic problems that face our country. Trump and Kiyosaki's target readers are average Americans. As such, this book is quite easy to comprehend.

These successful businessmen clearly explain dollar devaluation, excess government spending, skyrocketing energy prices, and more nightmares that threaten America. The 2008 – 2009 tumbling of the stock market and bursting of the housing bubble proved the accuracy of these men's predictions. The stock market has largely recovered, but the housing market is still abysmal, unemployment is high, government spending is out of control, and the dollar's value continues to plummet.

Ironically, neither Trump nor Kiyosaki would likely endorse recommendations to invest in index ETFs or index funds. These men made their fortunes investing directly in real estate and developing aggressive business ventures. Both men financed these operations with huge quantities of debt. Their book may inspire you to do the same. Until that inspiration leads to action, follow "Win the Money War's" recommendations.

"Retire on Less than You Think" by Fred Brock (New York: Times Book, 2008)

This book gives excellent advice on how to cut your expenses. Brock addresses nearly every expense associated with day-to-day living. Some of his proposals involve Draconian cuts. Though painful, all of his proposals warrant your consideration.

Brock emphatically espouses the idea that cutting expenses increases income. He gives detailed examples of how simply changing your state or city of residence can dramatically improve your household cash flow. Following Brock's advice will help you free cash for investing.

"How to Retire Early and Live Well with Less than a Million Dollars" by Gillette Edmunds (Avon: Adams Media Corporation, 2000)

I recommend this book more strongly than any other. Edmunds wrote this book, over a decade ago. However, his investing principles and strategies stand the test of time.

Edmunds discusses his concepts of target investment returns, non-correlated asset allocations, principal liquidations, and balanced real estate leverage in great detail. He discusses the nuances of the major asset classes and explains how to capitalize on those nuances, without accepting undue risk. His recommendations directly challenge the recommendations of typical financial advisors.

SMs will appreciate Edmunds' writing style. He quickly and clearly makes his points and then supports his points with convincing evidence. He accompanies his recommendations with deep analyses that verify his mastery of the material. Edmunds' honesty about his own mistakes in life and with money further supports the fact that his book is a "must read".

My own book does not precisely follow Edmunds' recommendations. Notable exceptions are my recommendations that you own a sixth asset class – a precious metals fund – and that you invest as much as a full one-third of your assets in REITs. Edmunds mentions gold but does not strongly endorse it. He discusses REITs but makes the point that REITs' returns bear a correlation with U.S. stocks' returns. You can achieve greater diversity (non-correlation) by directly purchasing commercial properties. However, his recommendation that real estate investors purchase commercial properties with 50% leverage will be difficult for most SMs to execute[xlvii].

I tailored my own book's recommendations to the idiosyncrasies of SMs' lives and to the compensation system that SMs possess. I also accounted for over a decade's worth of economic and political changes that transpired since Edmunds wrote his book. Nonetheless, Edmunds filled his book with timeless financial information that will greatly benefit SMs.

Chapter 26: Websites

This section lists websites that are available to assist you with establishing your finances.

1. www.morningstar.com The Morningstar website ranks the stocks and mutual funds provided by the various brokerages. For mutual funds, this website is especially beneficial. Among other details, the website lists funds' expenses, turnover percentages, and dividend payment schedules.

2. www.fool.com The Motley Fool website is an interesting source of financial information. The authors are knowledgeable and entertaining. The website covers a multitude of personal finance topics with a sarcastic humor that many SMs will appreciate.

3. www.dinkytown.net The Dinkytown website possesses an odd name but is very useful. This website offers a plethora of financial calculators. Mortgages, investments, savings rates, and tax estimates are just some of the areas for which multiple calculators exist.

4. www.bankrate.com The Bankrate website provides a number of handy financial calculators. This website is

particularly useful for comparing rates of return for savings instruments offered by financial institutions across the nation.

5. www.valoans.com The VA Loans website provides VA loan details, guidelines, updates, and calculators. It also provides the current 15-year and 30-year VA loan interest rates.

6. www.zillow.com The Zillow website offers comprehensive data about individual homes around the nation.

7. www.trulia.com Trulia is another website that offers comprehensive data about individual homes.

8. https://mypay.dfas.mil/mypay.aspx The myPay website is where you can access your LES. This website is also where you can set your TSP contribution percentages. To determine which funds those contributions will purchase, you must access the TSP website, itself.

9. www.tsp.gov This URL is the Thrift Savings Plan's login page. The current TSP website is a great improvement over the original TSP website. You can conduct much of your research and most of your investing actions (other than setting your contribution percentages) from this single location.

10. www.caranddriver.com The Car and Driver website offers detailed automobile reviews that can help you decide whether a given car lives up to the claims of its advertisers.

11. www.kellybluebook.com The Kelly Blue Book website is a great source for details about new, used, and CPO automobiles. Its estimates for cars' values tend to be a tad higher than the Edmunds.com website's estimates. As such, use Kelly Blue Book's estimates when negotiating to sell a vehicle.

12. www.edmunds.com Edmunds is another good source for details about automobiles. This website's True Cost to Own (TCO) calculations are particularly informative. Edmunds' estimates for cars' values tend to be a bit lower than Kelly Blue Book's estimates. As such, use Edmunds' estimates when negotiating to buy a vehicle.

Chapter 27: Financial Advisors

Following this book's advice will increase your net worth. The COAs that "Win the Money War" recommends are not difficult to execute. You need not be an expert in financial planning to create a reasonably effective portfolio of tax-advantaged and taxable investments. DITY investors who read this book will be able to quickly establish the genesis of sound, long-term investment strategies. Indeed, this book's target audience is SMs, and SMs pride themselves on being capable of independent operations.

Nonetheless, as your net worth grows, you may decide that the DITY approach is unmanageable, costly, and even risky. Your finances will have become so large and complex that small errors will lead to significant losses and failing to be aware of administrative requirements will threaten your estate. The difficulties of handling your personal finances will have become analogous to the difficulties that small business owners suffer. Small business owners cut costs by handling their own administrative tasks. So long as businesses are small, the DITY approach is tenable. Nonetheless, the DITY approach becomes untenable when small business owners become large business owners.

Large business owners can no longer afford the time that administrative tasks consume. To free themselves to focus on the primary goals of their businesses, large business owners pay other people to execute those administrative tasks. By spending small amounts of money, large business owners increase their odds of making much more money and reduce their odds of suffering financial calamities.

For similar ends, you may wish to hire professional assistance to better manage your wealth. Qualified financial advisors (FAs) can provide that sort of assistance. Most FAs will charge a fee that is equal to roughly one percent per year of your assets under their management. One percent is a sizable amount, but the reward for a FA's assistance might more than compensate you for the loss of her fee.

A FA will tabulate your assets and liabilities, will determine your short, medium, and long-term goals, and will assess your tolerance for market volatility. She will share this data with a team of financial technicians that her firm possesses. Each technician will specialize in a different financial area, such as insurance, investing, or long-term care. With respect to his or her area of expertise, each technician will determine how best to leverage your assets and minimize your liabilities to achieve your stated goals.

The firm's team will return a list of recommendations to your FA. Your FA will use these recommendations and her overarching view of your financial situation to develop a comprehensive financial plan for you. The aim of this plan will be to achieve precisely what you stated in your goals. Accepting the plan will result in a long-term relationship with the FA and her firm.

Your FA will be the interpreter that stands between you and the technical experts. She will be the financial person who most cares about your family and its goals. She will be your advocate and will ensure that the technicians fully address every aspect of your financial situation. To use another analogy, your FA will be to your financial health what your Primary Care Manager (PCM) is to your physical health. Her firm's technical experts will be to her what a hospital's specialists are to your PCM. Your PCM meets with you, face-to-face. He measures your vital statistics and asks how you feel. He determines what levels of care that he can immediately give you and then consults the hospital's specialists for those areas in which he requires more specific expertise.

Significantly, your FA will ensure that you do not derail your own plan. When the markets suffer their inevitable lows, she will dissuade you from precipitously shifting your holdings into "safe" investments, such as cash. When particular markets are "hot", she will dissuade you from selling your core holdings in order to chase those markets. She will clearly explain why both of these moves and other missteps that you might take will jeopardize your wealth. Most investors who have not hired FAs make these mistakes many times in their lives. The cumulative effects of these errors are substantial reductions in these investors' wealth.

Part VII

COMMAND AND SIGNAL

This section of the OPORD establishes who is in charge, when the assigned leaders are absent. This section also provides the methods by which the organization will communicate.

Chapter 28: Command

Declaring a household "commander" will likely result in one's spending the night on the couch. A better approach is to determine equal, yet distinct financial lanes of responsibility. A viable division of financial labor places one spouse in charge of the family's long-term investments and the other spouse in charge of the family's day-to-day cash flow.

The spouse that juggles the home, the kids, and, possibly, a sideline career is often the better choice to be in charge of the family's day-to-day cash flow. This spouse lives in the trenches. This spouse pays and tracks the family's bills. Of necessity, this spouse must know where the money is and where it must go. Hence, this spouse is more likely to ensure that the family remains solvent.

The spouse that goes to a job each day has less familiarity with the immediate financial needs of the family. This spouse is not in the trenches. This spouse is freer to focus on methods for increasing the family's income. One way to earn more money is to invest better. This spouse is the better choice to be in charge of the family's long-term investments.

One spouse should not perform both jobs. Both members of the couple should be involved in the family's finances. Both spouses should understand where the family's finances are going and what the current status of those finances is. Both spouses should feel as if they are contributing to the family's wealth. Lofty principles are not the impetus for this recommendation. Good business is. If both spouses have a stake in the finances, both spouses are less inclined to make frivolous financial decisions.

Chapter 29: Signal

Feel free to email me at the following address:
jgredwine@sbcglobal.net.

Find me on Facebook at Win the Money War.

[END OF FORMAL OPORD]

Part VIII

COFFEE BREAK

You have received your OPORD. Your mind is now spinning with a hundred implied, specified, and mission critical tasks that you must accomplish. As always, you fear that time is against you. Nonetheless, take a moment to breathe. Before racing back to your troops, grab a cup of coffee while we discuss a few final topics.

Chapter 30: Prepare for Changes

Our U.S. Government's shortsighted fiscal policies and expensive overhead threaten the economic strength of the nation. Economic trouble is as effective as bullets in destroying nations. Although American corporations remain formidable players on the global economic stage, they struggle under the policies of a nation that demands more and more entitlements. Paying for these entitlements weakens America's economy. We must change our ways, or we will go the way of previous super-powers.

The U.S. Government's writing of checks against an empty bank account must stop. To facilitate this paradigm shift, the U.S. Government must execute plans that refresh the nation's capitalist spirit. These plans must create corporate incentives that entice domestic industrial development. Simultaneously, these plans must spur individual Americans' entrepreneurial creativity. Enticing domestic industrial development and spurring entrepreneurial creativity may necessitate changing individual Americans' entitlements. Such changes will be unpopular.

The long-term solution for filling the nation's empty bank account is to increase the nation's productivity. Unfortunately, accepting this fact will require time, effort, and courage. Initially, politicians will focus on the low-hanging fruit. Politicians will cut Government spending, rather than institute policies that push the people to increase the nation's produce. Some of that low-hanging fruit will come from the Government's most obedient employees –

the military. Our inflation-indexed pensions that start immediately after our retirements from the military are easy targets. Our pensions are legitimate targets, because our pensions do, indeed, exacerbate the nation's economic troubles. To pay our pensions, Congress must levy taxes, and the IRS must collect those taxes. Those taxes come from the pockets of the people we defend. That arrangement may seem equitable, but it is unsustainable. The money no longer exists.

SMs should prepare for the extension of cuts to all public servants. These cuts will become deeper as the Government curtails more spending on our anti-terror wars. As we fade from the headlines, the people's appreciation of our sacrifices will fade. As the flag-waving subsides, voters will embrace the idea that SMs' retirements should be no different than civilians' retirements. The July 2011 proposal to change our military pension system is a clear sign that the flag-waving is already subsiding. The proposal moves the TSP from being a mere ancillary component of our retirement package to being the primary component. Alarmingly, the proposal seeks to apply this shift to current SMs, not solely to future SMs.

Socialism

Moving SMs to a more civilianized retirement system engenders SMs' frustrated claims that the Government is breaching their contract. SMs believe that civilians owe SMs for their sacrifices. While our service may warrant our belief, the nation's finances no longer support the honoring of our claims. We find ourselves in the same position that civilian employees found themselves, 30 years ago. The consequences of the IRS' 1981 401(k) ruling are rapidly making their way to us. We must either prepare for these consequences or become casualties of them.

Regardless of whether SMs like it, our current retirement system will almost certainly change. Our pensions and other benefits demand money from long-since empty coffers. This demand forces our Government to commit more acts of counterfeiting. An inexorable weakening of our economy follows. On the other hand, a more 401(k)-like retirement system would contribute SMs' money to the economy. We would fuel the economy, rather than drain it. Our investments would increase the nation's productivity, prosperity, and, consequently, the nation's security.

Nonetheless, SMs deeply resent politicians' attempts to change our benefits. SMs possess a visceral hatred for anyone who suggests that our benefits are too generous. We immediately question whether that individual has served in the military. If not, we deride that person as being too contemptible to warrant the serious consideration of his suggestion. In reality, we are simply tossing smoke grenades. Prior military service is not necessary to devise necessary changes to SMs' compensation packages. We are discussing long-term economic solutions, not short-term security measures.

Why do we get so angry? We nod in nearly universal agreement that our Government is fiscally irresponsible, yet we balk at the very suggestion that we bear complicity in that irresponsibility. Why are we so resistant?

The answer lies in our sense of entitlement that career military service engenders. We *deserve* our generous pensions that start long before we have passed our most productive years – pensions that onerous taxes, not mutually beneficial investments, must sustain. We *deserve* our families' subsidized health care plans that extend into retirement, for relatively insignificant costs. We *deserve* our tax-free housing allowances that permit us to live in homes that surpass the quality of the homes in which our civilian counterparts live. We *deserve* to remain at whatever rank we have achieved, regardless of whether our further usefulness is questionable. We deserve all of these things. Whether the Government must tax the American people into poverty to provide these things is of little consequence to us. If they resent it, they should have signed up.

In effect, we have become socialists. Indeed, we are more like the East Germans against whom we guarded the West than we are like the people we were defending. We demand benefits that taxes must provide. The people we defend struggle to provide the goods and services that enable the levying of those taxes. Each year, the Government's fiscal policies and excessive spending necessitate the levying of ever more taxes from the people. The people's pursuit of happiness becomes ever more difficult, and their resentment grows. Soon, our economy will become so severely strained that the people will demand changes. If we resist those changes, we will risk the outright refusal of the people to fund any aspect of our current benefits package. We must either compromise, today, or be left with nothing, tomorrow.

In order to compromise, we must embrace a more capitalist spirit. To change from a socialist to a capitalist mindset, SMs require financial education. Military leaders must passionately encourage and facilitate the pursuit of that education. Financially educated SMs will not fear a 401(k)-like retirement system, because they will know how to prosper within it. Armed with such knowledge, SMs will confidently accept the demands of the people we defend. In so doing, SMs will assist the Government in taking one of its necessary steps toward renewing America's economic hegemony. As for the SMs, themselves, they will have made a necessary compromise to preserve the existence of their benefits. Maximizing those benefits will require more direct involvement from the SMs, but those benefits will still exist, albeit in a different form.

Chapter 31: Investing Attitudes

Gambling

As a young military officer, my concept of financial planning involved little more than accumulating my salary in a checking account and paying cash for whatever I bought. This was better than what spendthrifts did, but it was still not good. I was more interested in playing Army than I was in learning how to make the most of my paycheck. I regarded the stock market as one huge slot machine and saw little point in wasting time on it. The only positive result of my contempt was that I avoided the 50% load scams that were rampant in the late 1980s. Nonetheless, my lack of participation in the stock market hurt me in the 1990s. I missed many gains that occurred during the bull markets of that decade.

Eventually, I grudgingly entered the game. I handed my savings over to a financial advisor who asked me the typical question about what level of risk tolerance I possessed. Unfortunately, I gave the same answer that I have warned you not to give. As such, my money wound up in investments that were too conservative. My belief that investing in the stock market was glorified gambling made me so contemptuous of investing that I put no effort into learning what was happening to my money.

Investing in the stock market is not gambling. When you buy stocks or shares of mutual funds, you are buying permanent, legally backed claims to the successes of the businesses that those stocks and shares represent. You are not buying lottery tickets that will be worthless immediately after the drawings. The money that you spend to receive those stocks and shares fuels the growth of those businesses. If your companies excel, your stocks and shares will grow. History clearly shows that, far more often than not, this growth is exactly what happens. In gambling, your investments do not grow. You may win a spin or two, but you will never win for long. If you did, casinos would not exist.

Unlike gamblers, investors are playing a truly lucrative game. Consumers want to buy good products. Companies want to provide those good products. Investors want to own shares of companies that are providing those good products. Your purchase of stock in those companies provides capital for the growth of those companies. When good companies grow, more good products are available for more consumers. Investors who own shares of those growing companies enjoy more dividends and larger capital gains. Every member of this circle wants every other member to be successful. No such unity of purpose exists in gambling. The casino wants you to lose and ensures that you do. Billboards that claim, "97% Payouts!" are being quite truthful. They unambiguously announce that, on average, for every dollar you give to the casino, you will receive 97 cents. Not even as a young lieutenant, would I have accepted such a return on investment.

Conservative Investing

In response to the 2008 tumbling of the stock market, a number of financial writers ratcheted back their claims of what the market's future returns would be. Recommended planning factors dropped from healthy double-digit returns to anemic single-digit returns. While adjusting a plan in response to changing conditions is good, failing to properly assess the situation before writing the plan is bad. When making their pre-2008 predictions of double-digit market returns, did these financial writers fail to account for such market crashes as those of 1929 and 1987? Did these writers think that such crashes would never reoccur?

If their old predictions did account for these crashes and these writers did believe that such crashes would reoccur, then these writers' new predictions are dubious. These new predictions are reflexes to momentary pain. The market recovery of 2009 to 2010 showed that the expected returns in the Asset Allocation Chart are accurate. This chart's returns account for a century's worth of market upheavals. Invest, accordingly.

Believing that a bad year or two has produced some sort of financial Apocalypse will lead you to unnecessarily damage your asset allocation. Undoubtedly, you will suffer some disappointing months and even a few disappointing years. However, after many years of investing, your average returns will resemble the expected returns in the Asset Allocation Chart.

Chapter 32: Wrap Up

This book contains four years of research. The COAs that I have recommended are the COAs that I am using. They are working for me, and they will work for you.

If you are a young SM, realize that this is the book I wish I had read when I was your age. If you will execute this book's recommendations, you will be financially successful. Time and the military's compensation system are your allies. Procrastination is your primary enemy.

If you are an older SM who lived the dream but neglected your finances, take heart. I became a student of business and finance much later than I wish I had. Nonetheless, in a relatively small number of years, I amassed a significant net worth, using little more than my military paycheck. I achieved this success while my wife stayed home with our two kids and our one dog. You can do the same.

About the Author

Jim Redwine became a commissioned officer in the Infantry in 1987. He has deployed for Operations Desert Shield and Storm, Operation Enduring Freedom, and Operation Iraqi Freedom. His training qualifications and combat decorations include the Parachute Badge, Ranger Tab, Expert Infantryman Badge, two Combat Infantryman Badges, a Valorous Unit Award, and two Bronze Stars. He has a Bachelor of Science degree from the United States Military Academy and a Master of Business Administration from Touro University International. He married Gina Maria Pagano in 1987. Gina and he have a son, Nicholas, a daughter, Elyse, and a dog, Charlie.

Endnotes

[i] Gillette Edmunds, How to Retire Early and Live Well – With Less than a Million Dollars (Avon: Adams Media Corporation, 2000), 6.

[ii] Definitions, Expected Inflation Rate, Bankrate.com, http://www.bankrate.com/calculators/savings/price-inflation-calculator.aspx (2012).

[iii] U.S. Bureau of Labor Statistics, CPI Inflation Calculator, http://www.bls.gov/data/inflation_calculator.htm/ (Jul. 8, 2011).

[iv] Pamela Villareal, Social Security and Medicare Projections: 2009, National Center for Policy Analysis, http://www.ncpa.org/pub/ba662 (June 11, 2009).

[v] Richard Wolf, U.S. debt is now equal to economy, USA Today, http://www.usatoday.com/news/washington/story/2012-01-08/debt-equals-economy/52460208/1 (January 9, 2012).

[vi] Morgan Housel, The American Consumer Is Back, Motley Fool, http://www.fool.com/investing/general/2010/05/05/the-american-consumer-is-back.aspx?source=isesitlnk0000001&mrr=1.00 (May 5, 2010).

[vii] Peter Sander, Personal Finance Handbook, (New York: Fall River Press, 2006), 90-91.

[viii] Bill Barker, Loads, Motley Fool, http://www.fool.com/School/MutualFunds/Costs/Loads.htm (undated).

[ix] Frank Nothaft, W(h)ither Home Values?, Office of the Chief Economist (Freddie Mac, Dec. 14, 2005), 1.

[x] Fred Brock, Retire on Less than You Think – Revised Edition (New York: Times Books, 2008), 104-106.

[xi] Janet Wickell, Discount Point FAQ, About.com,

http://homebuying.about.com/cs/mortgagearticles/a/discount_points.h
tm (undated).

xii VA Loans, VA Loan Guidelines – What is a VA Loan?,
http://www.valoans.com/va_facts_whatis.cfm (undated).

xiii Emily Brandon, 7 401(k) Mistakes You're Probably Making; U.S. News –
Money, http://www.usnews.com/money/blogs/planning-to-
retire/2010/04/29/7-401k-mistakes-youre-probably-making (Apr. 29,
2010).

xiv Thrift Savings Plan, Expense Ratio,
https://www.tsp.gov/investmentfunds/fundsoverview/expenseRatio.sht
ml (2011).

xv Social Security Online, Understanding The Benefits,
http://ssa.gov/pubs/10024.html#a0=0 (Apr. 30, 2012).

xvi Michael Astrue, Your Social Security Statement, (Baltimore: Social
Security Administration, Sep. 8, 2010), 1.

xvii Social Security Online, Average monthly Social Security benefit for
retired worker, http://ssa-
custhelp.ssa.gov/app/answers/detail/a_id/13/~/average-monthly-
social-security-benefit-for-a-retired-worker (Jul. 2, 2012).

xviii Social Security Online, Retirement Planner: Benefits for You as a
Spouse, http://www.socialsecurity.gov/retire2/applying6.htm#a0=1
(Aug. 3, 2012).

xix Social Security Online, Survivors Planner: How Much Would Your
Survivors Receive?,
http://www.socialsecurity.gov/survivorplan/onyourown5.htm (Apr. 24,
2012).

xx Social Security Online, Retirement Planner: Benefits by Year of Birth,
http://www.socialsecurity.gov/retire2/agereduction.htm (Jun. 19, 2012).

xxi Social Security Online, Survivors Planner: How Much Would Your
Benefit Be?, http://www.socialsecurity.gov/survivorplan/ifyou5.htm
(Mar. 30, 2012).

xxii Social Security Online, Benefits Planner: Income Taxes and your Social
Security Benefits, http://www.ssa.gov/planners/taxes.htm (Apr. 4, 2012).

xxiii Donald Trump, Robert Kiyosaki, Why We Want You to be Rich (Rich
Press, 2006), 73-77.

xxiv Defense Business Board Task Force, Modernizing the Military
Retirement System (Public meeting, Jul. 21, 2011), slide 12.

xxv Sander, 115.

xxvi Edmunds, 51.

xxvii Edmunds, 210-213.

xxviii Edmunds, 168.

xxix Edmunds, 165.

xxx Trump and Kiyosaki, 58.

xxxi Mark Hurlbert, The Index Funds Win Again, The New York Times, http://www.nytimes.com/2009/02/22/your-money/stocks-and-bonds/22stra.html (Feb. 21, 2009).

xxxii Dominic Wilson, Alex Kelston, Swarnali Ahmed, BRICs Monthly – Issue No: 10/03 (Goldman Sachs, May 20, 2010), 1.

xxxiii Jeff Opdyke, Rethinking Gold: What if It Isn't a Commodity After All?, The Wall Street Journal, http://online.wsj.com/article/SB10001424052748703908704575433670771742884.html?mod=WSJ_hps_sections_personalfinance#printMode (Aug. 21, 2010).

xxxiv Adam Blaser, Gold Vs. Dollar – Why Gold May Be The Best Coming Investment Attraction of The Decade, Articlesbase, http://www.articlesbase.com/investing-articles/gold-vs-dollar-why-gold-may-be-the-best-coming-investment-attraction-of-the-decade-1997587.html (Mar. 16, 2010).

xxxv Only Gold, Modern and Ancient Spot Gold Prices, http://www.onlygold.com/tutorialpages/prices200yrsfs.htm (undated).

xxxvi InflationData.com, Is Inflation Rising or Falling?, http://inflationdata.com/inflation/Inflation/AnnualInflation.asp (Aug. 15, 2012).

xxxvii Daniel Gross, U.S. incentives for renewable energy raise questions, The New York Times, http://www.nytimes.com/2007/05/27/business/worldbusiness/27iht-startup.4.5886367.html (May 27, 2007).

xxxviii Nick Murray, The New Financial Advisor (Library of Congress, 2001) 165-167.

xxxix Edmunds, 63-66.

xl Suze Orman, The Money Class (New York: Spiegel & Grau, 2011), 88.

xli Francesca Levy, Full List: Where Americans Pay Most In Property Taxes, Forbes.com, http://www.forbes.com/2010/01/15/property-taxes-high-lifestyle-real-estate-counties-assessment-taxes-chart.html (Jan. 15, 2010).

xlii Savingforcollege.com, The real cost of higher education, http://www.savingforcollege.com/tutorial101/the_real_cost_of_higher_education.php (undated).

xliii Jack Hough, Is a college degree worthless?, SmartMoney.com, http://money.msn.com/college-savings/is-a-college-degree-worthless-smartmoney.aspx (Nov. 7, 2010).

xliv Liz Weston, Is the Ivy League a waste of money?, SmartMoney.com, http://money.msn.com/college-savings/is-the-ivy-league-a-waste-of-money-weston.aspx?page=2 (Feb. 23, 2011).

xlv Jaime Pessin, How to Take Money out of 529 Plans, The Wall Street

Journal. Digital Network,
http://online.wsj.com/article/SB1000142405274870489360457620053240838361642.html (Apr. 3, 2011).

[xlvi] Utah Educational Savings Plan, Utah Educational Savings Plan Investment Option Performance as of July 31, 2012, http://www.uesp.org/pdfs/returns/2012/Investment-Option-Performance-as-of-July-31,-2012 (Jul. 31, 2012).

[xlvii] Edmunds, 132.

Index

·

CPSIA information can be obtained at www.ICGtesting.com
Printed in the USA
LVOW071933310113

318099LV00021B/1517/P

9 781480 229181